Managing change in schools

Change has been a major characteristic of education for the past few years as wide-ranging new legislation has been implemented, but practical advice on how to manage and cope with change in schools has been hard to come by. This book, written by two practising educational psychologists, seeks to remedy this situation by providing practical psychological approaches to the management of schools in general and the management of change in particular.

The book examines planning for the future, arguing for vision, intermediate and short-term objectives. It also looks at a number of key strategies in relation to bringing about change, including consultation, negotiation, research, project development, in-service training, professional and policy development. The authors point out the systemic links between policy, professional development and objective setting, and also explore methods of evaluating change and celebrating success. Most importantly, the book looks at how change affects the individual, how to safeguard the interests of staff and pupils during the change process, and how to be aware of the limits to the amount of change the individual and the organisation can reasonably be expected to cope with. The final section puts a case for asserting the school philosophy amid imposed changes. Each chapter offers information, evidence, theory and practical advice, and ends with an action plan.

Colin Newton is a Senior Educational Psychologist presently working for Nottinghamshire County Council's Educational Psychology Service, where he is engaged in active work with city schools, children and families. He also carries out research and development work which has included developing a special needs database, investigating preschool provision, and the training of Special Needs coordinators. **Tony Tarrant** is a Deputy Principal Educational Psychologist (Training) in the London Borough of Southwark, and contributes to the training of Educational Psychologists as an Associate Tutor at the Institute of Education, University of London. Previously, he taught in secondary education in East London for a number of years.

Educational management series
Edited by Cyril Poster

Managing change in schools

A practical handbook

Colin Newton and Tony Tarrant

London and New York

First published 1992
by Routledge
11 New Fetter Lane, London EC4P 4EE

Simultaneously published in the USA and Canada
by Routledge
a division of Routledge, Chapman and Hall, Inc.
29 West 35th Street, New York, NY 10001

Typeset in Garamond by LaserScript Limited, Mitcham, Surrey
Printed and bound in Great Britain by
Mackays of Chatham PLC, Chatham, Kent

British Library Cataloguing in Publication Data
A catalogue record for this title is available from the British Library.

ISBN 0–415–06548–8
ISBN 0–415–06549–6 (pbk)

Library of Congress Cataloging in Publication Data
Newton, Colin, 1957–
    Managing change in schools / Colin Newton and Tony Tarrant.
    p. cm. — (Education management series)
    Includes bibliographical references (p.) and index.
    ISBN 0–415–06548–8. – ISBN 0–415–06549–6 (pbk.)
    1. School management and organization – Great Britain.
    I. Tarrant, Tony, 1950– .   II. Title.   III. Series.
    LB2900.5.N48   1992
    371.2′00941–dc20

For Jacqui and Lorna.
Without their love and support this book would not
have been possible.

Contents

Foreword

Teachers at all levels of the profession may, with some justice, feel themselves overwhelmed with innovation, new legislation and change. A book such as this, which offers a great deal of practical help on managing change, will prove a godsend to middle and senior managers in schools and colleges, advisers, administrators and governors.

Written by two educational psychologists, whose collective range of experience covers county, metropolitan and inner-city LEAs, this book offers a refreshing new slant on a topic widely written about by academics, in particular over the past decade. Colin Newton and Tony Tarrant would not claim to be academics, though even a cursory glance at the pages of this book will reveal the breadth and depth of their reading. They are above all practitioners, as aware of the problems that arise in schools as any classroom teacher or member of a management team. All the situations used to exemplify their arguments derive from close contact with teachers, in support, advisory and consultative roles.

One outstanding merit of this book is that it brings to the issue of the management of change a refreshing new perspective, that of educational psychology. While some of the chapter headings might well be found in any book on the topic, the treatment within the chapters certainly will not. Working as series editor alongside these two enthusiasts, who have nevertheless throughout the book retained a healthy sense of realism over the needs and capacities of teachers in the limited time that they have available to them, has been for me both a pleasure and an educative experience.

Cyril Poster

Acknowledgements

We are grateful to a very large number of people. Our daily working lives bring us into contact with the processes of change and the need for change. Each person we meet at work contributes something to our perceptions and experiences of the change process, schools and nurseries, children, parents and many others. The situations we have written are real but contain experiences from more than one source so that no individual or school can find themselves portrayed here.

We would like to thank colleagues in Nottingham, Southwark, Essex and the Institute of Education, with particular mention of colleagues in the various Educational Psychology Services. Of course, our colleagues and employers bear no responsibility for the content of this book.

Among the many whose work has been especially valuable, Kath, Jonathan, Cathy and Sarah have made a particular contribution. Our illustrator, Christine, has been magnificent. Cyril our editor has given us plenty of detailed advice which has always brought improvement and Helen Fairlie at Routledge could not have been more helpful.

Introduction

At this stage in the late twentieth century, schools across the world face imposed and unprecedented change. Schools are uncertain about what they have to do, feel anxious about their ability to cope within tight time scales and find it difficult to allocate enough time to managing these problems effectively. At the same time expectations about the sophistication with which change will be managed and carried out have never been higher. Alongside this, incredibly competent and professional school leaders and managers are developing their own visions in relation to the education they want to see children receiving and in what form of learning culture they wish this to occur. Schools are wishing to develop and create extremely high standards for themselves towards which they continue to strive, increasingly in a context of survival in the market place of the community.

Change in such very real circumstances can be stressful and can easily lack proper personal support for the people involved. Feelings are regularly hurt and some individuals sustain long-term damage through efforts towards short-term change. Change can be both exhilarating and painful.

In this book we examine ways in which the reader can plan, and be proactive and assertive about change but at the same time we consider how this can be done while looking after the people concerned. We explore analytic areas such as evaluation and review and creative areas such as professional development, vision, and research and development. We examine leadership, the assertion of a school philosophy, how to carry out in-service training, the best ways to engage in consultation and negotiation and we look in detail at personal support and stress management. We attempt to provide a coherent framework from which major and minor change strategies can be planned and carried out, taking account of the links between objectives, policy, professional development, consultation, support and evaluation.

Some may see this book as a practical change manual like a car owner's workshop manual rather than an academic offering. We actually think that this is a psychology book. It might not look like one, but it is. We have attempted to use our shared experiences of change at individual pupil, family, school and local education authority levels to produce a book we hope will be informative but above all practical. The book reflects our own interest as educational psychologists in the way change at a whole-school level can have massive implications for individual pupils, parents and teachers and can bring about profound change even to those with highly complex difficulties.

Our jobs in the education system involve us on a daily basis in the processes of change: for children, for adults, for organisations and for ourselves. Our profession is arguably one of the most interesting and challenging in education because we have studied and work daily to produce change, even in extremely difficult situations and circumstances. The problems of others are our challenges. If we had no knowledge of the processes of change and simply had to record what we saw, our jobs would be among the least rewarding and most boring in education, and voyeuristic too. We started to look at the processes of change for our own interest and day-to-day needs and this book is the result.

Although we have rooted the book firmly in psychological theory and practice, we have tried to write it as a practical guide for schools, as a psychology book for educationalists. We feel there is a great need for guidance in this area to liberate the creativity latent in schools without the need for an academic or bureaucratic style or procedure. There is nothing very complicated about change; it is simply that the area has seldom been explored in terms that are practical, useful and accessible to teachers.

We take the reader through and beyond a structure of the change process which may not feel unfamiliar. Where are we now? Where do we want to go? How might we get there? What did we achieve? and How much change can we stand? We suggest that readers do not have to read this book from cover to cover but may simply dip into those sections most relevant to their particular needs. We have tried to make the chapters stand alone in their own right as well as link up in the *Gestalt* of the whole book, one consequence of which has been the necessary repetition of certain key ideas. If the reader is pushed for time we particularly recommend chapters 4, 5, 7, 10 and 11. We feel that the book gets more exciting the further you read into it, but you will have to judge for yourself.

The process of change has been the subject of many amusing tales, not least when it goes wrong. One favourite is the French comic novel *Clochemerle* (Chevalier 1955). This describes life in a sleepy, picturesque, happy French village, where life goes on in its own way much as it always has. The only minor dissatisfaction in this blissful community relates to the disgraceful state of its *pissoir*, a reeking, disgusting, medieval, unhygienic eyesore that all agree should long since have been replaced.

At long last the municipality funds a replacement, modern, hygienic, spacious and pleasing to the eye. Alas, the method of conducting affairs proves to be so lamentable and the potential for conflict in the community so considerable that the village becomes polarised over the issue of its precise location. Vicious divisions appear in this micro-society and the book ends with the blowing up of the new building.

Many innovators have felt that their projects have ended the same way as in the Clochemerle situation, with the destruction of something that was meant to be and was agreed to be of benefit to all. Innovators will often become the target at which all the tensions of an organisation strike. It hardly matters what the merits of the scheme might be. A psychologist might say that individuals with problems will try to project them on to others. We find it interesting that change is the focus of humour; but too much humour directed at change attempts may begin to sound like a defence mechanism against insecurity, very much a short-term and unproductive strategy. The processes described in this book will help to avoid replicating the Clochemerle scenario. That is where the psychology comes in and where we begin.

Chapter 1

Why change now?

'Mustn't grumble' was the most English of expressions. English patience was mingled inertia and despair. What was the use? . . . In America you were admired for getting ahead, elbowing forward, rising, pushing in. In England this behaviour was hated.

(Theroux, 1983: 15)

In this chapter we look at reasons for change and attitudes towards change which will help to sustain the change process.

While positive attitudes are commonly promoted as helpful or necessary to innovation, we attempt to look at attitudes towards change in a number of ways, from several angles, in depth and at a number of levels. As a result, the chapter is one that can be returned to a number of times and reflected upon, or it can be sampled parallel to later chapters which relate even more directly to action.

As individuals or groups may like or find it advantageous to depict themselves as conservative or radical, so we find that a school's attitude to change says something important about that school. In exploring the change processes and how a school might address them, deep issues about the essence of the school, what it is and what it does, can be addressed in a purposeful rather than a theoretical way.

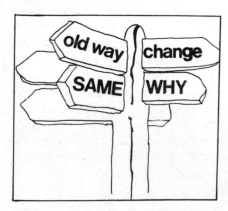

Why change now?

Living in the UK, we find this especially revealing and personally valuable. The novelist and travel writer, Paul Theroux, picked on a particularly English phrase: 'Mustn't grumble', used in answer to any enquiry like 'How are you?' Theroux found this irritating: a confusion between the need to speak and think positively and the need to acknowledge and face up to problems, producing a fatalistic, inactive view that, while things could be better, we have to comment on what the world does to us, not to make things happen. This is the opposite of being realistic about problems and positive in trying to work out ways forward; Theroux's grouse was that the English avoided acknowledging or specifying problems so that they did not have to try to devise solutions.

While you go through this book, and at the end, consider how this applies to your school. You may wish to find a phrase that expresses your school's reply to a 'How are you?' that is not a 'Mustn't grumble'.

RADICAL, CONSERVATIVE OR DON'T KNOW?

Change of some kind is a fundamental part of human existence. People grow and develop; they age and they die. Some aspects of human existence seem to have extraordinary stability. Religions can be identified as continuous over thousands of years, and cultural continuity is impressive. Humans take pride in aspects of their heritage that are ancient, reflected in family trees, traditions, and music. They also forget and/or reject these things. In Britain, some people like to call themselves *conservative* which can either mean a political view or a way of defining one's overall approach to life or both. Others like to feel they are *radical*, although the specific capture of that title by a political group is something now lost in the past. Both words have the effect of expressing something basic and important about people, and many people like to define themselves by these and similar phrases. For conservatives, this may mean that they like to feel that they are solid, competent, reliable, realistic, humble in the recollection of the great achievements of previous generations. For radicals this may mean liking to feel that they are breaking new ground, exposing the weakness of the status quo, challenging, a little daring, unafraid.

There are other positions relating to people's feelings about change, society and themselves. These can be interesting and complex. Some people can swing between two positions, indeed from extreme to extreme. Some people like to talk radical but act conservative, others talk conservative but act radical. There are many historical examples of radical change pushed through by essentially conservative figures: Charles de Gaulle, for example. In Britain we have over the last ten years been exposed to an extremely radical but supremely conservative government and our education system is still reeling from a number of imposed 'reforms'.

BREAKING THE HABIT . . .

Humans also settle into habits which can be limiting and store up long-term problems and contradictions. We like our routines but if we stick to them closely over a period of time we can become dissatisfied and bored. For some of our clients, anxieties have limited their lives to very set routines for themselves and their families; moving forward requires specific changes in behaviour to be made, usually in small steps, but steps which really will be taken and lead somewhere, together with a high level of reassurance to manage the anxiety.

Organisations and people need to address the issue of change to avoid settling into patterns of behaviour which may be comfortable and effective short-term, but may prove to be limiting and unhelpful over a longer time scale. A common belief in educational circles is that what is needed is more – usually more resources – if change is to occur successfully. However it is patently clear that more of the same can have the reverse effect leading to a maintenance of the problem or of the status quo. For instance, a child who is demanding a lot of attention may not be helped by being provided with ever longer counselling sessions after every incident or misdemeanour. When children receive more and more attention they may get worse because they actually enjoy this outcome. More, in this case, has the reverse effect. More of the same is thus not always the most effective approach to change. We may like to feel that we are dealing effectively with the real world but are we?

Our view is that in any change situation we need systematic, formal methods to ensure that we really are changing, developing or growing, and can show real progress which can be backed by resource changes.

At a group level, attitudes to change can reflect individual positions and contradictions. Our own profession of educational psychology has been depicted as talking radical but acting conservative (Quicke, 1982). A team one of us worked in once decided to dress conservatively in order to act more effectively as radicals. For individuals and groups, many positions and permutations are possible. Because of the variety in possible positions, addressing the change process effectively is a matter of concentrating on behavioural change. Changes in expressed attitudes will be interesting in their own right, but most valuable when behavioural change has been initiated. Development can be sustained as new and creative ways of thinking emerge and are applied.

Thus it can be counter-productive to give people your marvellous scenarios for their future. They need to be involved in the thinking through and planning of the changes so that they have the opportunity to react, then understand the need for change and then adapt to the future necessities. It is very easy to think that because you have worked through the issues and come up with a good solution, other people need only to accept the rightness of the solution and do not need to go through the thinking process.

(Hawkins and Shohet, 1989: 145)

Examining the process of change and reasons for and against changes is an activity that is fascinating and never to be completed. For the purposes of this book, some grasp of the practical processes of change for educational organisations, principally schools, is provided, together with some reference to broader perspectives. We start by looking at how the process of change is perceived, how it is construed.

SURVIVING THE DAY OR MOVING FORWARD?

It is naturally hard to consider innovation when the effort to keep things as they are is immense. Running hard in order to stand still is a valuable metaphor for how many of us feel and have to act. Pressures of this kind can be a feature of our own work and there are specific additional sources of stress which can affect the helping professions (see chapters 10 and 11). It is important not to undervalue past achievements or procedures that have been inherited, and not to sweep them away without having effective, well-thought-out and properly piloted replacements ready. Working to produce such alternatives at the same time as running hard to stand still is a daunting prospect.

The first stage in thinking about this is critical for the stages that follow. Adopting the philosophy that any system that involves immense stress to maintain the status quo is probably in decline or has serious malfunctions is liberating. Another liberating perception is that there are likely to be diminishing returns on high pressure work that is not regularly reappraised. Hard work and stress are quite distinct, but the harder an organisation makes people work, and the more stress they are experiencing, the more important it becomes to allocate time to consideration of the change process. Chapter 4 gives advice about the basic mechanism of change, but it is best to start with a consideration in some detail of why changes might be made.

We find it valuable to look at the reasons why people or organisations decide they want to adopt changes and at the reasons they give for wanting to change at a particular time.

The most basic decision of all is to decide whether to react or to proact, whether to devote most or all resources to surviving the day, or to planning to create better days. Will we allow events to change us? Will we be the initiators of change? Or what balance between the two will we seek?

PROACTING AND REACTING: WORTHWHILE ACHIEVEMENT OR GETTING BY?

The publications of Peters and his co-authors (1988; and Waterman, 1982; and Austin, 1985) and Peters (1982, 1985, 1988) are valuable sources for asserting that change is a natural and important part of an organisation. Peters argues a case for change in general and types of changes in particular to originate from within organisations in preference to reacting to external pressures.

Reacting quickly and effectively is something we all have to do. However, organisations which have effective innovation as a core activity will approach a situation in which reactive work is managed well, crises are infrequent, much of the activity is positive, planned and successful and quality of work is defended and maintained. The employees find their work leads to greater achievement and becomes more rewarding. People are on top of their jobs because the demands made on them are reasonable and part of a well designed, well run system.

At first sight, some of these points about proacting may seem obvious but we feel they are well worth looking at in detail. Peters (1988):

> gives a high priority to a change strategy which empowers employees at a basic level in the organisation;
> sees learning to love change, empowering workers, fast-paced inno-vation, and responsiveness as essential for survival in a fast moving world;
> focuses on quality.

We find Peters to be an excellent guide to certain aspects of the change process. He cites and describes organisations which pursue quality objectives yet also have great capacity for responsiveness. This approach is largely but not wholly rooted in the business sector, although Peters does cite some public sector examples. We feel that exploring in detail the reasons for adopting change as central to organisational planning and practice is essential for educationalists. Educational progress must be towards the highest possible quality, yet the need for effective evaluation, appraisal, optimal use of resources, may lead to the widespread and insensitive use of quantitative measures. This would be ironic at a time when attention to quality has seldom if ever been so salient in the business management literature with developments such as the quality circle in Western businesses based on successful Japanese experience (Hutchins, 1985). Since the rise of Japan as a leading industrial power, organisation theorists and managers have looked much closer at not only the issue of quality but also the links between management and culture.

> Gradually, but with increasing force, through the 1970s the performance of Japanese automobile, electronics, and other manufacturing industries . . . began to take command of international markets,

establishing a solid reputation for quality, reliability, value, and service.
(Morgan, 1986: 111)

Devotion to quality and responsibility to the public are at the core of accepting and promoting change strategies in education. High quality relationships and experiences are essential conditions for a successful school. Because schooling involves such a high number of interactions daily, keeping the quality of those contacts rewarding has to be addressed; quality is thus even more important in education.

We emphasise that change for its own sake or for the sake of appearing to be 'doing something' is not useful and is inefficient. It can also be, and be seen to be, critical of and punitive to the teachers and other workers. Peters firmly asserts the disadvantages of change in these circumstances. In contrast, giving all teachers and others in schools the security, encouragement, guidance and resource priority to pilot innovation successfully is the starting point for developing the unrealised potential of schools. Allied to this should be the real commitment to quality which teachers bring to the profession and which can be squeezed out of them by poor quality management or conditions.

Reactive modes of operating will fail to use much or most of the human potential of the school, and staff will feel and be undervalued. We now see how a school can start to look at the processes of change.

Which of these arguments for seeking change best applies to your school?

The world is a chaotic place; change now or your survival is unlikely. YES/NO

Changes in technology dictate changes for humans
(the computer says we have to . . .). YES/NO

Others are changing, change is essential to compete effectively (the school down the road has just produced a glossy brochure . . .) YES/NO

Parents, politicians and central administrators can be fickle; we have to have something for them to retain their loyalty. YES/NO

Our examination results are going to be published by law, so we have to make them as good as possible, certainly better than our competitors. YES/NO

If your YES score is zero for your school, read on cheerfully. If you scored even one YES for your school, also read on cheerfully, but make sure that you really take on board the positive reasons for change which follow to replace the negative ones above. We will see later in more detail how important the examination of the reasons for change in an individual school can be. Effective proacting is dependent on positive ideas from which specific goals can be derived.

The reasons listed above may be valid, but they are of limited value in promoting innovation and are inadequate as motivators. In addition, they can be construed negatively by others. Such reasons can foster defeatism and a sense of helplessness, which are obstacles to effective change strategies.

We believe that you will be able to look at the positive reasons for change that we list below, adapt them and apply them to your school and use them to empower your staff, to revitalise their commitment to quality and to develop their potential and your own to the full. You can of course add your own.

Are you changing the system or is the system changing you?

Positive reasons for change

- innovation can and should be interesting and exciting
- change creates more choice for individuals as consumers and as workers
- change can foster personal and professional development
- change brings different and more varied personal groupings to the workplace
- change helps keep things in proportion
- change encourages action research and helps integrate academic study and daily practice
- change creates confidence
- change can highlight the core strengths, ethics, skills and attributes which make up the school's ethos
- change is consistent with a tolerance of diversity, individual, cultural and organisational
- change can produce exponential payoffs from resource allocation
- change can help individuals in career progress
- change attracts interest and attention
- successful innovation usually takes time, so change can foster coherence and a sense of purpose, of working towards shared goals

We would like you to extend this list with respect to your own position and that of your school. When you have done this, check the positive reasons for change discussed later in this chapter, including those considered by 'Marion'. This is not a test, just an illustration of how easy it can be to miss fundamentals if personal space is not reserved for real consideration of issues. Naturally, there can be advanced many other arguments in favour of change and the application to schools in particular.

When you have considered additions to the list, we ask that you look through your new positive list of reasons for change and begin to plan how these and others might apply to your school. With a grasp of positive reasons for change, it is possible to begin to look forward from the day-to-day routine and the pressures that we have to deal with, towards achievable and worthwhile goals. As already mentioned, an agenda for change puts you and your school nearer the centre of the process rather than in a peripheral position, relatively powerless to influence what happens.

With these more positive views of why change is desirable, managers in education can begin to spread a little optimism among themselves and to the rest of the staff, and optimism is contagious. Optimistic attitudes add great strength to any organisation and can be communicated to all who are part of or connected to the school, especially the children. Indeed, childhood should be a time of optimism, realistically based; and one essential place to learn and to value optimism is in school. Reasons for doing things that are short-term and opportunistic are especially unhelpful for children; realistic but positive attitudes are important benefits in the school's hidden curriculum. These can be beliefs about people and their needs and rights, about having responsibility for one's own learning and development, working well with others and setting and reaching worthwhile goals.

THE BASICS: PROACTIVE CHANGE AND REACTIVE CHANGE

We feel that the most important resource in any organisation is its people and we feel even more strongly that this is the case in schools. This important resource is better targeted towards positive outcomes than taken up with responding when matters go wrong or need to be done immediately.

Reacting means that the people in schools are spending their time devising and trying to implement responses to others. These responses may be worked out on a case-by-case, event-by-event basis or taken from an existing repertoire of habits or by some combination of the two.

Proacting means that the school is devising and implementing positive plans. As schools have to devote a high percentage of adult time to direct teaching, the most important steps in setting out on the path to proacting are the allocation of time and the decisions about objectives.

We find it helpful to discuss planning for change and time allocation issues with some simple visual representation available. Pie charts are often used but we suggest that you begin by using a time allocation curve. The time allocation curve is frequently found in macro-and micro-economics and applied to resources other than time.

The reason we suggest schools begin in this way is that this kind of curve was and is widely used in economics to express changes within fixed resources, and to express difficult resource choice decisions. Although time allocation changes can be less of a problem in successful organisations as the use of time becomes effective, we like schools to start here, remembering that time is limited and humans are not inexhaustible. Change takes energy and can create new pressures; it does not have to create unreasonable or unplanned pressures nor always be an impossible or even substantial additional burden on our time. The curve is in a box with a fixed boundary; our assumption is that innovation will be conducted within existing work time. Other representations such a pie charts are compatible with unspoken assumptions about time being elastic and the size of the pie being changed. Until innovation has been piloted successfully we advise schools to use nothing more sophisticated than the curve in the box.

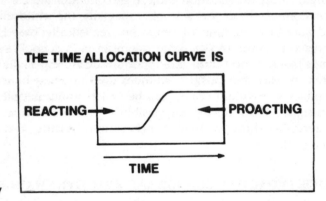

Figure 1.1

The shape of the curve is gradual at first, then steep and finally eases off to become flatter. The school plans to innovate initially in small steps, then the pace of change grows quickly, then the innovations are given time to produce their full positive effects in a period of consolidation, evaluation and relative relaxation. We see this representation as a helpful one in how we think about the change process; when we are discussing reasons for change it is helpful to have depicted change as smooth, planned, and with changes of pace. In the real world, life is never smooth, but good planning can help to create some steadiness in the turmoil, without avoidance of real issues.

In the school situation this type of curve has a clear logic, and depicts change as initially modest in its use of resources. Suddenly diverting resources away from reactive activities will produce crises. Equally, diverting resources towards proactive initiatives suddenly may produce a poor return because:

the school may not yet have identified its core strengths with precision and consensus;
the school may not be able to develop or apply the necessary skills at this stage – new skills cannot be acquired and applied effectively overnight.

Suddenly changing what is required of the staff will not only put stress on them but will make only a few of them the focus of the change process. Creating an ethos of innovation and sustained change requires the involvement of everyone.

If the quality of teaching in the classroom is to be enhanced, then headteachers must provide practical as well as intellectual and moral support and promote a climate in which teachers themselves can take ownership of and responsibility for innovation in practice.

(Day *et al.* 1990: 135)

The initially cautious move towards a positive mode of thinking and away from reactive thinking reflects the need to maintain all that is working well before new procedures and projects are introduced or running effectively. This means that limited piloting is undertaken before much time is committed. It should also mean that those who are most involved in the innovations are not given sudden substantial increases in expected performance and are not expected to carry the organisation while others disclaim responsibility. Effective innovation does not put the most enthusiastic workers in exposed and overworked positions.

We now examine a situation which may be common; we look at some basic issues, and at some that are less evident at first sight.

Situation 1:1

Marion is in a middle-management post in a high school for pupils aged 11 to 16. She is responsible for the pastoral care of 200 children aged 14. In practice this means that she does some counselling of children she believes to be troubled, acts as the lead person on formal occasions such as assemblies, refers children to support agencies, and tries to make sure that staff complete and collate reports within specified constraints: time, level of detail and style. Her post has many other aspects which arise from her being perceived as the person responsible for the 200 children and their schooling, and many other tasks fall to Marion.

To fulfil these functions, Marion receives a salary enhancement of about 20 per cent and her post is generally regarded as an important stepping stone towards promotion to a senior management post.

Marion has a team of seven teachers assigned to act as class tutors, with one additional teacher who usually substitutes for any teacher absent or late. Only one of these teachers is paid anything additional for this responsibility and this amounts to an enhancement of 10 per cent. The eight teachers Marion leads have been assigned to their tutor role as part of the timetabling of the school with little if any time for consultation with them about this role. They vary widely in age, experience and attitude, although nobody in their first year of teaching becomes a tutor. Marion has eight 40-minute periods a week when she does not teach, and is able to meet her team for 20 minutes weekly in school time.

Marion is just about coping and is not enjoying her work. The problem that is giving Marion many sleepless nights is simply that the 200 pupils for whom she is responsible behave badly for a number of teachers across the school. Three of her form tutors have serious problems managing their classes as well as their tutor groups and two of these teachers seem often to be absent or late.

When pupils behave badly, teachers either send them to Marion or send for her. Either action disrupts her own lessons. In addition, Marion finds that most teachers, other than some of the younger ones, do not seem to be very grateful for her help in dealing with behaviour problems. Marion finds that teachers regularly come up to her in the staff common room and criticise the behaviour of the children for whom she is responsible. They go on at such length that Marion feels herself to be criticised on behalf of the children she is responsible for, and regards this as very unfair. She tries hard to help and feels that staff might occasionally show some gratitude for her efforts. She spends a lot of time following up other people's problems and feels that her own lessons are consequently not as good as they used to be. She finds it hard to complete other tasks in school and has to take a great deal of work home.

Senior managers in the school seem unimpressed or openly critical of the way things are going. Some of the heads of department in the school have said at meetings that Marion's children are poorly controlled and the deputy head has said that there are complaints from parents who say that she always accepts the teachers' version of events without listening to the child. Other parents are reported to have said that they are thinking of transferring their children to a school where the classes are better behaved.

The situation described is of a teacher behaving reactively, within a school system which is also reactive. Sadly, we think that this kind of situation may be found quite frequently in schools for children of all ages. It would be all too easy to list negative, reactive reasons for seeking change in this situation.

Such negative reasons might be:

• Marion's lessons are being disrupted

- staff seem to blame Marion for the problems she tries to solve for them
- the same problems occur regularly
- parents are reported to be complaining
- colleagues have voiced criticism at meetings
- Marion is having to take too much work home
- staff in the school as a whole, and in Marion's team in particular, seem to be absent a lot or late
- Marion is finding her post unrewarding.

Many other negative reasons could easily be imagined in this scenario to give good grounds for the introduction of changes. It might help Marion to realise that teachers are projecting on to her their own stress and that is why she herself feels so stressed. This explanation might enable her to see the situation differently and more creatively. She might conclude that change was required to reduce the stress on herself and her colleagues and to reduce her visibility as a convenient receptacle for their stress. These reasons would be valid. However, we do not believe such reasons should be central in seeking to change because they are neither positive nor proactive. They have a limited scope and vision.

This need not mean simply asserting the power of positive thinking. We believe that positive thinking is valuable and try to think positively ourselves; but, in a difficult situation, where people are feeling that they are putting in a lot of effort for little reward, exhortation alone may well be perceived as less than helpful. In chapter 11 we study ways of looking after ourselves and the management of stress during change processes; at the present stage, we explore positive reasons for change at two levels. The first is the level referred to above, the adoption of a positive mode without any further exploration.

Before Marion looks at the kind of strategy that would begin to improve matters and examines how her personal skills and energy could be applied proactively and most productively, we list some of the positive reasons for promoting change she might consider.

Such positive reasons might be:

- Marion wants her own lessons to run smoothly. This will begin to give a model to the children, teachers and parents of the standards that can and should be attained. It will also enhance her personal reputation. In addition, lesson continuity will be more likely to be seen as important. Marion has rightly been critical of those on her team who are absent with minor ailments, yet her own behaviour has been to disrupt the continuity of her own teaching in reacting to every problem.
- She wants to work on non-teaching tasks systematically and to do them well. This means working out a strategy for ensuring that priorities are established so that essential paperwork, discussion and planning is done

within a set time and that routines for monitoring pupil progress and behaviour are established and maintained.

- She wants to relax in her break times and to enjoy them.
- She wants to have friendly and co-operative dealings with colleagues on the staff.
- She wants parents to support the school.
- She wants the children to do well in school and to go on to college where possible.
- She would like to learn more about counselling and to promote the application of counselling within the school.
- She wants to enjoy her job and to help other teachers enjoy teaching too.
- She would like to give encouragement and support to children, many of whom may have serious problems out of school.
- She would like to move into a senior management position in the future, ideally in three to four years.
- She would like to help new teachers.
- She would like to develop more leisure activities out of school and to build personal relationships.
- Above all, she would like her work to be appreciated and would like some appreciation and support herself.

These and many uncomplicated but positive reasons will lead to more rewarding activities and to greater success. They represent a first step forward in thinking usefully about sustainable change. They will help Marion to think more creatively and to have a sense of purpose and achievement. They allow for agreement that change is necessary and hence positive, but are limited in working out directions for change and may not promote much of a consensus. We might agree that change is desirable but have different views about the direction in which to move. Thus we give a limited role to such reasons. We find that many people try to follow the exhortation to be positive yet would benefit from exploring the implications of this in more depth.

These positive reasons can also be developed to a second and more fundamental level. Many of the reasons for change listed above relate to personal and professional fulfilment. Others relate to a desire to help people. These positive reasons go to the heart of why Marion and so many teachers enter the profession in the first place, usually accepting worse working conditions and lower lifelong earnings than in comparable fields.

Above all, these positive reasons begin to express the constructs that Marion shares with her colleagues on the staff, even or perhaps especially those who appear to be critical of her. Exploration of this level will begin the process of establishing real consensus, not over details but of mutual concern to work at a highly professional standard (Pope and Keen, 1981).

Shared constructs are fundamental in seeking to solve problems, to relate on a person-to-person level and to further one's own fulfilment and that of the group. Exploration at this level opens up many creative opportunities, especially in improving the human side of the organisation. As schooling is concerned with humans, intensively so, these opportunities are particularly valuable for schools. What is especially useful at the start of a change cycle is the shared construct that each human brings assets to a situation and the best outcome is obtained by developing those assets and applying them fully. Such a perception is likely to promote an equal opportunities ethos in the school; seeing people as assets is not easily compatible with institutional racism, sexism or other discrimination and is certainly incompatible with personal racism or sexism.

Expressing and sharing constructs about personal and professional growth may sound a formidable task and it is dealt with at some length later: developing and asserting a school philosophy in a changing world is dealt with in chapter 10.

Readers may have been habituated by society at large and by the organisational culture of their school either to be cynical or, perhaps more insidiously, to become overawed and to assume that such approaches must require years of complicated study. It could also give rise to assumptions that one can confront colleagues with sensitive, fundamental issues and expect them to be on the same wavelength.

As psychologists we recognise these levels but increasingly find that schools new to us are often able to take on change effectively and without fuss. Their needs are for practical starting methods and for follow-up and support to sustain and develop the innovations. They also often need strategies to identify and deal with their own negative feelings: we deal with issues of resistance to change in chapter 10.

The time allocation curve and the view of change as a process of variable momentum, beginning slowly, takes account of these issues, giving a cautious start to an important process which can be sustained.

Positive reasons need a positive context

Look back at the positive reasons for change that Marion could be considering privately, to improve her own satisfaction with teaching and educational management. How could they be perceived by others? How might she share them with others?

You will soon come to realise that it is not really feasible to put these forward reactively, in response to some incident, without making them seem less positive. The context of proposals is an important element in how they are interpreted and received.

An innocuous phrase such as 'wanting to have friendly and co-operative dealings with colleagues on the staff' could be interpreted as 'I like people who don't come to me with problems, and I don't much like people who do' if articulated in the context of requests for help or problem-solving. In this kind of context, a colleague who is already feeling stressed may feel criticised in addition, and is likely to become more resistant to Marion's proposals as a result. We mentioned earlier how Marion was having other people's stress projected on to her; comments of this kind can project her stress on to others. Positive proposals are best initiated with their own timetable and with consideration of the strategies to adopt.

In an organisation that is only just coping and in which there are some difficult professional and perhaps personal relationships, habits of attributing actions to cynical motives are probably common. For Marion to propose an in-service session on positive behaviour management might seem to her helpful. The planners of Clochemerle had similar positive intentions. Her proposal might be interpreted as implicit criticism of colleagues, as an abdication of responsibility, as an admission that she cannot control children or in a number of very negative ways. Working out a programme which covers a range of essential professional skills, which will be delivered over a cycle, which will be of a very high standard and which will be piloted in favourable conditions will help to avoid some of this negative attribution.

Shared constructs and shared change

Moving forward is best achieved by beginning the process of using the human resources available to address positive issues and by looking at the human resources in positive terms. This is the first step to more fundamental levels. Marion's positive reasons for change begin to express her core philosophy, to say something about herself, her choice of career, what she knows she once found satisfying. Yet they begin to provide areas in which short-term, small-step objectives can be worked out quite easily. They also give clues as to how to begin the process of building a consensus for progress and change, and can be easily and precisely related to a system of time allocation.

This can begin to link daily concerns and progress with the examination of the development of ethos and organisational culture (Sarason, 1982; Gordon 1984). There is a fascinating literature in this field which attempts to identify what positive organisational culture consists of, how it can be developed and maintained, and how theories of psychology can be applied to these processes (Morgan, 1986). Without discouraging anyone from exploring these and other valuable texts, we like colleagues in schools to have made clear practical progress from the basic principles of the change process as a preparation for study. One innovation successfully achieved is a rewarding experience adding more motivation and skill; referring to the literature at this stage after some practical experience of promoting change will be especially valuable. Working with others to achieve some progress allows the sharing of constructs about education in the light of joint success and effort.

How might Marion begin on these processes to best effect? As the original reasons why Marion herself sought change were largely negative, it is likely that her colleagues, the management, parents and children could start from the same negative premises. A strategy is needed to translate these negative reasons to embark on a process into positive terms.

One at a time

Marion identifies the colleague – or manager, or child, or parent, but we will start with a team member – who is most likely to share specific constructs. Marion might ask her team who was interested in counselling. She might try to elicit individual responses rather than superficial and largely negative 'groupthink' by asking people individually or right at the end of a meeting or in writing. When a colleague responds, an individual, planned discussion could be set up to explore positive reasons to learn more about counselling and to promote its development throughout the school.

All at once

Marion starts to introduce her positive reasons for change through the regular team meetings. She should do this if she is confident that no team member will deliberately heckle the process. She will need to practise what she preaches; what she does is more important than what she says. She will need to articulate a philosophy of education but to link this with specific actions and decisions.

Springboarding

Marion sets up a more lengthy meeting, elicits negative reasons for change, then has the meeting define the opposites or polarities to the negative reasons. This way the negative reasons act as the springboard to identifying positive reasons. Although this may miss some of the deeper reasons for change, it is a useful place to start.

Reflecting back

Marion listens to some of the negative reasons for change people are articulating. She then defines the opposites or polarities herself and devises positive targets that are thereby useful to her colleagues and consistent with their thinking. Somewhere in what is being said is some genuine information about what is going wrong.

Empathy

Marion tries to imagine how others feel: the teachers who come late to work, the ones who moan at her during break. She considers what their feelings are and translates them into opposite positives. She decides to meet them regularly to discuss strategies and concerns, and then insists on a grumble-free break time, as much for them as for her. They have not been helped when they start back to lessons after a break time with negative emotional perceptions and feelings swirling around inside, likely to be projected on to the next class.

Consultancy

Marion asks an outsider with whom she shares trust to advise her and her team on positive reasons for change. This may involve an exercise to identify shared constructs, to team-build, to set precise and realistic targets, to identify assets more clearly, to start processes of action research or team teaching.

The hierarchy

Marion discusses positive reasons for change either with new teachers or with her deputy. Precise objectives are worked out, time allocation is agreed and resource allocation is made according to progress along the critical path to the objectives. A key feature of this is that those senior in the hierarchy pilot the changes themselves and have high profile work directly with children, taking on the most difficult situations.

All of the above strategies can be used quickly, efficiently and pleasantly, but picking the best strategy is not something anyone can do for you. With a team that is generally well-meaning, Marion could use the direct approach or springboarding; with a more difficult or demoralised team, Marion could use empathy or one-at-a-time.

Although this chapter looks at reasons for change rather than at the details of change strategies or objectives, we would like to give just one or two quite obvious examples of how Marion's reconsideration of reasons for change from largely negative to largely positive reasons might have worked out.

Marion wants to relax in her break times:

- She decides to set up a cakes rota with her team and they eat them during a break time.
- She decides to sit outside on a school bench when the weather is nice and talk to the pupils or to friends on the staff.
- She tells the office staff that she will be taking phone calls only at the end of the afternoon and that they should take messages when calls come

during break time. Problems with pupils or organisation at break time go to the teacher in charge at these times, not to Marion.

- Once a week, she decides to treat herself to an exotic snack.
- She sits next to team members at break time and chats to them about social events out of school.

You will see that Marion is proacting even in her relaxation. She has decided to relax as a positive series of measures and strategies. She involves others in almost every instance, opening up social opportunities and opportunities to discuss ways forward, breaking down barriers. Children will also see her as available for purely social talk and will see her and her teacher colleagues as friendly and mutually supportive.

Had she looked at relaxing as the avoidance of interruption, most of the focus would have been on the way interruptions prevented her from really relaxing. We all want to be left alone on occasions, but that is not the same as relaxing. With her positive strategy, Marion is spreading the message that she can be relaxed and content with pupils and colleagues and on top of her responsibilities.

Most of the changes are easy and quite superficial. What will change the way matters go in the future is the adoption of a model of change like the one in the time allocation curve. The initial changes noted above are not the whole of nor even particularly important parts of the change process, merely the first small steps of a much more fundamental process. They are rewarding for all concerned: creating a more rewarding work environment is a good way of preparing for more positive and purposeful discussion of changes for the future. Another important element in moving to sustained, cumulative, effective change is the articulation of a philosophy of education – what we are trying to achieve and why – and seeing the change process as something to follow systematically over time, perhaps a cycle of three years.

Perhaps the most important element in moving towards deeper reasons for pursuing positive change strategies is the exploration of a school's understanding of what it means by education. Fostering learning, development, personal growth and success are all central to a definition of education. The further a school goes in developing precision about its own aims and skills in helping children, the more easily will it be able to apply those skills and follow those aims in developments for the adults.

Considering positive reasons for change on a number of levels will help schools start to implement change effectively; how to proceed is covered in later chapters. Creating positive attitudes towards change will help considerably in implementing the advice provided later.

Most of the changes noted above are at the first, more superficial level of those which will take a school forward. Beginning to open up areas of discussion and work will lead to exploration of deeper levels as progress is made, aiming to build on the initial steps. Examining positive reasons for change will also assist in setting achievable goals: more about that in later chapters.

We feel that promoting change for positive reasons will help bring about a new sense of realism that will go far beyond the immediate issues of the school, but that is something you will need to discover for yourselves.

Learning and changing

Exploring constructs about change and reasons for change will begin the process of looking at what a school means by and understands by the concept of education. There are many models of the change process in organisations and many theories about change in individuals and groups of various sizes. However, for a school it is highly appropriate to start with a model of education, applying this equally to the teaching process and to the organisation's development. This means that the model of education for a school is clearly articulated, reviewed, amended, applied and researched.

How Marion proceeds with innovation, with moving from a reactive stance to a proactive one, might be considerably different depending on the educational philosophy or paradigm of the school in which she works. In a school which sees the purpose of education as the imparting of received knowledge the reasons for change and the tactics of change might be primarily derived from management literature, with an emphasis on specified roles and responsibilities. A school which owed more to progressive ideas might adopt a joint problem-solving approach such as that described by Aubrey (1988). A school that looks in detail at applications of personal construct theory (Kelly, 1955) to counselling might want to explore relative views of the situation and possible changes (Pope and Keen, 1981). This might lead to specific exercises, such as triangulation: looking at perceptions from three points of view. In a school that is very achievement-oriented rather than pastorally-or humanistically-oriented, target-setting might be the more suitable major strategy.

We have looked in much more detail than is usual at reasons for initiating change and have attempted to show how a teacher in a difficult situation could revise her thinking about change to help her to become more creative, more imaginative and more fulfilled personally and professionally. The initial reasons for change may have seemed well thought out but provided only one starting point for thinking about change at successively deeper and more productive levels. We believe that it is possible to link the practice of a school in its teaching approaches to the development of strategies for change at an organisational level.

We assert that many types of educational processes could be applied directly and successfully to an organisation. A grasp of personal construct theory could be particularly revealing (Kelly, 1955) and helpful in setting positive goals that express the way people see and understand situations and themselves. While a variety of models of education can be used, as schooling is an activity that necessitates intensive human interaction, drawing on or at least having some basic knowledge of insightful, humanistic theories and techniques will be helpful.

There are also many techniques that can be called upon to begin to develop creative potential (Adams, 1986). Perhaps the best known of these is brainstorming. We have chosen to focus on the starting point of expressing positive reasons for change, and, once these and positive attitudes towards the change process have been established, then specific techniques can be called upon productively. We do not feel that such techniques are quite as essential for schools as for other organisations, given that schools already have and can further develop expertise in processes of learning and development. We find that the resources of creativity unlocked through positive tasks such as brainstorming can be followed with and for children as well as at an adult level, so schools can become quite expert in their use. One example of an activity to help organisational creativity is well described by Hawkins and Shohet (1989):

> It is possible to ask staff to carry out a guided fantasy in which they travel forward in time, one, two, or even five years. In this fantasy they can look at what is then happening . . . within the whole organization, their part of it, and also in the wider environment that impinges on them. What will be different? What conditions will they have had to adapt to? Will they still be with the organization? Sometimes groups find it helpful to produce both positive and negative scenarios of their future. The material can then be worked on with brainstorming and problem solving techniques creatively to produce an action strategy that is owned by the key staff whose energy and commitment will have to make it happen.
>
> (Hawkins and Shohet, 1989: 151)

Positive thinking and positive action

The process of thinking positively about change goes beyond exhortation, and the need to set objectives for action is something we see as a core requirement of the change process. What teachers ought to remember after they retire or on social occasions should be the achievements and changes they were associated with, not the daily problems, however difficult the basic conditions may have been. Discussions have to be reflected in action to give any sense of achievement.

There are many alternative explanations for change or lack of change and there is a helpful and detailed literature referring to organisations and their social psychology (Katz and Kahn, 1978). An essential point is to be aware of broader perspectives but not to substitute this for looking positively at change short-term.

There are associated areas which are not central to the theme of this book which have valuable additional information to complement the core innovation strategies we cover, such as assertiveness, personal effectiveness, management and leadership studies. They can be applied in the same way as the areas covered, and again the starting points are some easy piloting and processes of looking at positive reasons for change. These additional areas are relevant in themselves once the basic processes have been understood and worked through, although the basic application of an educational model should not be lost or confused. We refer briefly to one example: leadership. Kouzes and Posner (1987) see the core function of leadership as change. What leaders are remembered for, they argue, are the changes they pushed through. These are attained through the long-term visions that allowed them to pursue change consistently and enthusiastically in spite of difficulties, the pleasure they take in the change process, the genuine optimism they have about the feasibility of change and the perception of change as a team achievement. In addition, the sampling the authors conducted led to the conclusion that the leadership characteristic rated most highly by employees was honesty. Effective innovators know where their organisation is going to go, are honest about the objectives, enthusiastic and generous in building team engagement in the process of change. We now look at a parallel source of positive perceptions of the change process.

Listening to children

We are very interested in the reasons children give for improvement and change. This is an area we would recommend for schools to research themselves, for there is a great deal to be discovered. We have found useful guidance from listening to actual comments made by children and young people. Children we have talked to in our work have made a number of points, including the following:

- I behave well now because my work is a lot better.
- My work's a lot better because I made up my mind to do well.
- I'm different now, more grown up.
- I decided that I'd change and be a different person starting from my 14th birthday.

There is a large and fascinating psychological literature in this area; indeed the relationship between attitude change and behaviour change has been one of the core areas of experimental psychology this century. The reasons given for success or failure have been of particular research interest in the last twenty years with important intervention studies addressing gender differences which skew success and failure.

What might be the adult equivalents for the statements of these children in a school that has changed for the better?

- We really do some teaching now.
- There is no way we would ever settle for second best.
- The children know we're interested in them, but we have a job to do and we do it.
- These children sometimes come from tough homes or they are very poor, but we believe they can do just as well as anyone, for they are really hard workers once they have a little success.
- When we went on the study trip for a week, we had to have a rule that nobody worked after ten o' clock at night, otherwise some of them would never have stopped at all.
- Some of our best teachers are the new ones who are finding it hard to keep discipline, because they are trying to teach in ways that really interest the children and excite them, while some of us older staff go for a quiet life.

All of these comments have been heard from teachers in schools situated in areas that are as tough as any, in schools that had many positives in a difficult social context. They reflect a basic confidence that the people are assets, whatever their problems, that learning and development is a shared process, and that personal decisions to look forward positively can be turning points in personal and professional development. Such attitude changes open doors to better relationships with colleagues, children and others, place the teachers' confidence at the centre of the change process and reflect a co-operative view of achievements, rather than giving or taking credit individually. They embody the confidence that individuals can and should promote change without undue stress, and that change is best achieved in co-operation with others.

The comments of the children and of the teachers give reasons or are based on reasons for change that:

> give credit to individuals but use collective comments
> recognise positives in others
> assume excellence is the only standard worth attaining
> accept that total, fundamental change is possible
> assume that excellence can be attained in any situation and that the situation will be improved by first class work
> accept the need to learn from newcomers
> give credit to those who seem to be struggling for what they can contribute.

Above all, they reflect a successful attitude towards work completed. There is work to be done and it is being done well. We are on top of what we are doing and it is worth doing well, because it helps us realise our own potential as humans (Rogers, 1961).

In later chapters we give guidance on how to keep the desire to move forward within boundaries in order to manage and prevent stress and confusion and we look at the need for core organisational objectives. At this stage, we note that reasons for change usually and usefully relate to the core task of the individual or organisation. Perhaps Marion could begin by seeing her job in terms of children's progress rather than their behaviour, and begin to work with colleagues on a course of study and examination skills?

We also note that reasons for change when progress has been made seem to claim credit for the individual or group but seldom if ever relate progress to personnel changes. The *we* who started the process of change are the ones who have seen it through, not excluding or denigrating individuals, implicitly or implicitly blaming them for what went before. Children whose behaviour has improved seldom if ever say to us 'My behaviour has improved because the other children in the class behave better now the main trouble-maker has been expelled.' Staff in schools which have moved forward don't seem to say: 'My teaching is better because one or two bad teachers have left.'

The recruitment of high quality personnel to an organisation is a considerable bonus, but usually the starting point for innovation may be as favourable in any other school in terms of potential, although it may be worse in terms of performance. The problem is more likely to be that staff members have been deskilled and demotivated by working in a poor environment, with inappropriate leadership and management, seldom if ever that of worthless personnel. This does not rule out staff changes; it does rule out the easy answer of equating change with change of personnel.

We appreciate this is not received wisdom and we work in organisations which are immensely careful, rightly so, about whom they appoint. However, monitoring progress in the large number of schools we have visited led us to change our minds or at least reserve judgement. We found that some of the less likely candidates implemented the changes thoroughly. We found that tightly defined and worked out innovations were accepted and applied without much variation between what we saw as 'good' and 'bad' schools. This does not mean that there were no good or bad schools; it means that our attitudes towards innovation were unduly pessimistic in certain situations. Perhaps we made too many assumptions about the 'good' schools and gave them less specific guidance, and took their motivation for granted. Perhaps the thoroughness of the planning and implementation owed something to the anticipated difficulties in certain schools. Would the quality have been there in easier circumstances?

We feel that moving away from a personalised view of innovation to a universal view that everyone is capable of successful innovation strikes many chords with teachers who can relate this to their expertise in fostering the development of all children through the design of activities. The creativity of teachers in their basic work is currently an underdeveloped resource for innovation. In this chapter we have given reasons why this might be so and attempted to show how restrictive some apparently helpful reasons for change can actually be. You will see far more creativity in a system in which reasons for change are genuinely positive. We cannot think of a better, more productive activity than identifying positive reasons for change. It may take no more than a few hours a year to do this in depth, yet it will play a significant role in liberating the creativity of schools.

How is Marion doing? As a result of re-examining her reasons for wanting to change, she has introduced the following innovations:

The team treat Her team are envied for their regular leisure activities; this month they're off to a health club for the evening, for a work-out, or a sauna, or just a drink.

The support for learning policy Marion and her team went to the Special Needs Department and were helped in working out learning programmes for children and groups which they now run three days a week. They also use tutor periods to help children who are having trouble with homework or coursework. About once a month they use tutor periods to look at every child's written work in every subject, to give encouragement, help, or to give positive comments to teaching colleagues or to parents. They and the children and the parents call it the *Success First* policy.

Marion and her team are so frequently talking to children about their work that issues of behaviour seem less important. The support for learning allows Marion to predict when behavioural problems are likely to occur and to intervene before escalation occurs.

Leisure and counselling Marion and her team sit in the staffroom and have a reasonable break most days of the week if that is what they want. Any colleague with a concern can raise it with almost any team member because it really is a team. Most of the time there are few concerns raised at breaktime because Marion's positive policies have implemented positive preventative actions. Most of the time she is gently pursuing others in the staffroom to see where they have progressed to in setting appropriate work for her year, for example.

Critical friends Marion uses probationary teachers in this role for her team. She asks them to report on what she and her team are doing and asks for a long list of suggestions for improvement. Time is allocated from probationer induction for this to be done professionally. This produces excellent suggestions and gives new staff a genuinely important role in innovation in the school. They sense that problems can be worked on and that their views are important, whatever the current pressures.

Discussion She talks about real issues of stress, organisation, success and problems regularly and has house rules that these discussions focus on strategies and personalities do not come into it. They talk about best and worst experiences as a voluntary group and have begun to support each other through the worst, but spend more time celebrating the best. They are also looking at what is shared among the best experiences as a way of discussing what they most value in school.

ACTION PLAN

- Consider reasons for change in detail.
- Translate reasons for change into positive terms.
- Positive reasons for change open up issues of personal fulfilment and effectiveness and can be addressed on deeper levels. Follow these issues to deeper and valuable levels.
- Adopt an educational model of the change process.
- Start with action as well as discussion; make the time commitment specific and modest and start with easy tasks.
- Disseminate a perception of the change process as cyclical with a time scale of three years.
- Perceive the change process as necessary in seeking to realise the human potential you have, and that of others.
- Perceive people as assets and change as a co-operative process.
- Record and remember achievements.

Chapter 2

Evaluating your organisation

> Before you go on a journey, you must know where you are starting from or you will become hopelessly lost.

Evaluation is used in many contexts and with a range of shades of meaning. There is now legislation requiring British schools to publish or make available certain types of data so that the public in general and parents in particular will be able to make judgements about a school. That is one way of interpreting the word *evaluation*.

We are looking at evaluation from a different point of view: so that schools and others may decide where they are in order to select appropriate and effective ways forward. In chapter 1 we looked at attitudes towards and reasons for change; in this chapter we look at how a school can prepare to move forward.

In relation to organisational change it is crucial, before planning your next step forward, to be clear about where you are coming from and where you are at present. The process of finding out where you are is often referred to as self-appraisal or evaluation. We will be referring to just such a process and will be terming this *organisational evaluation*.

We do not see this as a bureaucratic or cumbersome task. To do so would

Evaluating and monitoring

be to delay the innovation process. We also note that there is some evidence relating to individual children that establishing a baseline prior to starting an intervention is less critical than other aspects of a positive programme, such as having a record system and follow-up discussions, to give two examples (Miller, 1989). Effective baseline definition does however ensure that the intervention is appropriate and can help to make it efficient. Similarly, evaluation is likely to be most productive if it is a part of looking ahead and moving forward. Although there are many aspects of evaluation, many potentially complex issues to consider and many levels of sophistication to delve into, the basic purpose remains to prepare for effective and smooth progress. This it will be if those assets which the organisation already has are fully recognised and applied to the change process. The most important assets are human skills, motivation and attitudes. As such, evaluation is a specific rather than a global process, looking for particular ways forward rather than pointers as to where a school might be on a 'good-bad' spectrum. While global conclusions can be sought and made, the emphasis of this chapter is on the specifics.

School reports for children have developed substantially over the last twenty years. At one stage, it was thought to be adequate to give a comment, 'could do better' or 'must try harder' or 'good' and a percentage mark or rank order in the class. Now reports on children are detailed, include advice for progress and can be built into a cumulative, formative record of achievement with a contribution from the child and/or parent. The principle is that the detail and the parent and child's contribution are likely to lead to optimal change in the future. The principle of providing every child and family with the same quality of evaluation information and suggesting individual targets is also powerful and increasingly supported by legislation in the UK and elsewhere.

As educational psychologists we feel it important that evaluation of the performance of individual children includes information about context, as we believe it is not appropriate to assess children as though they existed in isolation: the quality of the strategies used to help them is a major factor in the assessment of the child (DES, 1978). The most valuable aspects of assessing children are those that give detailed guidance about the best ways to move forward, and the use of curriculum based assessment and individual educational programmes have been powerful in promoting change for in-dividual children. We feel that the same principles are robust and should be applied to assessing or evaluating and reporting on schools as organisations.

Evaluation is an important part of the development cycle for teachers. Teaching is a human-intensive occupation, and to sustain quality and purpose over several years in these relationships can be demanding. For an excellent teacher, this means building positive and purposeful relationships with children and their families and achieving high standards in all aspects of the occupation. An annual feature of a teacher's life is that as one cohort of children moves on, a new start has to be made with a new cohort. This going back and starting again may militate against striving to achieve new and different aspects of excellence, without some specific exercise to support this striving. A clear development cycle with an element of evaluation is helpful to move teachers forward, so that they are not doing essentially the same things with successive groups of children, however excellent those things may be.

To move forward some kind of objectively validated account of the progress made is important as is the context of that feedback. Evaluation can threaten and undermine self-belief or it can create and build it, in the same way that a teacher's insistence on high standards can add to children's confidence or undermine it, depending on the skill, attitude and humanity of the teacher.

On several occasions in this chapter and elsewhere we refer to self-fulfilment in teaching and to the work of Rogers (1961). We believe that successful teaching should and can be rewarding, but we are also aware that the perception that working with children should be rewarding can in itself become a source of stress when difficulties arise. The context of evaluation should be the overriding school philosophy that hard work is important for children and for adults; but there are limits, and one aspect of evaluation is the need to balance working successfully with a sustainable life style. Seeing development as a cycle, with a period of taking stock of progress so far and making precise plans for further development is compatible with meeting this need for balance.

Perhaps too, teachers can adapt Piaget's (1950) classic developmental model of stages to their own professional and personal development. Development does not need to be at a constant rate: it can have its crises, sticking points and overlapping stages. Moving to new levels of complexity can be difficult and performance may not always in the short term be smooth. Evaluation which takes account of qualitative as well as quantitative data will recognise this kind of progress and development. There are other models of education and development which can be adapted to the development cycle. An evaluation stage will help to keep the cyclical model in mind and reduce the likelihood of repetitive functioning which seeks to reach the same level with successive cohorts of children, eventually reducing the creativity of the teacher.

Evaluation is particularly important for the exploration and planning of progress towards equal opportunities and rights. Because the wider society reduces life chances for certain groups, progress in schools towards these objectives cannot be expected to occur automatically. In these areas, the tightest strategies and evaluation will be appropriate. This suggests a model of evaluation that is dynamic rather than static, that records where the organisation has come from as well as where it is now and where it is going, and also includes reference to achievements that can be built upon.

We noted in chapter 1 how individuals and organisations can become limited and too comfortable in their habits. Evaluation will act as a safeguard, linking objective and subjective evidence: as with a journey, we may find that we are not where we thought we were, and perhaps not even close. The sooner this kind of discovery is made the better, so that we can be back on course and travelling to our destination once again.

The map metaphor is one that we employ because of its value in reminding us that no person or organisation should ever be lost. We need to know where we are and where we are going, not just where we think we might be or think we might be going. Attitudes and beliefs are important and dealt with at length in this book, but there can be no substitute for objectively defined positions from which to progress. For programmes to help individual children, our definition of whether an intervention is rigorous enough to be defined as a programme is whether or not there is a chart of performance. Nothing cheers children and parents more than the progress that records of this kind will pick up. We advise a similar precision at an organisational level. The metaphor of mapping is helpful in relating our view of the situation with the need to be in the right place.

The map metaphor is also capable of some additional complexity. Map makers depict the same reality in different ways, depending on the needs of the user. On French Alpine Club maps, climbers' refuges are shown very clearly and much larger than their real size and the scale would require. In this example, the safety of climbers is seen as more important than accuracy. Different projections can depict the world in different ways and the reason maps are drawn in certain ways reflects the priorities of the map makers and their perception of client needs. Different maps have different countries at the centre of the map, and, to be diplomatic, the UN picked the North Pole as the centre of its projection. Children's maps show the features of the location that they value. Record systems, charts or maps, have subjectivity as well as real-life objective value. In evaluation the issues are to keep more objective recording in key areas, and to make the subjective elements part of the articulated and debated philosophy of the school.

The map metaphor will remind us of another caution in our realism. Map making has historically expressed power and dominance, racism and conquest. Medieval map makers had Rome at the centre of their map, usually drawn larger than scale, and sometimes included religious or mythical figures or places on the map. Without a full participative element, a management map will be inaccurate in its emphasis, in its reductions and its omissions. The school map could easily overstate white, male management concerns and priorities and omit or reduce the skills, contributions and priorities of workers at junior or manual levels, women, black people, the disabled and other groups. If evaluation is to approach accuracy, equal opportunities means equal input into and power over the mapping process.

It follows that the primary function of headteachers and leaders in schools is not to identify need for others, *but to involve others in identifying needs*. This indicates that change based on the teachers' perceived need is of prime importance.

(Day *et al.*, 1990: 129)

EVALUATING THE ORGANISATION: MANAGEMENT AND PARTICIPATION

We refer here to the process of building up a critical picture of an organisation's strengths, needs, metaphors and other domains of meaning. This process will contain both quantitative and qualitative elements and may be directed at specific parts of an organisation or may be more global in purpose. The direction and orchestration of such a process will usually be carried out by senior managers who are key participants in the organisation itself, although the composition may be provided by an outside consultant or adviser. We saw in chapter 1 that the key aspect of leadership was honesty. Extending this to the organisation leads us to suggest that an organisation that is honest about where it is and employs evaluation techniques to provide information about this puts itself in a good position to move forward purposefully.

Evaluation needs the co-operation of the whole organisation to be effective and accurate. Workers in all departments and at all levels can give accounts of what is really going on; management may be denied access to some information, especially the negative aspects. This is not only because some of these may be so negative as to introduce the risk of dismissal or other disciplinary action if revealed. It is also because there are many instances of employees who disclosed problems and then found that the management was not interested in what they had to say or was overtly hostile to their message and to them. In psychological terms, treating the whistleblower as a scapegoat allows the managers who created or colluded in the scandalous situation to believe that the activities of the whistleblower caused the problem or contributed substantially to its extent.

Later we look at how a school can develop, disseminate and assert a common philosophy to those within the school as well as the broader community. At this stage we note that ownership of the evaluation process and procedures may be a good indicator of the school's real power relationships and now move on to discuss some of the practicalities of evaluation.

Evaluation and development

Evaluation requires the systematic collection, by those within as well as those outside the organisation, of data or information which is then analysed and synthesised.

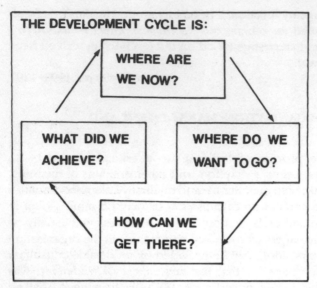

THE DEVELOPMENT CYCLE IS:

WHERE ARE
WE NOW?

WHAT DID WE
ACHIEVE?

WHERE DO WE
WANT TO GO?

HOW CAN WE
GET THERE?

Figure 2.1 Development cycle

Evaluation occurs at the beginning of the process of change and again at the end, forming a complete development cycle, a concept familiar to those who have been involved in action research, in planning programmes for individual pupils, in curriculum development and so forth. Within a school, there will be staff who are very familiar with this kind of approach, especially in science or technology faculties. Models of this kind can be traced to Dewey (ed. Sidorsky: 1977), who drew on engineering procedures, and need to be made explicit. They are conventional and helpful ways of focusing evaluation on planning development, rather than as an end in itself. While mechanical models are crude representations of reality, those following such models will ensure change is undertaken and not merely discussed.

Planning the evaluation: some questions.

It is important that, before embarking upon a substantial evaluation exercise, you are very clear as to your purposes. What exactly do you need to evaluate?

- What areas do you need to be most clear about before you plan change?
- What areas of your school are you most concerned about?
- Which areas are likely to be open to some degree of change in the near future?
- Which areas of change may be the easiest to implement?
- Do you need to carry out a wide-ranging review of your organisation?

- Have you gained agreement for the evaluation process from other key persons in that organisation?
- What time scale are you operating on?
- What resources do you have at your disposal?
- How much time will be needed from key personnel to complete the evaluation?
- How exactly will evaluation data help the school to move forward?
- Do you wish to draw upon prepackaged materials or will you be drawing together your own methods and systems of investigation?
- Will a consultant be involved?
- What technology have you available for managing data?
- Have you made sure that responsibilities with regard to the evaluation are absolutely clear and that all know exactly what they have to do?
- When can you begin?

Having clarified the answers to the above questions it is likely that you will wish to begin your evaluation by seeking information from within your school or organisation, both quantitative as well as qualitative. By this point you will have decided whether or not you are using a prepackaged evaluation system or whether you will be pulling together your own set of methods. You will have clarified the time scale and the requirements of time and personnel. You will also have begun to think about the boundaries of what is to be done and how the results will be used. You will also have dropped certain aspects of the evaluation as they may not have yielded information that helped progress.

Collecting quantitative data

Typically, quantitative data gained in schools has tended to relate to what have been considered *hard* indicators such as:

- attendance figures
- exclusion figures
- exam results
- assessment data, such as reading/maths/reasoning standardised test scores
- number on school roll in relation to capacity
- pupil turnover
- data about pupils' social status, number eligible for and taking up benefits
- number of parents attending school events, concerts, parents meetings
- number of pupils with a statement of Special Educational Needs, (known in the USA as Exceptional Students)
- attendance by governors at meetings, number of visits to school by governors, inspectors and others

- operating indicators: class sizes, staff-student ratios, space usage, equipment and assets
- financial data, including money raised at school events
- data on buildings, maintenance cycles, upkeep and vandalism
- equipment data: books bought, books borrowed and returned through school library, number and type of computers
- staff data: stability and turnover, sickness and punctuality, mean number of years experience, number of applicants per post, levels of qualification, gender/race/age and other data, teaching load, formal commendations or disciplinary reprimands, references sought to apply for posts elsewhere.

This data has the appeal of being countable and easily converted into descriptive graphs or statistical analysis. Undoubtedly this kind of information will have a place in many evaluations, but the careful evaluator should be cautious about the interpretation of such figures. Numbers when used in evaluation reports can appear spuriously scientific and may seem to the reader to hold more validity than other, softer data. This may be extremely misleading. For instance, examination and pupil performance assessment data can be highly unreliable; correlations between such outcomes and factors as the quality of teaching or home environment have been shown on many occasions to be quite insignificant.

The way the data is collected can also affect the figures, so that one school may enter all pupils for examinations, whatever their likelihood of obtaining good grades, while another may have a policy of entering only those likely to pass. The so-called success rate of the two schools will be markedly different.

There are situations in which reliance on hard data may have negative effects. If the number of pupils excluded for behavioural reasons were regarded as an important performance indicator, and particularly if some resource allocation were to depend on low exclusion rates, then a school might admit as few problem children as possible or may even persuade parents as an alternative to exclusion to remove their children or seek special school placement. Hard data is helpful but needs to be interpreted with caution. Researchers sometimes give additional rigour to the collection of hard data by the *double blind* method, by which neither those collecting the data nor those providing it know why it is being collected. Even events apparently easy to define have some inter-observer differences, and researchers will give a percentage range that allows for inter-observer unreliability. We do not see any particular need to attempt this level of rigour for the hard data collected by schools in most instances, but a caution in interpreting data and against over-reliance on hard data is required.

If the collection and interpretation of data is going to have particular significance, then the use of consultants is likely to be necessary, or at least reference to those on the staff who have knowledge of the issues mentioned here. Quantitative data is seldom formative in nature and, although it may provide some useful summative information, it tends not to provide a useful platform on which to build or plan next steps. For example the results of a battery of verbal reasoning tests used on a group of pupils might provide very little helpful information about specific attainments or about suitable programmes of study that would help these pupils learn more effectively.

Specific methods for carrying out quantitative evaluation include time sampling, event recording, record analysis, seasonal adjustment and other trend analyses, assessment and testing activity combined with aggregation of results. Auditing and accounting processes may also occur, together with different forms of statistical analysis.

Commercial balance sheets also try to give hard data accounts of all assets and liabilities, but a strong note of caution is always urged in reading any evaluation of an organisation based on its hard data. Balance sheets give values to property based on what it might realise if sold, on equipment, on the value of well-known brand names, and customer knowledge of the product. Other accounts may emphasise opportunity cost, that is, the income from investments not just as they turned out but also in comparison with what might have been earned from alternative investments with hindsight.

In some instances, expenditure on long-term research and development is hard to define and the return on this is equally elusive in many cases. Occasionally, the concept of benefit-cost accounting will be used, looking in particular at expenditure that does not have a profitable direct return but which may promote other benefits which are then given a value.

We advise a conservative and cautious approach to the collection and interpretation of quantitative data which involves random sampling and consultants.

Later, we comment on the most important aspect of data for evaluation: how effective and accurate do the predictions based on that data turn out to be? Data credibility should be earned and tested and the most attractive and impressive looking statistical analysis has to go through this process, and may not always prove to be as useful as apparently less rigorous items.

Qualitative evaluation

Quality is the dimension we urge for educationists, having noted the high priority given to quality objectives in the commercial literature. Quality is often thought to be wholly subjective and hard to turn into data but there are ways of addressing this concept, many of them in common use in business. In school systems, we feel that qualitative data is likely to have long-term value because of our belief that self-fulfilment is part of a successful school's philosophy. Quantitative data may be especially helpful in starting the school off in its innovation; the further it goes the more the qualitative aspects will be the focus of attention in evaluation.

When carrying out qualitative evaluation of your school organisation you will find that you will be able to gather extremely rich and detailed information that will enable you to probe a number of areas that you would usually find inaccessible to quantitative investigation. Qualitative evaluation methods, which have been described in some detail by Patton (1980), provide the contemporary evaluator with a set of systematic methods previously unavailable to social scientists. Philips (1990) more recently supports this position arguing that traditional approaches which include faith in experimentalism, careful measurement and sophisticated techniques involve a number of compromises and that such measures must be augmented by newer methods. These methods include action research, *thick description* and *contextualism*. By *thick description* Philips is probably referring to the process of gathering large amounts of rich, detailed information about a situation without being interpretive or judgmental. By *contextualism* he is no doubt meaning processes and methods which are embedded in and take full account of the social and cultural contexts of all situations studied. Let us consider how qualitative evaluation may proceed simply.

To start with, to carry out qualitative evaluations systematically, you will need to ask the following questions:

What is the context of your evaluation?   Here you need to consider for whom the evaluation is intended, what questions you are going to focus on, and what actions or decisions are anticipated as a result of the evaluation.

What methods will you use and how do these follow from the evaluation questions?   You should consider the strengths and weaknesses of the methods to be used and be aware of the consequences of design and sampling decisions that you make. You will need to consider which people and situations you are going to sample and over what time periods.

How will you present the data that you find out?   Recipients of your evaluation will wish to know what occurred to produce your findings and exactly what these are in relation to your initial evaluation questions.

You may wish to analyse your data using a selection of the many qualitative approaches available. If so, you may provide an analysis of the data, presenting patterns, themes, tendencies, trends and motives that emerge. You may list other dimensions, patterns, categories, classification systems and typologies that you elicit and even go on to explore linkages and relationships between these. Some workers go on to interpret their findings or to offer tentative explanations for them. Others are prepared to suggest possible causes and likely consequences of the findings. Certainly it may well be a good idea to arrive at your own hypotheses about what you think is going on in relation to processes observed and outcomes noted.

Most researchers and serious evaluators are concerned with ensuring that their work has high levels of validity and reliability. Validity means that the measure is looking at what it claims to; reliability means that it has robustness and will not be changed significantly by different circumstances. One type of reliability to accept and perhaps include from the start is a measure of inter-observer reliability, the percentage figure of agreed event recording. Unless substantially the same results will be obtained with different observers, then the data is not reliable and becomes largely subjective opinion. Managers need to check that their recording of an evaluation of events has some good degree of inter-observer reliability otherwise the evaluation becomes an exercise in self-justification by the management. Another approach to improving reliability is to attempt to replicate the evaluation results using different methods and/or evaluators. Replication is increasingly seen as perhaps the only way that research outcomes and evaluations can achieve true significance, validity and generalisability (Philips, 1990).

There is usually little or no reason for there to be data that is sensitive or confidential, but this issue does need to be reflected on and decided from the start. One necessary safeguard against qualitative data becoming corrupted by biased collection and/or interpretation is to keep the raw data for examination and second opinion. Another is to make the procedures part of the school's research expertise so that ideally there is no reason why individuals cannot replicate procedures if they wish, and replication in either identical or slightly different situations is a valuable indicator of how robust the conclusions are likely to be.

Robustness may be particularly important when using qualitative methods. You may, for instance, have to validate and verify your findings by providing details about the actual implementation of your methods and any departures made from these. You may need to reflect on the credibility of your findings and even be prepared to discuss rival hypotheses and explanations. Finally you must reflect on the effects you have had personally and professionally on the outcomes and their interpretation. Your role and your particular perspectives and personal constructs will all have some influence on what is done and finally reported. It will be best to declare these openly. We look at empathy and looking after oneself and the others in the organisation in chapter 10, but it is necessary to remind oneself that there are often different and equally valid perspectives on a given situation. This is something that educationists are likely to be aware of anyway because of interest in the way that children learn to see things from other people's points of view (as in the classic three mountains experiment of Piaget (1950) and the debate this set off).

Specific methods which might well be considered appropriate for the qualitative evaluator include the following:

in-depth interviews
questionnaires with opportunities for full responses
individual case studies

observation of specific situations
video and video analysis of specific situations
shadowing pupils through part or all of their school day
staff appraisal/peer appraisal schemes
cluster analysis
ratings and preference, in open and limited choice situations
open-ended exercises, extended writing about ideal experiences
use of pictures and other visual representations.

Evaluation methods that seek to explore aspects of quality and to help plan improvements of quality need to reflect that same concern for quality. We have expressed some caution about the use of quantitative methods; with qualitative methods we feel that they put the onus on the evaluation team to begin to pilot high quality work, to have the evaluation match or lead the organisation. If a school is trying to find out what the image of the school is with parents, the method of investigating this is itself part of the parent/school interface and its quality is part of that which it is seeking to evaluate. This is an opportunity rather than a problem in that it is an aspect of evaluation that immediately addresses and initiates action and progress.

The qualitative evaluation can have some variety of purposes, mentioned briefly above. Is the quality measurement to record the highest quality, or reliability, minimum acceptable quality, average satisfaction with service or range of satisfaction, or lowest acceptable level of satisfaction by any individual? We believe that many headteachers are concerned about the performance of the least competent teachers and the most competent pupils and may use quantitative methods to monitor these. This might involve looking closely at examination results at the higher grades or the punctuality at lessons of certain teachers. Without disputing the importance of these aspects of school performance, we find that systematic attention to high quality teaching and to the feelings of children who do not find attainments easy are valuable early steps forward for schools and excellent areas in which to pilot the use of qualitative methods.

A number of products are now available to the would-be school evaluator. There are those aimed at the evaluation of public policy and performance (Dror, 1973), those that review most aspects of a school's functioning, such as GRIDS (McMahon et al., 1984) and SSI (Myers, 1985), and those that zoom in on one area of concern such as PADS, the acronym for Preventive Approaches to Disruption (Chisholm, 1986). These approaches can be followed to enable your school to go through processes which may 'develop a rigorous approach to analysing, evaluating and improving [policy and practice]' (Dror, 1973: 25).

When using these it is important to reflect on whether your purposes, values and beliefs match those of the package designer. You might face considerable conflict within yourself and potentially with the rest of the school staff if there is too great a clash of ideologies, or even the style and tone of the package. We have also looked at the need to match materials with well considered and shared reasons for change. This allows the rigour of the engineering approach to act as the framework within which positive relationships can best lead to progress. In general, packages are valuable sources to aid the processes, skills and attitudes of evaluation and are valuable once the process has been started; they can be much less valuable if used from the start without significant internal contribution.

We noted above that qualitative evaluation had the advantage of not losing data that did not fit a conception of rigour. We do feel that impressions and feelings are important in building up qualitative pictures of a given situation. However, care must be taken that they do not form the only basis for major decision making because they may be affected by a range of factors including feelings or personal meanings being projected onto situ- ations or other people as if this is where they really existed. This may be aggravated by feelings of stress, frustration or pain. These perceptions need not necessarily be considered negative factors and they can be very meaningful and rich. In practice they do not have to be lost or repressed. Opinions about whether the children seem happy in school, how cheerful the teachers are, if the atmosphere seems so settled as to be unexciting and so forth can provide the hypotheses for more formal evaluation, especially of quality.

Pre-change and post-change evaluation

It is likely that, having decided on answers to the questions outlined at the beginning of this chapter, you decide to adopt a 'mix and match' of approaches to pre-change evaluation. If so, you are likely to draw upon a mix of those qualitative and quantitative methods mentioned above to suit your own evaluation questions.

A particular approach that the authors have been working on is for schools, with some help from outside agencies or consultants such as educational psychologists, to create their own set of performance indicators or objectives for success in a range of key areas. School staff then set about measuring whether or not the school has achieved the stated objectives. Sequences of objectives set out developmentally facilitate pre-change and post-change evaluation and provide a ready framework for monitoring and reviewing successes as well as failures and for effective, formative planning and new objective setting.

One approach we have worked with successfully is to set out a model of phases of development for the meeting of special needs in a mainstream school, setting out a map of desired end points or objectives to which a school might aspire. Users are encouraged to audit the progress their own school has made towards these objectives as well as to those set out in earlier phases, and to use this as a basis for future planning and ongoing evaluation.

Evaluating the school culture

Organisations such as schools can very usefully be thought of as cultures. They are mini-societies with their own distinctive patterns of culture and subculture. There will be patterns of belief or shared meaning, such as 'we are the best school in the town, and always will be'. These may be fragmented or integrated and more or less supported by operating norms and rituals, but they will influence how effectively each school handles change. Attempts to understand how a school is functioning cannot afford to take this cultural aspect for granted or to ignore historical explanations of present behaviour and ways of being. Morgan (1986) reflects on this, making the following very useful point, pertinent for any would-be school evaluator:

> One of the easiest ways of appreciating the nature of culture and subculture is simply to observe the day-to-day functioning of a group or organisation to which one belongs, *as if one were an outsider*. Adopt the role of anthropologist. The characteristics of the culture being observed will gradually become evident as one becomes aware of the patterns of interaction between individuals, the language that is used, the images and themes explored in conversation, and the various rituals of daily routine.
>
> (Morgan, 1986: 121)

Other sources of evaluation information

Parents

An extremely important source of evaluative information is present outside your organisation and will be constantly encountered whether sought out or not. Parents will make very definite evaluations that will or will not lead them to send their children to your school, even though their judgements may be based on information that is highly unreliable. Your organisation will constantly be judged and critically evaluated by those within the walls and all those who have any dealings with it including parents, pupils, advisers, inspectors, support services, area administrative or education officers and, of course, other schools. The choice you face is whether passively to receive the constant flow of evaluations and judgements in an unfiltered ad hoc fashion or whether actively to seek out and structure the evaluative information that is out there.

We began this chapter by stressing the importance of knowing where you are before embarking on a journey in any direction. One of the best ways to find this out is to ask someone who knows the locality well. It helps if you do this in a pleasant and friendly manner so that there is some incentive for that person to help you. You are surrounded by a myriad of individuals and other groups and organisations with a personal or social construction of reality (Kelly, 1955) as it applies to your school, a view, an angle. The secret is how best to access and use this rich source of information intentionally and most helpfully.

In the 1990s parents are becoming more involved in and more powerful in relation to their children's education than ever before. In Britain and elsewhere, government legislation has increased parents' level of choice of school, rights to information, involvement in school government and access to comparative data on which to hold a school accountable with regard to their child's progress (DES, 1981; DES, 1988). In Australia and in the United States, parents are involved in decision-making processes on school councils, principal selection committees and so forth and are much more concerned about the quality and perceived value of the instruction being received. As a consequence of a range of factors, including the bad press on state schools, the increasing influence of market forces on education and the attitudes and influence of central governments, in many countries an increasing number of children are attending non-state schools, particularly church and independent schools (Beare *et al.*, 1989).

Increasingly, with changes in administrative funding towards decentralised school-based budgeting, the strong link between cash resources and the numbers of pupils on roll has become even more critical. Local Management of Schools, a consequence of the 1988 Education Reform Act, has sent many British schools into a flurry of activity to sell their schools to prospective parents. In short, parents are increasingly important and what they think about your school, however biased or misinformed it may appear to be, is ultimately crucial to the survival let alone the development of your organisation.

Parents also share in the central task of schools in delivering education to their children (Topping,1986). Parents' aspirations for their own children and what they know about their children's aspirations, experiences, strengths and perspectives on schooling not only greatly affect children's learning but are also a source of extremely valuable educational information. Parents will often present negative as well as positive feedback to a school through structured channels, such as the typical parent consultation evenings or open days. Special kinds of meetings and communication include home–school diaries, invitations to parents for shared problem-solving about their child, and parent groups. Forums of a more political nature include parent–teacher association meetings, meetings involving parent governors, school council/committee meetings and governor elections. Information that has been made available through these channels may, if recorded carefully and communicated to the evaluators, be open to systematic evaluation along the lines described earlier.

More informal channels will also provide a rich source of data in diverse forms. Communication events may include parents approaching school with a personal crisis, letters of complaint or compliment, spontaneous comments, praise, criticism or even the extreme acts of physical or verbal attacks on members of staff.

Contacts like these are often less easy to monitor effectively for evaluation purposes but are none the less extremely important sources of information. Such information may clearly expose aspects of the school culture and how it does or does not offer support to those it impinges upon.

More systematically, projects can be set up specifically to evaluate parental perspectives on a school. These may take many forms including the following:

parents randomly selected and interviewed in depth
parents of a whole year group sent a questionnaire
group of parents invited in and engaged in group discussion which is then qualitatively evaluated for main themes, values, patterns and essential personal constructs emerging
parents home visited and interviewed using a structured or open-ended interview technique
parents on a consultation evening, each asked three pre-planned questions.

The possibilities for such evaluative endeavours with potentially your most powerful and influential set of allies and resources are enormous and have been known dramatically to change school cultures and practices. It is worth remembering that effective work with parents is one of the only ways we can be truly confident about dramatically improving basic skills such as reading and the child's behaviour in and out of school (Newton and Taylor, 1991).

The other key area for qualitative research is into the experiences of pupils and we feel that every school will benefit from a regular evaluation of this. The quality of experience of pupils is the basis of what the school is trying to achieve and evaluation of the pupils' perceptions of this will help to inform the development of a school's philosophy and to move towards it. Ultimately, the experiences and interpretation of these by the pupils is the essential source of performance indicators.

Situation 2.1

The headteacher of a large primary school in south east England carried out a piece of evaluative research that focused on parental involvement in the school. She sent questionnaires to the parents of all the pupils in her school and a separate one to all her staff. She then interviewed in depth a selected number of parents chosen at random from across the age range of the school. This involved her in home visits as well as in school meetings.

Making use of the outside support of the Open University and her links with the educational psychology service, she analysed her results in some detail. She also carried out a search of relevant literature to provide context to her work.

She used a computer to map out graphically the results of her survey as well as to type up her findings. This involved bar and line graphs, grids, lists of key factors and so forth. Even though the school had already adopted a very positive policy of parental partnership and involvement, her results revealed blind spots that could be linked to issues raised in literature and research studies carried out in Britain and elsewhere over the last ten years.

The results raised many questions with which the school made considerable efforts to grapple, including the following:

- Why did parental involvement decline so dramatically in the junior department?
- Was the parent–teacher association being perceived as a clique and therefore having some negative effects on parental involvement?
- What could be done to overcome the numerous anxieties which still existed in relation to entering the school building and speaking to teachers?

She was soon actively to follow up the concerns raised by this piece of work. An INSET strategy was embarked upon which was intended to improve teacher skills in relation to communicating, counselling and problem-solving with parents.

Policy documents were reviewed and new approaches to parent meetings and consultation were tried out. The headteacher gave additional support and encouragement in areas where this was needed and reviewed the role and purposes of the parent–teacher association.

The community

Beyond the parents of pupils attending the school is the community. Again this will be a source of judgement and positive and negative evaluation of the school. Local businesses, companies and other potential employers are a part of this community and will all have a view and a perspective on schooling and on the local schools. The community includes local shops, youth clubs, youth organisations, churches, groups, clubs and amenities such as parks and amusement and sports halls. Information actively sought in a planned way from these sources will not only help build useful links and public relations but will also provide rich information to help make the school increasingly relevant and meaningful to the community of which it is an integral part. That elusive element, the reputation of the school, is to be traced through the community. Remember that businesses will sometimes give a substantial value to a brand name: the public knowledge of a product or company and public association of that product or company with high quality is to be prized. Evaluating the current situation regarding the community's perception of school quality is important. It even helps to be proactive rather than wait for something to appear in the media which may or may not be positive.

Outside agencies

Inspectors, advisers, educational or school psychologists, school nurses, educational welfare officers, special needs support teachers and other educational consultants are a large body of professionals often working from widely different paradigms, all of whom either visit schools or work for periods of time within schools in given areas. They bring to schools their own perspective, set of skills, knowledge, level of confidence and objectivity. They may themselves attempt to engage you in an evaluation exercise to further the goals of their own work in your school or of the education department which employs them. Alternatively, you may wish to harness their skills and knowledge, particularly where they are experienced in school evaluation activities. At a minimum you will be well advised to collect information from them systematically as their perspective will have its own professional quality as well as a contribution to the context of the community and local education authority or administrative area in which they work and which the school itself impinges on. They may well have much to gain from identifying positive areas to develop and may have perceptions that are not bound by hierarchical factors, or too closely influenced by the culture of the school. Critical friends can have advantages and disadvantages. If skilled and trusted they can facilitate observation, offer comparisons, be constructively critical and act as a resource. If not skilled and not trusted, their interpretations may be out of context, they may be reacted to untypically by staff and pupils, and working with them can be time consuming (Day *et al.*, 1990).

In chapter 5 we look further at how to get the best from outside consultants, but for now it may be worth reflecting on how best to involve them in your evaluation process. You might find out whether your school inspector could be involved in some form of focused curriculum review. You might request that a team of psychologists explore aspects of the way your school looks after its members in areas such as support, communication networks, stress management, counselling for teachers, pupils and parents, supervision and appraisal arrangements. It might be worth asking for specific feedback on aspects of the school's functioning from visiting agencies such as school inspectors, advisers or psychologists.

It is often found helpful to invite a psychologist, adviser or member of another outside agency on to your evaluation working team for specialist advice. Even if they are not involved from the outset it may be valuable to share your work with them for critical, creative, or simply constructive feedback to help improve the quality and value of the final report.

Other schools

We all compare ourselves constantly to others and the greater part of learning is by imitation. It may therefore be worthwhile to follow the same procedures in the interests of evaluation and development.

There are many ways of making the best use of contact with other organisations that are similar to your own. One well tested idea is that of teacher exchanges and this can be especially valuable when there is detailed evaluative debriefing between all involved at the end of a given period such as a school term. Visits to view positive practice in other schools and discussion with other colleagues at local meetings, in-service training events and conferences can all prove rich learning opportunities. Reading and analysis of literature and reports and of evaluation work done elsewhere can sometimes be as useful as direct observation of other teachers working in their classrooms. Cross-phase links in evaluation can be valuable. Membership of inter-school associations, working groups and support groups can yield useful information and ideas for self-evaluation and development. This is best achieved by building a co-operative, non-competitive relationship with other schools.

Finally, it may in some circumstances be valid to design an evaluation device, such as a checklist, to use when visiting schools further afield, of questions, observation and opportunities to analyse records and so forth.

ANALYSIS AND SYNTHESIS OF EVALUATIVE INFORMATION

Having collected your data, you have next to consider what to do with it. It is important to be able to lift out of your mass of data a picture of:

- what is happening
- what has been discovered
- what patterns, themes, trends and relationships have emerged
- whether we can safely make any interpretations or explanations
- whether any hypotheses are emerging
- what rival explanations and hypotheses there might be
- problems and priorities that have emerged
- the implications of our findings and options for development.

To create this picture you will need systematically to analyse and synthesise the data you are dealing with and find useful ways of summarising your findings. Numbers will often slot into graphs and tables but constructs, patterns, relationships and other more qualitative data will require more imagination. You might consider using relationship matrices showing, for instance, outcomes along one dimension and processes along the other, continuum lines, rich pictures, conceptual models, video clips, and quotations to highlight typical responses. With qualitative data, presentation of randomly selected elements, video and children's comments will be necessary to give a flavour of the data to those who will not be able to go through all of it.

What is finally presented as an evaluation report will need to be succinct, and considerable attention should be paid to the communication of its content to the target audience. It is often advisable to try to present information in a form that the listener can visualise. The use of story, analogy and metaphor become essential at this stage, as do good quality visual aids.

The ritual significance of presentation is especially important for evaluation data and comment. If the presentation is led by senior managers and the content is mainly about the performance of staff on lower grades, then the hidden agenda will not be a positive one. If the presentation is shared and not hierarchically dominated, then the data is more likely to be considered on its own merit. The audience is also important. If a presentation is made to a group of people not subject to any evaluation, then they will be perceived as sitting in judgement and the attitudes engendered are likely to be defensive by the presenters and critical by the audience. Where possible we suggest that the audience/presenter distinction is blurred to focus attention on ways forward. This means considering interactive presentations, with everyone having the chance to look at and process raw data and to come with data of their own. Data about time devoted to various activities is important and this is usually dealt with in group activities, in which the evaluation of time spent, strategies employed and outcomes can be discussed at an important and practical level.

Evaluation will be an important ritual in the school's life and very much a positive experience. It will bring recent achievements to be recognised and celebrated. It will provide information about what is going on that will be fascinating. It will provoke comment, discussion and a sense of purpose. It will inform all who make up the school and will have a major effect in helping to create a picture of where the school will be going next. It will be efficient in terms of the time and resources taken and it will also justify these by allowing the school to make the most of its positives and maximise its opportunities to avoid crises. It will help to keep change as a high-priority and positive item on the school's agenda, and will help the school to select worthwhile and realistic targets.

Evaluation should promote a real confidence that the school has the capacity to move forward and to influence its own future. Earlier in this chapter we referred to the motivating power of charts and similar record systems for children, which are our operational definitions of individual educational programmes. Children and their parents see that these detailed records show progress even if it is in very small steps indeed. As a result they become motivated and excited by the entries on the records, confident that there will be progress and involved in discussions about the teaching and learning strategies to be employed.

THE TIME SCALE

Much of what we have said about evaluation has been intended to promote evaluation that leads to action, to the identification of pilot projects, at least. This means that we are suggesting a cycle of evaluation and development of three years or so. However, evaluation should be built into the organisation to empower and inform the change process and short-term evaluation time scales can be employed usefully.

In contrast there is a growing interest in long-term outcomes, either through the measurement of *sleeper* effects, or through longitudinal study, which can be qualitative as well as quantitative. Sleeper effects are effects that may not be apparent at the time or shortly after, but which may be evident many years in the future. These effects can be statistically significant, although this is usually only picked up by large sample sizes. Longitudinal study is the following of a particular group or cohort right through the school and at pre-set intervals after. It is unlikely that schools will be able to devote much time to investigating evaluations of this kind, but they should be aware of them, perhaps discuss them with researchers or at the very least should take care not to destroy data which may have long-term significance. We are finding more and more schools using their own longitudinal data as the source for research work by their pupils or by members of the community. Apart from its intrinsic interest, it will help to keep a sense of context, of what we are trying to do and why, in the consciousness of the school.

ACTION PLAN

When involved in evaluating your organisation remember the following steps:

- Be clear what you are doing and why.
- Spell out your evaluation objectives and focus.
- Set out your evaluation questions to which you wish to find answers.
- Form an evaluation team and clarify responsibilities and roles.
- Decide upon evaluation methods and link these to your questions.
- Clarify when and how the outcome of the evaluation will be presented.
- Decide which information you will seek from within your school and which from outside and from whom.
- Carry out evaluation along an agreed time frame.
- Analyse and synthesise data to state what has been found out.
- State implications and ways forward.
- Plan carefully the communication of the evaluation to its target audience, making full use of communication aids.
- Deliver your report and agree next steps.

Chapter 3

Children learn – so can schools

> Think and act systemically: more self-reflection, less self-centredness.
>
> (Morgan, 1986: 246)

In the first chapter we saw how a teacher could look at the basic reasons that would form the basis of effective teaching and personal development. In this chapter we wish to take this idea further by considering whether there are any useful parallels between the way schools and children function. Similarly we will be reflecting on some of the similarities between adults and children, with help from concepts from Transactional Analysis (Berne, 1964). We will be looking at ways of unlocking teachers' abilities to foster organisational growth and development. Thus we will be attempting to take a systemic look at the circularity of change in schools by exploring the triangle of pupils, teachers and organisation.

THE CIRCULARITY OF CHANGE IN SCHOOLS

Traditionally schools as organisations have been thought of as open systems in constant interaction with their environment. Changes coming from the

Children learn – so can schools

outside have been viewed as challenges to which the organisation must respond. Most of the major problems faced by schools are thus usually seen as stemming from changes in the environment or context. In other words schools are affected by legislation, by parental choice, by the nature of the pupils attending, by the community's perception of the school and so on. This idea, that most change originates in the environment, has been traditionally held about all organisations, not just schools, by both contingency theorists and population ecologists. This basic idea has been challenged by two Chilean scientists, Maturana and Varela (1980), who have developed a new approach. They argue that all living systems are organisationally closed, with autonomous systems of interaction that make reference only to themselves. They argue that living systems are characterised by three principal features:

autonomy
circularity
self-reference

These features lend systems the ability to self-create and self-renew. They use the term *autopoiesis* to refer to this capacity of systems for self-production through a closed system of relations. How can this be true?

> This is the case because living systems strive to maintain an identity by subordinating all changes to the maintenance of their own organization as a given set of relations. They do so by engaging in circular patterns of interaction whereby change in one element of the system is coupled with changes elsewhere, setting up continuous patterns of interaction that are always self referential. They are self referential because a system cannot enter into interactions that are not specified in the pattern of relations that define its organisation. Thus a system's interaction with its 'environment' is really a reflection and part of its own organization.
>
> (Morgan, 1986: 236).

Living systems such as schools seem to close in on themselves to maintain stable relations and it is this process of closure or self-reference that distinguishes the identity of a system as a system. Maturana and Varela maintain that there is no beginning and no end to any system because they are in a constant closed loop of interaction. We can recognise this circularity in schools, can we not?

> A child makes silly noises to gain attention from his teacher. The teacher shouts at him, annoyed at the unacceptable behaviour. The child pauses but then resumes with a different way of gaining attention kicking a nearby child. The teacher shouts more loudly still, even more concerned at the unacceptable behaviour and inadvertently gives the child what he wants – and round we go again . . . .

This is not just cause and effect. The child and adult are caught in a circular relationship of mutual causality. The child behaves as a result of the teacher and the teacher behaves as a result of the child and round and round they go triggering each other, caught in a repeating cycle.

At an organisational level:

> Members of a senior management team push hard to set up a new system of appraisal. They recite the positives, are very encouraging and actively promote the initiative with staff. The staff resist and put up counter arguments as to loss of professional integrity and power. The management presses still more enthusiastically and assertively. The staff consult unions and prepare to take political action to resist what they see as a negative imposition that will further demean their status – and round it goes . . . .

Neither party can really be said to be in the wrong, but both parties can easily be caught in a circular pattern where the behaviour of each has a knock on effect on the other. Both parties appear caught in a closed loop of interaction from which they seem powerless to escape. We find systems of relations, rather like Russian dolls or Chinese boxes, being made up of wholes within wholes.

Systems approaches to schools are based on this concept of mutual causality and from the familiar notion that the whole is bigger than the parts (Gorrell-Barnes, 1985). When considering change, a holistic rather than a reductionist emphasis can be extremely rich and useful. One such approach developed by Checkland (1981), called *soft systems methodology*, typically focuses not on a presenting problem but on:

> the situation in which there is perceived to be a problem, or an opportunity for improvement. The initial task is not to converge on a definition of a problem to solve, but to build up the richest possible picture of the situation in question, drawing on the disparate perceptions of those involved.
>
> (Frederickson, 1990: 2)

While in this book we emphasise the importance of vision and objectives, we would not wish the reader to lose sight of the circularity of change processes in schools. We do not wish to overemphasise the linear nature of change or reductionist approaches to breaking down processes into small steps or goals even though this may make many tasks more manageable. It is clear that progress can be made but there may well be complex circular reactions occurring simultaneously to which we wish to alert you. Thus a school may improve its record in relation to not sending so many children into special education but at the same time may increase the number of pupils permanently excluded. This would be a paradoxical but eminently possible approach to the inclusion of pupils with special needs. It is crucial to be aware of such paradoxes and mutual causality which may be particularly evident in communication, decision-making and patterns of power within a school involved in change.

In the rest of this chapter we wish to explore a potentially unopened circle of causality. We wish to bring to the surface a circle of learning and behaviour that involves adults, children and school organisation with the hope of maximising and increasing the positive impact of their mutual causality.

Schools can behave and learn just like children. Teachers and parents can behave and learn just like children; and it is their relationships with children that evoke this at the same time as children are learning and behaving just like adults. The circle is completed by teachers and parents using what they have learned with children to help the school to learn and behave in its own way, but are at the same time influenced by how the organisation treats them.

> An individual or organization can influence or shape change, but the process is always dependent on complex patterns of reciprocal connectivity that can never be predicted or controlled. As in nature, significant combinations of chance circumstances can transform social systems in ways that were never dreamed possible . . . . Individuals and organizations have an ability to influence this process by choosing the kind of self image that is to guide their actions and thus to help shape their future.
>
> (Morgan, 1986: 246)

THINKING OF SCHOOLS AS CHILDREN

Organisations can be viewed as machines, organisms, information-processing brains, cultures, political systems or even psychic prisons (Morgan, 1986), but let us think about organisations as children. Specifically let us reflect on schools as children.

- Children are complex and sophisticated; they learn and develop. So do schools.
- Children behave in acceptable and unacceptable ways at different times. So do schools.
- Children develop their own sense of identity and self-esteem. So do schools.
- Children have relationships that involve parents and teachers. So do schools.
- Children have social relationships and learn to communicate with others in and out of their family. So do schools.
- Children are vulnerable to the power of others for good or ill. So are schools.

This metaphor may be useful when thinking about managing change effectively as well as when attempting to understand the circular nature of school systems. Schools and the adults that are members of them have learned a lot about children over the years. We believe that this learning could be used more effectively in relation to thinking about organisational development. Can you think of any new ways of applying what has been learned about children to your organisation?

Perhaps the following might provide some starting points:

listening
encouraging
meeting them at their level
ensuring success by setting sensible achievable targets
providing a stimulating environment
assessing needs in detail
reporting about progress accurately to others
sensitively dealing with personal and social issues
developing independent, active learning
managing firmly but fairly, with clear limits for behaviour
praising specifically and genuinely
planning meticulously for success but using the spontaneous moments to advantage
making sure that input is relevant and meaningful
maintaining a sense of humour at all costs.

These and many more skills are well developed in work with individuals and groups of children but are not always evident at such a high level of quality in the way the school organisation operates. Essentially this brief list reflects an excellent set of recommendations for leaders, managers, change agents and consultants wishing to facilitate change in schools. We can so often forget that teachers and parents are involved in a daily process of bringing about change in the young. Much of this change will occur incidentally but a lot is planned and thought out by adults; and it is this very rich source of knowledge that schools should be drawing from on a regular basis to create an effective culture of change and ongoing development.

In the 1980s, when we first began to explore some of the parallels between our work with individual pupils and with staff working towards whole-school system change, we were particularly interested in what we would do and advise for a pupil with learning difficulties (Newton and Tarrant, 1988). We began to imagine that schools in many ways had their own learning difficulties and required systematic interventions in the same way as children. We began to explore and work out the practical implications of setting targets for school change that involved achievable small steps. We were soon rewarded, and senior managers and heads often welcomed the opportunity to agree with an outsider on a small number of discrete objectives. We were struck by how easily these could be achieved and by the positive ripples that such achievements had on other areas of school functioning. Our pleasure was probably similar to that of the original teachers and psychologists who researched and proved the value of teaching pupils with learning difficulties in small steps. We also found that praise, encouragement, listening, counselling, supporting, and meaningful intervention strategies and relevant learning activities were just as powerful for schools as they were for individual pupils. The problem-solving model, we found, as others have (Stratford and Cameron, 1979), to be particularly generalisable from pupils to whole schools even in areas as complex as managing emotional and behavioural difficulties. We have found immense value in switching between individual and whole-school focuses at different times, while adopting essentially the same methodology. We have found that it is possible to switch between working with staff to set up a programme to reduce the number of tantrums that a child has in the playground, to working with the same staff on increasing the amount of constructive play that is occurring on the playground among *all* pupils. We will go on to extend this idea further in the next chapter as we emphasise the need for vision and medium and short-term targets for pupils and schools.

If you have been involved as a parent or teacher in the education of children, then you already have a wealth of knowledge about how to bring about successful change and learning. It would be worthwhile taking the time to write down a list of what you think makes the difference in bringing about positive change with children and then to reflect on this list in relation to the change process you may be involved in or about to embark on within your own organisation.

Thus the circle becomes clearer; schools are in a number of ways like children and need the same approaches if change is to occur. Teachers and parents working in and with schools have knowledge and skills in relation to these approaches but may not be using them for the benefit of the organisation. A break in the circle?

THINKING OF TEACHERS AS PUPILS

Staff meetings at their worst can seem a bit like nineteenth-century classrooms. The head takes the droning and monotonous role of paternalistic authority and the staff adopt the roles of petulant, passive or rebellious pupils. Teachers can find themselves caught in circular relations with their managers, in relationships that have all the hallmarks of those of parent and child. Some want obedience or conformity or a change in behaviour, others feel the need to draw attention to themselves, to rebel, or to be given the security of knowing what exactly is expected of them.

Teachers are not alone in this. All adults, whatever their status, can be thought of as children and will behave on occasions with their personal 'child' dominating. All of us carry with us our Parent, Adult and Child who are dominant at different times.

> Continual observation has supported the assumption that these three states exist in all people. It is as if in each person there is the same little person he was when he was three years old. There are also with him his own parents. These are recordings in his brain of actual experiences of internal and external events, the most significant of which happened during the first five years of life. There is a third state, different from these two. The first two are called Parent and Child, and the third Adult. These states of being are not roles but psychological realities.
>
> (Harris 1970: 18-19)

There is a universally shared experience, then, of all the adults working in a school: that of having been a child and of continuing to experience child-like responses to some events and situations. When people are in the grip of their feelings it is said that their Child has taken over. These feelings may include a replay of frustration or anger, or feelings of rejection or abandonment. On the brighter side, in the Child reside creativity, curiosity, the desire to explore and know, and all the good feelings associated with first discoveries.

When leaders or managers plan for change they need to reflect on the Child that will be present in every member of staff and themselves, and at the same time need to consider how they can nurture this child but also ensure that successful development takes place. This is not to say that teachers should be treated as children, but rather that this aspect of their psychology needs respecting and reflecting upon. Leaders and managers must also keep a very close eye on their own Child. They may quickly be put back in touch with it when their ideas are rejected or they are criticised by staff even when they thought they were doing their very best. Transactional Analysis (Berne, 1964), with its reference to the constant interaction between the Parent, Child and Adult in us all, may be found to be an extremely useful tool for improving understanding of yourself and your relationships with others.

CONSTRUCTS AND SCRIPTS

Psychologists who study social and learning processes have been pointing out for decades how individuals and societies construe reality. The way we see or do not see things becomes more than a habit; it becomes the way we protect ourselves from trying to process each new experience or event. Whatever the world throws at us, we have a set of 'scripts' already formed which allow us to classify, react to or ignore with no fuss. This helps us cope, avoid stress and be personally effective within limits. Researchers are now trying to copy these scripts in computers.

However, psychologists have also been pointing out for decades how wrong some of our scripts can be. Early psychologists were often fascinated by the study of illusions which demonstrate that we often see things as we have become used to seeing them, not as they are. Necker's cube, for example, illustrates how a figure can be seen in two ways, but it takes time in looking at it for the second way of seeing to emerge.

Socially, psychologists showed sixty years ago how racial prejudice was not something that sensible argument was likely to change. At first hearing, the arguments which disadvantage black people may not sound racist: 'Some of my best friends are black, but even they agree . . . '. Yet arguing successfully against one racist statement simply leads to another. The basic position is not being changed; the facts are being fitted into pre-existing scripts. We will see at a later stage how one might go about influencing arguments like these.

Failure constructs can be used by us all to fall back on, to externalise failure, which is an important defence for the individual. However if a person or school is using this kind of defence frequently, this becomes cause for concern. The kind of constructs schools fall back on to explain difficulties with children or parents often utilise theories of psychology, not always explicitly and not always accurately, to give what is essentially justification for failure. Assumptions of low intelligence, of parental mismanagement, of 'disturbance' within the child, are translated into ways of helping the child which usually seem to involve moving the child away from the teacher who is giving the 'helpful' advice. We find that these attitudes exist where there has been no access or limited access to positive, interventionist psychology. Where this has been made available as part of a school ethos or with a substantial input over a period of time, few if any comments or assumptions are made that label children negatively.

At times the organisation may well feel and be construed to be more like a patriarchal family than a school and issues of gender may surface:

> In the view of many writers on the relationship between gender and organisation, the dominant influence of the male is rooted in the hierarchical relations found in the patriarchal family, which, as Wilhelm Reich has observed, serves as a factory for authoritarian ideologies. In many formal organizations one person defers to the authority of another exactly as the child defers to parental rule. The prolonged dependency of the child upon the parents facilitates the kind of dependency institutionalized in the relationship between leaders and followers, and in the practice where people look to others to initiate action in response to problematic issues. In organizations, as in the patriarchal family, fortitude, courage, and heroism, flavoured by narcissistic self-admiration, are often valued qualities, as is the determination and sense of duty that a father expects from his son.
>
> (Morgan, 1986: 211)

ADULTS LEARNING IN SCHOOL

In the same way that children have needs for physical, social, communication and intellectual development, so do the adults working in schools. Analogous to the situation within business, there needs to be a recognition of a variety of needs and levels of need for development and innovation. Not all businesses need to spend high levels of their budgets on professional development, training and basic research and development; few are able to spend negligible amounts and survive.

In a school situation, the negotiation process should aim to bring together the needs of the school and the needs of the individual. If the school is to move coherently and systematically towards its objectives, professional development will need to be targeted on these objectives with some precision. However, the needs and perceptions of individuals will broaden and deepen the development agenda for the school. A development programme for a school or other educational organisation will benefit from precision in order to allow the individuals to define their own learning needs in context. More of this in chapter 7.

Positive and negative learning experiences

Activity 3.1

> Close your eyes and recall a time when you really enjoyed learning something. Stay with the feelings and write down exactly what you felt and what helped your learning to be positive.
>
> Close your eyes again and this time think about something you have found difficult to learn. What were the feelings? How did you behave? What made it difficult for you? How could the learning experience be made more positive?

As psychologists, we view learning in behavioural as well as emotional and cognitive terms, and it is useful at this stage to look at the implications of this for adults in schools. Behavioural definitions of learning describe it neutrally: learning is the acquisition of a repertoire of specified behaviours. Such learned behaviours may feel very positive or negative. The environment influences the acquisition of positive and negative behaviours. In addition to the formal occasions of adult learning planned by the school, it is worth analysing the informal, habitual and environmental aspects of adult learning. In a young person presenting negative and severely challenging behaviours, an analysis of the setting conditions, the conditions in which these behaviours have a high frequency of occurrence, is essential. This might well complement an analysis of how best to manage these behaviours or to extinguish them once learned. This can sometimes be achieved by sampling the conditions in the school, by tracking pupils, teachers and others, by questionnaire, by structured interview. Behavioural observation and analysis can be helpful, but need to be freely and openly negotiated to be ethical and accepted.

An example of this can be seen in effective and experienced teachers of teenage pupils. To manage effectively, one needs a good set of assertiveness skills, to be able for example to close conversations to prevent the flow of a lesson being disrupted. However, if this is done as a routine for five or more hours a day, the repertoire of other social skills which are less directly or routinely useful can atrophy. We find often that teachers cannot easily use listening and eliciting skills without explicit instruction to re-establish these skills of facilitating the development of another's line of consideration. This seems to us to be perfectly natural and can be changed quite easily either by formal learning opportunities or by the scheduling of particular activities.

The behavioural approach also allows precision in beginning to identify what kind of experiences and range of experiences will best support adult learning in school. Examples might be:

assertiveness with children
assertiveness with adults
listening and eliciting skills
time management skills
room design and management skills
the skills of task devising
the skills of feedback
participating in meetings
leading meetings
record keeping
writing skills
planning skills.

With some idea of the range of skills and experiences, the formal professional development agenda and consideration of the environmental factors can be empowered. What kind of meetings will be attended? What kind of good practice will be observed, how can it be specified, articulated, practised and passed on to others?

In schools we see children with learning difficulties provided with programmes and strategies to overcome their problems. Schools can have or develop expertise in promoting positive behaviour, excellent attendance and punctuality, motivation and a sense of purpose. Perhaps schools will find it a helpful starting point to consider which skills and strategies transfer easily and which less easily to the organisation from applications to children. Perhaps, too, the hidden curriculum can be revealed through further study of this issue.

We all can develop fixed habits which may reduce anxiety and make us feel content in the short term, but which may create a situation of becoming progressively out of touch. Schools make systematic and generally successful attempts to prevent children limiting their development in this way; at an organisational level this involves building an ethos of questioning and changing practices and beliefs which are strongly held. To do this, recognition is necessary of the threat to individuals that this can constitute. A basic mechanism for this is the triennial cycle of review. The strategy for changing habits is to have small, well defined steps for change which are insisted upon, but with a high level of reassurance and recognition for progress made.

The environment for adult learning

An audit of assets may provide detail of the formal and informal skills, knowledge and experiences in a school. Creating the optimum environment to maintain these existing skills, to disseminate them within the organisation, to refine them, to ensure that induction of new staff into the organisation includes effective exposure to these skills, are objectives not only for the formal professional development processes but also for the learning environment. Consideration of how best to do this, and piloting and implementing it, is for each school to consider, for it is a process of assessing the school's own fundamental skills.

Examples are easy to provide. Early years teachers are expert in creating activities in which children learn co-operatively and in which skill acquisition is linked to positive activities. The room might have a number of display and activity areas with rules and guidelines for each area; children are directed to such areas in groups with particular activities in mind and the teacher moves among the groups to facilitate this. Consideration of the physical environment and its effect on the children's learning experiences is a high-level skill and there is a wide range between best and less good practice in our experience. To disseminate the skills of room design and management among teachers and others, activities such as joint room design, joint literature searching on room design, observation of children's usage of particular designs can be devised. The objectives are to work co-operatively on related tasks and then to articulate the principles involved in the relationship between design, usage and learning. Once the principles have been articulated, it is easier to apply them to adult learning. One principle that emerges for the adults is the need to separate working space and leisure space and the ownership of space.

Finding the right environment for adult learning exposes conflicts of interests in the same way that access to classroom space has to be managed for children in order to avoid, minimize or resolve conflict. This will take the adults towards consideration of the ground rules appropriate for adult learning.

A learning environment is not just the room space; that is the beginning. Devising individual, group, large group experiences and how to allocate time to plan and work these out effectively merit serious consideration and piloting.

Creating an effective learning environment will involve looking closely at developmental objectives and activities, and at daily, weekly, termly and annual routines, and allocating time and expertise to events and routines to build in sharing, learning and exploration. Creating the time for this, as with any development, is never easy as innovation creates short-and medium-term pressures to complete currently required activities and to develop new ones. However, the priority given to an activity can often be assessed by the time allocated to it and we urge consistent time allocation over a substantial period. The consistency of allocation rather than the amount of time at any occasion is important, as the changes resulting from the application to adults of a school's skills should ultimately be the easiest and most rewarding of all. However, the reader will gather now, and later in the chapter on research and development, that we feel that the time allocation across the school system and in initial training should reflect these priorities.

Thus we find teachers and other adults caught in the circle of mutual causality, sharing similar feelings and needs with children. They may think that they behave in response to children. Adults may unconsciously switch into their own Child and its needs and this can lead to behaviour that triggers the actions of children in their care, and round and round they go. While staff will to a greater or lesser extent recognise and be able to reflect on themselves and their own needs and behaviour some may tend towards instinctive, knee-jerk reactions rather than thoughtful responses to situations. We all need space to reflect on what is going on in ourselves as well as the adults and children we work with. This will be returned to when we consider the human factors of change.

UNLOCKING TEACHERS' ABILITIES WITH CHILDREN TO SUPPORT ORGANISATIONAL CHANGE AND DEVELOPMENT

In this section we attempt to unlock the circle, or to encourage its rerouting to allow the closer linkage between teachers' skills with pupils to be generalised into working for the organisation. Here we are including all teachers, from the head to maingrade staff.

We believe that schools have an enormous reservoir of skills and creativity which is seldom drawn upon as fully as it might be. In poorly managed schools, these skills keep the school going against all odds. In well managed schools the potential is used much more extensively.

As the purpose of schools is to foster learning and development, there is great potential even in less successful schools. A simple example is valuable in starting positive discussion and thought about how these skills can be specified and then transferred. We often hear what teachers do or are trying to do for children but we like to ask what do children do or try to do for teachers? This twin tracking of sharing positives brings up some important points which are worth following up by asking or listening to children or through observation. Children:

like the teacher's attention. To what extent does the teacher need or like the children's attention?

like to play and will often do so for long periods in ways which act out situations. To what extent can teachers learn from this?

ask a lot of questions, even when we think they ought to know the answer.

talk to themselves about their activities.

learn skills at a fast rate and enjoy performing their new skills.

are good at peer-tutoring and like to help other children with work, and to work collectively.

respond well to positive contexts and badly to negative contexts.

need boundaries and clear routines.

like a variety of activities but also set routines.

like records of progress.

like to have something of their own to contribute to the classroom: pictures on the wall, their own tray, for example. They like adults to know their name and to use it from the start.

like to show their school attainments to parents and others.

The first step in applying these skills is to identify them. That is why we see evaluation as a key part of the development cycle. At the start of a process of planning change it is helpful to ask the teachers for an account of how they came to be there, and to share these experiences.

We try to find out why teachers went into teaching, what kind of college course or other induction they had, what were their strengths, the gaps, what kind of post-experience, evening or other courses they have followed or are following. We find out about their interests, their experience and something of their motivation.

Every day, parents, other adults, and often teachers themselves, ignore or undervalue the miracle that takes place as part of the daily routine. With just one child or a few children at home, most adults feel the reward of children but will also begin to feel how demanding children can be, to feel tired, and to long in many cases for the end of the school holidays. Often we find ourselves spending money that cannot easily be spared to keep children sufficiently interested to avoid major problems. The thought of managing 30 six-year-olds for a day or teaching 200 teenagers in shifts throughout the day is a daunting one. Yet this feat that teachers perform every day is so routine that it is worth looking at how best to use these skills in other situations and at different levels. Teachers themselves can be modest or so fluent in what they do that it is not easy for them to explain exactly what they are doing in a way that is easily coherent to others, and precise enough to pass on. Yet we find teachers of immense skill in promoting change for children, directing it, facilitating it and requiring it, for individuals, groups and large numbers.

A first step is to look at the kinds of skill teachers might have. This proves not easy to do. As noted above, excellent teachers can be so fluent and unconscious in skill performance in many cases that they cannot easily specify their expertise. This does not help them to apply it to the school as an organisation. We might begin to break into this closed world by:

an in-depth study of excellence
asking children and parents
looking at how teachers arrange their rooms
looking at the tasks they set
asking them about the useful things they learned or did while training to be teachers
discussing their social and interpersonal skills
examining the teaching materials they use or create
asking about their organisational routines
asking them what they have found useful and adopted from the practice of other teachers
asking them about the best teachers they have ever come across, what they were like, what they did.

You might reasonably criticise this on the grounds that there are many studies of excellent teachers. However, we would point out that the process of discovery is as important as or more fundamental than the list of discoveries; and, as advocates of action research, we are careful about taking things at face value and are ready to be surprised by valuable insights from practising teachers.

What areas of expertise might we find?

Interpersonal skills
Assertiveness skills
Listening skills
The ability to empathise
The ability to give encouragement
Group leadership skills
Team-building skills
Motivational skills
Questioning skills
Lecturing and exposition skills
Skills in answering questions

Other communication skills
Paper skills: writing worksheets, policy papers
Task design and implementation skills: setting tasks to help children learn
themselves
Seriousness
Humour
Reporting skills
Academic or other curriculum skills
The ability to give useful feedback to children
Room management and design skills, environment skills
Curiosity and its communication

When we asked headteachers about the very best teachers they had encountered, they all said that they had had the privilege of teaching with at least one person who was absolutely outstanding. Yet those teachers usually had not been told in so many words how highly they were esteemed. Rarely were processes of study set up to find out how their skills might be disseminated and made part of the whole organisation rather than specific to individuals.

> 'I do some pretty incredible things', was not an English expression. 'I'm fairly keen', was not American. Americans were show-offs – it was part of our innocence we often fell on our faces; the English seldom showed off, so they seldom looked like fools.
>
> (Theroux, 1983: 15)

Before looking at ways of liberating these skills, it is necessary to explore possible explanations of why they seem to be under-used at an organisational level. The management of schools which fail fully to use their human potential need not be unintelligent or inadequate. Yet for the visiting educational psychologist, meeting teachers who outperform any reasonable expectation of what might be accomplished is as common as finding hard-working, competent headteachers who do not seem to realise just what potential they have within the organisation. We have seen teachers in the most difficult circumstances produce thriving, learning mini-communities within the classroom but having little or no influence on the school as a community.

As psychologists we find this interesting. Initial teacher training contains significant input on educational and psychological theory and much of this focuses on why and how children develop, the process of change and progression by children. Our experience is that teachers absorb and practise such theories, but are less often able to describe a range of psychological theories or work out their practical applications. We find teachers describing children and situations in terms that illustrate models of psychology deeply absorbed into the popular and educational culture, but without articulating the theory, or necessarily being able to work through the theory systematically. If such descriptions refer to theories of intellectual or personality structure and assessment, deviancy theories of behaviour and other deficit explanations of problems, we feel there will be limits on the application of teaching expertise to the organisation.

Such ways of describing situations, constructs of what teachers experience, can be articulated but are less often evaluated. They are the scripts which allow the rapid processing of new experiences, but which can operate to limit change rather than to prepare for it, to work efficiently within limits.

Moving forward

To move forward in the process of using teacher skills with children effectively at different levels within the school, as we saw in chapter 1, reasons for change need to be explored in some depth, although this need not be a lengthy process. Similarly, the processes by which teacher skills begin to work on the school's organisation need to be understood, although this need not be a time-consuming or complicated study.

An audit of assets

We are usually aware of problems, because they produce complaints, crises and stress. We need to be aware of assets on a day-to-day basis to develop the positive initiatives to give a positive impetus and ethos to the school. The use of the word *appraisal* can be unfortunate, because it may embody a top-down, pass–fail meaning, relating to individuals rather than emphasising collective achievement, and because it may not convey a sense of evaluation linked to innovation reflected in the work of some writers and trainers, Poster and Poster (1991) for instance. An audit of human assets takes the positive meanings as central. It need not set out to be exhaustive, although it should stimulate motivation to be exhaustive, for identifying assets is a rewarding activity.

In chapter 2 we looked at evaluating an organisation and at how an organisation can best reflect back on one cycle of change before starting on another. In contrast, in this chapter we invite schools to reflect on how they search out and develop the assets the children bring with them and how these daily applied skills can be made explicit and generalised.

This is a global task, but we feel that identifying just some of these skills can be a most valuable part of the processes of empowering staff in the process of school development and making the process of change positive and exciting. Focusing on problems within a school is not a way of moving forward: it may be necessary for other reasons such as to specify an acceptable level or type of professional behaviour or to investigate and address complaints. Preventing crises or minimising them by rapid and effective reaction is not constructive but prevents the positive policies from being further disrupted by escalating crises. Our positive approach to school innovation is not at all incompatible with tackling negatives as a matter of urgency. In our own work we seek to challenge negative practice or poor quality work but do not see it as a way forward of any particular value. Rather it is something that has to be done, is preferably done so as to take up as little time or other resources as possible and not interrupt or delay the positive agenda for change.

The way forward is a positive one, even with ineffective schools and poor teachers. This reflects the practice that will give children the feeling that they are supervised and that going off task will be anticipated, dealt with and the child will be back on task without fuss. Above all, the flow of routine in the classroom will seldom if ever be interrupted in order to address negatives. Good managers set behavioural targets and give positive expectations and challenge poor standards but do it without deviating from establishing positive momentum in the classroom. With many age groups they impose a positive momentum by insisting on the early production of an excellent piece of written work, a demonstration of a behavioural target established and met. With ineffective teachers, change is achieved as part of school change; the time allocated to them need be no more and indeed can be far less than the time spent helping good teachers become outstanding, and similarly with schools. However, all need some time, to receive and be seen to receive some positive input even if the consultant or manager feels this is unlikely to be a valuable use of time. Otherwise, ineffectiveness can become outright hostility.

The audit of assets is an excellent way to start this process and to begin to put problems into their place, into context and perspective. It will also show up some assets in unexpected places and begin the process of people in the school feeling that they have something positive to offer and that they are all part of the school. Some of the unexpected assets we have found are:

- a number of teachers who have done highly relevant evening courses in education and/or psychology but have not applied this new knowledge across the school
- teachers and others who have counselling skills and experience such as running church groups
- supply, new or temporary teachers who have skills or training in, for example, writing and running individualised educational programmes
- experienced teachers who know rules, laws, procedures, resources and how to reach goals with less bureaucracy and time wasted
- leisure-related interests and expertise which can be a valued part of the school.
- expertise in creative processes and performance.

In all of these cases, the school initially either was unaware of the asset the teacher embodied or had made nothing of it within the school context. In each case, more use was made of this asset and in all instances, the person concerned was pleased to contribute. However, in each instance, the contribution was not to take responsibility for an additional task, but to act as a consultant to the person or persons whose formal responsibility it was.

Where can a school start?

Study success

Schools benefit from developing the habit of looking closely at what they are doing well. We urge this on schools as the first step in liberating and being precise about their skills and making it easier for others to acquire or improve their skills.

Use the skills of good teachers in adult settings

If politeness is valued for child–adult communication, apply it to adult–adult communication. If the environment of the classroom is important, then the environment in which adult discussion and work takes place is important. If child learning is to be activity-oriented, then adult learning can be planned in similar style. If participation is achieved by all children, then it can be achieved for all adults.

Respect teachers as academics

Talk about what colleagues have studied, what they have found interesting, what they have done to apply this to their teaching. Not only does this show your interest, it also opens up conversations of the kind discussed in chapter 1. It leads naturally to discussions of why teaching had appealed to them, what skills were seen as available and valuable. This should not be seen as something exclusively or largely for management.

What kind of theory might the teachers have studied?

Have a group session or individual discussion to find out what kind of scope the teacher training and other qualifications had. We find that on most staffs there are teachers who have excellent qualifications, or other highly useful backgrounds or experience. We also find teachers who have qualifications that they have gained since their initial teacher training of which their headteacher or colleagues are unaware: and often these teachers undertook this extra study in order to throw more light on what happens in the classroom or more generally in the school. However, in such cases, the application to the real life of the school may have been limited. Where there are teachers from other countries, the mixture of qualifications and experience is often particularly powerful, yet these teachers may feel insecure and marginal within the school and may not offer to share their skills. Schools need to ensure that they are asked and feel confident enough to do so.

Such discussion and study will help to articulate the philosophy of the school and will also begin to link theory with practice in a way that does not always happen at college, or stays as an issue after college. Yet the relationship between theory and practice will be what gives a school its ethos, its consistency combined with flexibility across situations. It will help to give a school confidence to succeed in uncertain and difficult situations, to give a structure within which events can be interpreted and put in their context. Finally, the school will be sharing more than one model of education and psychology and can draw on alternative paradigms and perspectives in different situations without undermining the basic model it adopts.

This will also promote consideration and adoption of models for change. The one used most frequently is the problem-solving model, derived from an engineering metaphor and outlined by Dewey. More recent developments of this are applied to pupil or organisational problems (Stratford and Cameron, 1979). It is both efficient and creative for schools to adopt as their core model an educational view of the change process, using others only as appropriate for different aspects of the school. These may draw from social psychology, developmental theories, organisational theories, systemic ideas, industrial models and others.

Discussion and enrichment of a basic educational model will have benefits at a number of levels. By having a single core model, school leadership can be strengthened. The ethos of the school will be overridingly educational; even though the daily routine of the school may present it with many change concerns that are financial or essentially non-educational, if the model of change most commonly used and articulated in the school is educational, then learning will not be pushed down the agenda by expediency.

> Work environments will be more collegial, status will be more fluid, authority will come from peer recognition, and stake holders will be decision makers. People are seen as assets, capable of development and commitment, and organisation members are shareholders in every sense of the concept.
>
> (Beare *et al.*, 1989: 256)

Learning will also come to be seen as learning for life rather than solely for academic or school-based activities. This should assist in building an ethos that values all skills and all learning and promotes tolerance of individual differences. It will value practical skills as well as book learning and will build an expectation that teaching and learning have direct practical applications.

From a Piagetian perspective, the school could be depicting change and development as uneven and irregular. Development can be accompanied by difficulty, by hesitation, by uncertain performance, until the move to a greater complexity of performance and understanding is completed. This model can be applied to the school's development to give some space and tolerance to staff during attempts to move forward, while giving a clear expectation that a more complex and sophisticated level of performance and understanding is to be arrived at. Such development could be supported by planned activities rather than through formal presentations. Applying such a model to the organisation would also respect developmental differences in currriculum areas while creating a shared agenda for common progress. It would also foster a belief that most of the development would come from within the school.

Other models could also be used analogously. From a Vygotskian perspective, evaluation would have the purpose of attempting to define a zone of next development (Vygotsky, 1962). It would also give particular importance to the language of progress and to the recording of how progress is described which would be helpful for those new to the school. A school could look at ways of using concepts such as emotional projection to describe what is happening both for children and teachers. Finally, a school could use a radical behaviourist model to look at targets, motivation, task analysis and the development of routines.

- Be open about the philosophy of education of the school and the implications of this for adult interactions.
- Talk regularly about professional development and how it will help the individual or apply beneficially to the school.
- Use the skills of the staff on small, defined objectives. Have joint work across the staff on small defined objectives.
- Look at the quality of written materials produced. Celebrate those of top quality and use them for staff documents to spread the use of this quality.
- Look at interpersonal skills: when activities are planned, what is done to encourage silent or shy non-contributors, or to damp down the dominators?
- Identify the range of positives on the staff and bear this in mind when planning joint projects.

Situation 3.1

St Just's First School has made much progress in recent years. Initially, staff sickness and absence was high, and the school was not an easy place to teach in.

The process of change and development was positive and considerable, although it took immense work and commitment to keep going in the early days. Some use was made of general management techniques, not specific to education, and some to methods designed with schools in mind: GRIDS, for example, and Handy's work on school management.

However, the headteacher and staff were not overawed by these sources but developed the confidence to make their own development part of the school ethos and practice.

The school is a denominational school and much of the mission statement (see chapter 4) reflects this. However the desire by the headteacher and staff to make religious beliefs and instruction something much more than a space on a timetable led them to consider the principles they would use for themselves, for adult–child and child–child interaction. This meant examining what the children brought into the school in terms of religious and moral beliefs and constructs. The staff believe that all children, however young, have a richness of belief and morality that is well worth exploring and sharing among the adults. The methods they use for releasing this richness of feeling and thought are being explored in a number of ways and discussions have also raised the issue of how action research might assist in this process. A staff group has piloted this process of exploration to inform the school's development for the forthcoming year, engaging in large group discussions with the children, exploring moral dilemmas, discussing how positive beliefs need a behavioural expression and to be asserted positively within a community. The teachers are fascinated by what the children are saying and doing and it seems that the fascination is at two levels:

• what the children say and do
• how best to facilitate these processes and share them at an adult level.

It seems in this case that the teachers are learning from the children although obviously the children are also learning from the teachers.

Looking at this in more detail reveals the scope of the teacher discussions about how best to facilitate this process. Points which have been of particular interest to the staff have been open-ended questions used in succession, and hence:

• an interest in the interpersonal skills of counsellors as distinct from the basic social skills of teachers
• a strong belief that a high degree of organisation is needed to promote creative discussion (Adams, 1986)
• a belief that all are included in this process and that extended discussion sessions will promote inclusion and contribution
• an interest in projects that are conducted by children in cross-age and cross-phase groups
• an interest in what theories of personality have to offer today

- a curiosity about how best to promote high achievement within the school, while recognising the wide range of ability
- an interest in promoting this through the exploration of basic principles and their application rather than the massive task of material-based curriculum extension
- an interest in the process of creativity and change
- an interest in how best to involve in this process children and adults new to the school
- a recognition of how tolerant children can be about the beliefs of others and of their undogmatic approach to belief and theory
- a recognition that those within the school and those who work with the school may have a significant contribution that it is advantageous for the school to seek out
- a cheerfulness and curiosity.

Thus we have come full circle. The challenge remains for all involved. Can teachers be facilitated in the releasing of their abilities in relation to pupils to use these for organisational change? Can a healthy loop of mutual learning and causality be formed that can encompass teachers, parents, pupils, managers and organisational change itself? We think so.

ACTION PLAN

- Reflect on the circular relationships that exist within your own school.
- Consider situations that you are involved in where you can perceive the occurrence of mutual causality.
- Measure the usefulness of the school-as-child metaphor in your own organisational situation. What has your organisation learned so far? Where does it stand in developmental terms? How does your organisation behave and relate to others?
- Consider your own personal Child and that of other staff members. What development needs do you and others share? What degree of nurturing and positive learning is already occurring? Can you build on existing strengths?
- Audit the assets of the school staff. What special skills and abilities are being under-used?
- Attempt to unlock the skills teachers use with children for the benefit of the organisation.
- Build on creative spontaneous moments of individual or joint work, treasure these moments and be careful not to crowd them out by overplanning the use of time.

Chapter 4

Visions and objectives

In this chapter we examine some of the literature that refers to change in organisations; then look at change in educational organisations; and finally focus on objectives for change, looking at the kinds of objectives that are likely to promote change most effectively. The literature contains a range of perspectives from considerable optimism to pessimism about the ease of creating change in educational systems, and in particular in schools (Leithwood, 1979; Gordon, 1984).

Currently, there is particular interest in the relationship between the research work on school effectiveness and the literature on school improvement (Reynolds *et al.*, 1989). As researchers try to move closer to identifying what makes schools effective independently of intake, so there is a growing pressure to find out the best ways of implementing these and other findings. If we can find characteristics shared by effective schools, perhaps we can begin to induce all schools to adopt these characteristics of effectiveness. Possibly, too, effectiveness characteristics vary and effectiveness may be due to an interaction between intake characteristics and school characteristics, although the evidence suggests this to be unlikely.

As it becomes clearer that the findings of the school effectiveness research are quite complex then it becomes important to find ways of promoting

Targets and visions

school openness and interest in new ideas, in research, in experimentation and in self-appraisal. It is unlikely that some simple idea is going to have substantial value in school effectiveness, or that some simple set of characteristics can be prescribed for all schools to make them effective. It does not seem as though substantial improvements in school effectiveness can be achieved by having more small schools, or through streaming, or through types of pastoral organisation. These large ideas might be thought to be easy to introduce, to have a time span that would have political appeal. It seems as though school effectiveness may be like economic growth, made up of an infinite number of micro-components, and with differences in the outcome related to differences in quality that permeate the organisation. This gives a less clear-cut agenda for change. The research has looked in detail at the issue of expressing this in terms that are objective and precise enough to have rigour and meaning while attempting to maintain a sense of what is going on at a personal level.

The complexity of what may make schools effective also entails looking at change as a process to be worked out co-operatively with schools rather than imposed from elsewhere. If there had turned out to be a simple list of characteristics, top-down change may have been attractive at a political level and imposition without consultation might have seemed feasible.

This leads to a long-term objective of equipping schools with expertise in the change process and working to build a positive interest in the research relating to change and innovation. At the root of successful change for schools lie positive attitudes. In many political and local climates, these attitudes may not be easy to adopt for schools and there may be risks perceived by schools in taking steps to change. There may be a gap between a relatively sophisticated literature which attempts to disentangle the effects of schools from the effects of society as a whole and the pressures and perceived pressures on the schools.

These issues have political importance and use; the articulation of objectives for schools is something that is occurring on a regular basis in the political arena. In research circles, there is concern that it may be hard to change the behaviour of ineffective schools (Mortimore, 1991) so the political dimension may be missing an important issue, of how to promote change within a range of political or ideological views about education. We referred earlier to the differences at a micro-level that different educational purposes might bring to change strategies. The exploration of these issues can be productive, but to ensure optimal outcomes, the debate has to progress in parallel with practical and successful experience of change.

It may seem daunting to try to devise objectives for change where there is no political or professional consensus about school effectiveness or what kind of school should be aimed for. This is an international and permanent feature of education. It is an issue we address in chapter 11, dealing with how and why a school should assert its philosophy at a time of pressure to change from outside. It is also the same issue that faces change agents seeking to promote positive and lasting change for individual children in school. At the start of the process there may be no consensus about the desired direction of change. The success rate and speed of progress is improved by the existence of a consensus and the use of that consensus to devise mutually agreeable objectives; yet, in some circumstances, progress has to be made where no consensus areas seem to exist. Expertise in these difficult situations exists in schools, in psychological services and in educational support teams and elsewhere and can be applied at an organisational level.

There have been criticisms of psychologists within school systems for taking a limited role in promoting the process of change in schools (Reynolds, 1987). There have also been suggestions about ways forward in developing such a role (Gale, 1991) and broadening the expertise that is brought to bear on the school change process. We feel there is scope not only to develop a role as a profession but more importantly to develop expertise in schools in the use of psychology in the change process. In particular we will look at how psychologists help clients to select and work towards objectives for change.

We note that some of the techniques used by psychologists to influence the behaviour and performance of children are adaptable to organisations and are well rooted in the theory and practice of psychology. One of the basic methods is to identify precise objectives for progress. We often work to address this at a child level and then look at the process of devising objectives for schools. As in *Alice in Wonderland*:

'Would you tell me please, which way I ought to go from here?'
'That depends a good deal on where you want to get to,' said the cat.
'I don't know where . . . ,' said Alice.
'Then it doesn't matter which way you go,' said the cat.

CHANGE IN ORGANISATIONS

An educationalist seeking guidance in promoting change effectively who carries out a review of the literature is in for some serious thought and weighty, sometimes sombre reading. There are brief, dynamic, go-getting paperbacks which relate specifically to business, and to the hire-and-fire end of the spectrum in some cases. Broader-based texts tend to be lengthy, couched in rather general terms, and might leave the reader less, rather than more confident about the feasibility of change.

Pfeffer (1981) holds that organisations possess a lot of inertia: the degree of inertia is such that the prime mechanism for change is selection *between* organisations or departments within organisations, rather than *within* departments or organisations. As one structure and range of activities becomes set through habit, others need to be set up to fulfil the functions that the first could perform, were it less rigid. This process tends to lead to the creation of inefficient overlapping units and/or the painful process of sporadic crises involving the whole organisation or the destruction of individual units.

> Power, once acquired is maintained . . . . Change is not frequent or easily accomplished.
>
> (Pfeffer, 1981: xii)

Similarly, Hord, referring specifically to education, states that change 'takes support and a great deal of energy' and that 'innovation and its successful implementation take time' (1987: 164).

Kanter goes so far as to list ten rules for stifling innovation derived with ease from observations of unsuccessful businesses. They include:

> regard any idea from below with suspicion . . .
> treat identification of problems as failure . . .
> make decisions to reorganise or change policies in secret . . .
> express your criticisms freely and withhold your praise.
>
> (Kanter, 1983: 101)

We found the literature to be focused on the apparent problems of producing change, couched at quite a high level of generality, and identifying resource shift as a prime agent of change.

On a more positive note, Pfeffer reports that a very small resource shift within a mature organisation can lead to a large change, as the resource change is given greater salience by the background of resource stability in the organisation. Stable organisations *feel* greater effect from even quite small resource changes in contrast with more unstable situations in which freer fluctuations of resources are occurring.

Interestingly, The Audit Commission (1986), in looking at common factors in successful community care initiatives, emphasised the importance of individuals with vision and stamina who would not take no for an answer. These were referred to as 'strong and committed local champions of change.' Yet strong and well-known arguments refer to the 'myth of the hero-innovator' who will be swallowed by the dragon of the system, and suggest more subtle and thoughtful approaches to innovation (Georgiades and Phillimore, 1975).

CHANGE IN EDUCATIONAL ORGANISATIONS

UNESCO's survey suggested that change in organisations in education was not easy to attain:

Research on the process of educational innovation was rather limited . . . . The process of educational reform was clearly a very complicated one.

(Adams and Chen, 1981: 7)

The twelve propositions for change which emerged from this major international survey focused on power and resource issues. The authors were critical of the literature and expressed this in strong terms:

There appeared to be unfortunate gaps existing in education between research and policy making and educational practice. This has led us uncomfortably to the conclusion that present paradigms and procedures are inadequate for addressing today's problems in 'live' social systems and that the time may well be ripe for innovatory approaches to educational planning.

(Adams and Chen, 1981: 5)

Baldridge and Deal (1975) provide some rules for consultants who aim to promote change in educational organisations, for example *Assess needs and problems seriously*, but these need to be interpreted with a high level of detail. Buchanan and Huczynski (1985) have referred to four basic features that can be expected of organisational change however it occurs:

Triggers Changes started by some kind of 'disorganising pressure' or trigger arise from inside or outside the organisation.
Inter-dependencies Change in one aspect of an organisation creates pressures for adjustments in other aspects.
Conflicts and frustrations Technical and economic objectives of managers may well conflict with the needs and aspirations of employees resulting in conflict that creates pressures resistant to change.
Time-lag Change rarely takes place very smoothly and usually happens untidily, some parts of an organisation changing more rapidly than others, with certain groups and individuals needing time to catch up with everyone else.

We found these and other studies interesting and useful, but found advice which was often general, or rather unclear, with some key words and broadly phrased rules. These seldom, if ever, sought to connect with the drive and enthusiasm of individuals. Objectives for schools appeared to be expressed on a long- or medium-term basis, with the schools being expected to plot a path towards these general objectives. Performance indicators for schools may be expressed in more concrete terms; if the school has the skill to break these down into specific and attainable steps, progress may result. An analogy is with pupil behaviour. A school may be well aware of a pupil's need to change to positive behaviour, may well be able to define positive behaviour by describing it in other pupils, but may or may not be able to define appropriate and attainable steps towards the general target or strategies to promote and maintain progress through these steps.

There are many accounts in case studies of promoting change with children, but fewer which relate the individual case to the organisation. Gregory (1988), for example, describes his own exhaustion as a psychologist and that of the teachers he worked with in promoting innovation while fulfilling the existing functions they had. He cites Walker *et al.* (1986), suggesting that innovation can increase the workload of teachers, start by undermining their confidence, create unpopularity with colleagues, and even create a career risk if the innovation embodies aspects which might be seen as in opposition to the prevailing establishment.

Promoting change: psychological tools

In contrast, we as educational psychologists are involved in promoting change in and for individual children, often in situations in which change seems unlikely, for instance when children have severe or long-standing learning or behavioural difficulties. Our work with children gives us access to the theory and practice of promoting change with families and children. The initial sources we draw on are those which psychologists use in their work with individual children.

Situation 4.1

Christopher has been a cause for concern since he came into the education system at the age of 4. At 10, he has been excluded from school on two occasions and his mother has been told that he is likely to be excluded permanently. His mother finds him difficult at home and the school has suggested to her that she should request placement for Christopher in a special residential school. Christopher's father is no longer in touch with the family; the school has been told by his mother that the boy is becoming just like his father, who was reported to have been violent, had time in prison for assault and has been described by her as schizophrenic.

If the headteacher tries to talk to Christopher about his problems, he says nothing, or denies that there is a problem. He will sometimes say of any incident that it was another child's fault and it is unfair that he is the only one in trouble. He says he thinks his work is good and that his behaviour is good too. The main concern of the school has been Christopher's aggression towards other children, which has been serious; he has also hit a lunchtime supervisor who tried to stop him hitting another child. There have been complaints from other parents and from staff.

The support teacher advises and helps the school to start looking for positives in what Christopher does and for areas in which positive targets might be shared. This does not prove to be easy. The programme that is arrived at simply uses a system of tokens to be won for good work and positive behaviour. When Christopher has achieved certain work targets and has behaved well for a specified period, he is given a token which can be cashed in for privileges in school or pocket money at home. This works well and after one month, Christopher has produced good work and has not been involved in any violent incidents.

At this stage, with a more positive atmosphere, the teachers are able to open up discussion with Christopher and his mother. They try to address the basic conditions that are producing the problems in the long term. They also try to give Christopher and his mother opportunities to discuss their views in more detail. The headteacher asks his mother to try not to see Christopher as a younger model of his father and suggests that Christopher could be the scapegoat for the hurt she feels from his father. The teachers talk to Christopher about the importance of good relationships being based on safety and talk to him about how upsetting violence can be, how to make restitution, and how to be assertive rather than aggressive. The support teacher asks the school and parent to stop threatening Christopher with being sent away. The school spends far more time on work-related issues with Christopher than on behaviour. As aggressive behaviour is so attention-seeking the teachers keep to a strong positive system of behaviour recording and reinforcement for some months but introduce change every three weeks. They do this to provide more ambitious targets for Christopher, to prevent the original system from becoming routine, familiar and less rewarding.

As Christopher's problem behaviour had been established for many years, a tight system of targets and rewards was kept to for six months after the last significant violent incident, to ensure that the improvement was maintained. His kind of situation relates to certain clear skills in finding objectives that will be appropriate in promoting change:

- looking for and finding positives
- looking at areas in which agreement is most likely
- keeping precise records which are easy and quick to use
- closely linking change with reward
- finding rewards which are rewarding
- being precise in defining targets
- setting targets that are achievable and realistic, and hence setting up a realistic possibility of reward
- updating, maintaining and changing the system, but keeping to the same principles
- moving forward once initial targets have been achieved, to more ambitious ones with a focus on education rather than behaviour
- suspending discussion of bigger and long-term issues until progress has been achieved and then addressing these in a positive atmosphere

- adopting a neutral, non-judgmental tone
- involving child and parent in discussions and implementation of the day-to-day arrangements
- specifying changed arrangements for all parties concerned, not only the child
- changing behaviour of all concerned in ways that were specified rather than discussion of attitudes
- keeping up arrangements to establish long-term change
- involvement of an outside support teacher with a specific role
- building dialogue on big issues on the basis of success, rather than right at the start
- optimism and positive attitudes balanced by determination to achieve change
- teaching and discussion on key issues once progress had been established
- recognition of a need for attention
- keeping core educational issues central to the targets
- accepting and articulating the view that progress towards small targets will lead to the achievement of more substantial success
- believing that the child is not qualitatively different from other people.

In looking at the types of psychology that were being applied to the educational process at an individual child level that could be adapted or transferred to an organisational level, we identified a number of influences. We were influenced by the ideas of stage theorists in developmental psychology who have described the growing and changing child reaching set stages or learning goals naturally or with encouragement (Piaget, 1970; Bruner, 1975; Vygotsky, 1962). Equally the work of systemic family therapists such as Minuchin has affected our perspective on human factors which maintain homeostasis as well as promote change in family systems.

We are also interested in the work of key philosophers and psychologists that have encouraged us to attempt to reflect on and elucidate the meaning implicit within all social situations, a perspective some have termed hermeneutic (Gould and Shotter, 1977), whereas others have focused on qualitative evaluation (Patton, 1980). All such psychological and philosophical work has a bearing on organisational and systemic change and those who wish to achieve this. Effective educational psychology draws on this extensive and sometimes complex literature to provide intelligible, practical and straightforward guidance which will promote effective change. With individual children, whatever the complexity of the problem, we seek to obtain initial behavioural change, as this provides early, unambiguous success and provides a basis for effective attitude change.

Interestingly, we found that the methods we used in setting objectives for children were paralleled easily at school organisation level and also emerged in our literature search as the single most important factor in organisational change. Thus we feel that the sources we use at child level can be applied at a number of levels. These sources are very specific and optimistic, and, combined with our own practical experience, have convinced us of the importance of setting clear, unambiguous, realistic and useful targets for change and devising precise strategies to maximise the probability of reaching these targets.

We have become convinced that success breeds success, that small steps lead to big changes, and that involving people in agreeing objectives and working towards them leads to a high degree of success. We have been influenced in particular by problem-solving models (Stratford and Cameron, 1979) and curriculum models that stress the importance of setting clear performance-based objectives (Ainscow and Tweddle, 1977).

These approaches are well known to educational psychologists with respect to individual children and many other professionals are aware of the need for precision in setting targets. Many businesses set clear sales or other targets which may well be linked to salaries. Our experience has been that even though we are very familiar with the process of devising objectives in our work with children, a formal structure for organisational change proved very valuable indeed and provoked a lot of thought about optimal strategies and objectives for change. The process of building and then transferring the skills of devising objectives did not seem to be something that could be done routinely without some examples and discussion. In contrast to much in-service training on behavioural skills, which start with instruction and practice in distinguishing between vague and precise descriptions of behaviour at a micro-level, we feel it works well to look at the three levels, from the most global down to the more detailed objectives. Articulating the vision came before providing the detail. Perhaps the analogy with our work with children is the need to assert a confidence at the child level, to be able to project a sense of importance to the techniques of change and to the achievement of change for an individual child.

Thus, inspired by these successful ideas in relation to children, who are most certainly very complex, we adapted the same ideas and models to our work with educational organisations, namely the schools we work with and the educational psychology services we are part of.

Detail and vision

We argue that promoting effective change may be less difficult and complex than a literature survey implies (Leithwood, 1979). We reached this conclusion as a result of practical work in our schools and became aware of the potential to increase our skills and those of our schools in the process of change. We have become increasingly impressed with the need to supplement short-term and intermediate targets with visionary, exciting objectives. We believe that successful organisational change in education can be accelerated with visionary, attainable and immediate objectives.

Visionary objectives are often looked upon initially as too theoretical, unattainable or abstract, yet they have led individuals and organisations to some remarkable accomplishments. They have the power to inspire and spur by providing a vivid picture of what a team is trying to achieve, an image of what it stands for, challenge and excitement as well as a common direction for a its activities. Most workers in education begin with enthusiasm and an ethic of service to the public. Articulating a vision strikes a chord with teachers in particular, presents change and development as shared processes and transmits optimism. There has been increased attention in schools and other organisations in recent years to mission statements. Visionary objectives have specific advantages. They can be expressed with enough precision to give guidance to action and to be easily analysed into smaller steps. Sustaining steps towards the visionary objectives will lead to their realisation. Without this they are in danger of becoming meaningless.

Visionary objectives give guidance and direction to action at any level of time-scale or size of step. Secondly, they give impetus to the change process before all the steps are worked out and without a long period of delay while discussion goes on. Discussion should never be completed, and we have suggested a time scale of three years as a cycle to focus the discussions on levels of objectives. An appropriate visionary objective gives direction to the school, and greater meaning to daily routines and actions, while leaving room for strategies to develop and debate to occur.

The attainability of visionary objectives is an interesting point. By definition a vision should be of something very special, around which myths and rituals can be constructed. Daily life is not like that, unless we bring more vision and importance to it. Perhaps the point is that we will bring a substantial improvement if visions are articulated in ways in which attainment becomes possible. This will lead to the enrichment of daily life, will encourage us to value daily work and remind us of the worth of what we do. In education, it will help to support the high quality we seek to attain. There is no reason to put pressure on ourselves by feeling that we have to achieve legendary standards. The articulation of high-level objectives is a necessary condition of reaching such standards.

Looking at objectives at this level can have other benefits. They can be an important part of creating a shared and mutually supportive ethos in school. This also relates to the sharing of objectives with students. Childhood and adolescence is a time for considering and making life choices which need to be practical, but also a time to form and follow ambitions. Putting visionary objectives on the main and hidden curricula sends important messages to pupils and opens the school to the views of the children and their families, their values and their hopes.

There may be some immediately practical points arising from this process of sharing with the students. Some structure may be required to elicit their views as distinct from a repetition of what they feel the teacher may wish to hear (Gaine, 1988). They may need encouragement, confidence and personal space to begin to be open about what they feel for the future. As well as dreams they will have fears, especially fear of failure and fear of ridicule. Creating the atmosphere in which this quality of discussion can occur will be an important achievement for the school, and will begin to address peer group mores at a useful level. One school began to articulate for pupils, staff and parents the motto: *be reasonable*. With hindsight the positive effect this had could have been developed in other directions.

Sharing objectives at a visionary level with students may also reveal that both staff and students need to be more ambitious. If there is a lack of vision, of known objectives that provide inspiration, then beginning to discuss this issue is a starting point for success. With goals couched at a visionary level, expression in achievable terms is important in matching action to intent. As with religious ideals, if they are not linked to any possible actions, then they become at best superfluous, at worst hypocritical. The process of renewal of objectives at this level is not one that need be constant, hence the three-year cycle we suggest. With this kind of time scale, preparation, discussion and choice will occur frequently enough for there to be debate and renewal within the time almost all pupils and staff spend at the school, and time to achieve progress towards objectives of the highest level.

Attainable objectives are found to lie between short-term and visionary objectives and are stated in such a form that a time scale for accomplishment can be worked out. Our initial steps in devising organisational objectives used termly and annual objectives. These can be expressed in an annual organisational plan and will include items which reflect likely pressures on the organisation from outside. Discussion of the number of objectives will need to occur, with care taken that there is a focus on core activities and not too much of a range or dispersal of energies. Organisations which try to be all things to all people and try to go in all directions at once will reduce their chances of successful outcomes. As schools have relatively little time for planning and other management tasks (Handy and Aitken, 1990), maximising the use of this time suggests careful boundaries to the objectives, their scope and number. This may seem dissonant with the encouraging of visionary objectives, but, within the infinite range of possible objectives, limitation is a necessary but not sufficient condition of substantial progress towards the high level goals.

Intermediate goals can be expressed in behavioural language and can be used as performance indicators and it is at this stage that the issues relating to appraisal need to be addressed (Poster and Poster, 1991). At this stage the who and the how of the change process need to be stated with precision, so that the organisation is supporting the individual and has objectives shared among the individuals. Where organisational objectives are to be addressed primarily by individuals, we question whether these should be classified as goals for the organisation, unless these are primarily piloting exercises.

Objectives at this level can be to achieve new goals or to maintain existing practice. Maintenance goals can constitute up to half of the annual objectives and are helpful to new people entering the organisation, to ensure standards of performance, and are valuable in giving the organisation stability and reliability, a reputation in the community for getting certain things done well. In the time allocation curve in chapter 1 we implied that the time taken on new projects can increase after piloting to implementation, but still a large percentage of the time available is left to effective maintenance; sustaining activities and standards cannot be expected to occur automatically. Time allocation gives priority to what is seen as important and it is hard to argue that something is important but that no time needs to be allocated to it.

At this level, questions of time allocation need to be addressed. Goals need to be couched in positive terms and to be seen positively, perhaps most essentially by those most immediately concerned in their attainment. It is a necessary condition that time is available, and is made available, to attain these objectives. As discussed in chapter 1, if the change process is seen as taking place within the resources the school already has, especially human resources of time, realistic goals are more likely to be set and hence achieved. Some allocation of time must be included for the inevitable mishaps. Planning needs some flexibility for the expansion of aspects of work that were not properly predicted.

The allocation of time can be discussed in more detail at this stage and related to short-term objectives. However, it is perfectly possible to continue with the discussion of annual objectives without going into detail about short-term steps, simply ensuring that time is available regularly throughout the year. How that time will be used in achieving short-term steps which represent a task analysis of the overall objective can be decided later.

As noted briefly above, annual or similar objectives need to involve everyone in the organisation, especially new people. This will also ensure that the whole potential of the organisation is used and developed. Otherwise the potential of those groups in the school who are liable to be undervalued by reasons of status, race, gender, disability and so on may not be realised.

Immediate objectives or short-term objectives are those precise actions or achievements which can be accomplished in the near future or in a given situation. There is a large literature in behavioural psychology about task analysis but we do not propose to say much about this here. Analysis of annual objectives into short-term steps is best discussed in the light of practical experience. The principle to follow is that the best task analysis uses the smallest number of steps that can be followed without risk of failure. To have too many discrete steps slows down progress and may make the achievements relatively unimportant; to have too few creates risks that the steps may be too great to give a high and reinforcing success rate.

The short-term and annual objectives are the levels at which progress is clearly seen and a school should expect and plan for the same level of success for the organisation as it does for individual learning programmes and positive behaviour management programmes. It should be reaching approximately 80 per cent of the annual and short-term objectives. Were the success rate better than this might well mean that the objectives represented steps that were too small and unambitious. There has been some concern in the USA that target-setting in individual education programmes has become unambitious in some instances to prevent litigation and to give the appearance of success. One concern about top-down appraisal schemes is that they may foster the same preoccupation with easily attainable goals, rather than with the value of the goal.

Seeing progress at these levels is vital for many aspects of the organisation and for schools in particular. We refer in this chapter to the mixed view in the literature on the feasibility of change in schools. We note well researched concerns that change in schools may be hard or especially hard to achieve. It is at the level of setting and reaching annual and short-term objectives that the problem needs to be addressed in more depth using some of the approaches that prove effective for children. Such approaches were devised for individual and group situations in which change seemed difficult to attain and hard to sustain. Learning from the kind of steps to success in situation 4.1, some points which will help promote an expectation of success arise:

- Articulating visionary objectives will promote positive thinking among staff
- Visionary objectives have meaning for all who are part of or associated with the school, so promoting co-operation and involvement
- Discussing visionary objectives and general principles first is motivating, and helps to promote a positive consensus and sense of involvement
- Stating objectives in precise terms increases the probability of achievement
- Looking for all to take easily attainable steps forward, no matter how small, begins to make innovation a successful and enjoyable new habit
- Linking steps to recognition and reward as closely as is necessary to motivate effectively is possible if the steps are defined in precise terms
- Starting with shared goals establishes habits of joint change and progress
- All parties involved change their behaviour in clearly defined ways
- The steps are reviewed and new targets set, with more demanding targets being devised after initial success
- Explicit positive records are kept which link progress with recognition and reward

- Extrinsic and intrinsic rewards are linked; the change process may start with material rewards linked to the first steps forward but is sustained by developing a consensus about what is valuable to achieve in itself
- Personal judgements are suspended; individuals are regarded as of worth while the need for progress is asserted independently of this.

Stating immediate objectives in precise terms will also identify those areas in which the school is making progress without undue difficulty and those which pose more problems. This is valuable in overcoming the difficulties identified in the literature. Without this kind of detail it is hard to see how the development process in schools can be effectively promoted. With areas in which progress seems relatively easy, celebration of success can be linked with some key questions:

- how can we move forward to build on this success?
- how can we generalise this success to all parts of the school?
- how can this success be maintained?
- how can we ensure that this success is not taken for granted?
- does this mean we have particularly effective staff?
- do these successes relate closely to the core visions of the school?
- can we progress in larger steps?
- do we need to set smaller objectives in other areas of development?
- do we need consultants, more piloting or a more generous allocation of time in other areas of development?
- when we succeed, what are the key variables?
- how did the management and organisation of the school contribute to this success?
- what resources were devoted to this and what was the input–output relationship?
- what does this mean in our prediction of future progress? Did we predict this success accurately?

Experience and skill in devising short-term steps is something that we expected would come easily to our schools, but they welcomed the devising of lists of possible annual objectives which related to our work with school and/or to issues of special educational needs. This may reflect some of the difficulties that Hargreaves (1991) and others have reported that schools are facing in effectively completing and carrying out school development plans in Britain.

Perhaps it would be easier for schools with histories of engaging in in-service training in learning and behavioural interventions for children if they were able to generalise what they have learned to their organisation. Once the skill of stating goals in precise behavioural terms has been attained, the need for such lists and menus is reduced or become almost superfluous. Fluent performance does not need these supports; they will be useful to ensure that successful innovation is a basic feature of the school rather than something a number of individuals achieve on behalf of the school.

The need to have available objectives with this degree of precision is something we urge on schools. This is in order to translate intentions about education into practice. Without the skill of expressing visions or basic beliefs at a level of precision and with a short time-scale for attainment, it is hard to see how visionary objectives will ever be approached or achieved. Without this, they can be seen as reminders of what ought to be rather than as goals that are being approached, and as such can be a source of stress rather than of inspiration and satisfaction.

Developing this expertise may also help to take some of the pressure off the managers. If the educational change model is applied at a detailed level to children and to the organisation, a basic confidence can be built that the school can grow and develop by positive processes. This allows senior management more opportunities to look strategically at the change processes and to conduct negotiations at the boundaries and with respect to resource needs and usage. If the change process is an integral part of the school's philosophy, if the skills of the school are strong on implementing change at a number of levels, then other management functions can be addressed more effectively. Above all, the organisation can deliver and the energies of the staff can be used to pursue success rather than excuse failure or to try to blame others for failure. An organisation that can demonstrate its capacity to change, to innovate, to respond effectively is much more likely to be seen favourably in resource requests and at a policy level. Building a reputation for getting things done, for delivering the goods, is an excellent and fundamental step forward for any organisation. It can open many doors and create many favourable attitudes which can make future development much easier. It will also make it easier to assert the school's basic philosophy in difficult times.

We argue here that for change to occur successfully in organisations, leaders and managers of the organisations need a vision of where they are going, as well as a clear plan of attainable and short-term or immediate objectives worked out in some detail against a clear time-span. Our own experience suggests that the role of the consultant may be to help inspire the organisations' leaders and managers or persuade them of the value and nature of shared visionary objects for their organisation and then to help them plan in more specific terms attainable as well as immediate objectives. For the consultant, as well as the manager, going through this process has many benefits as well as facilitating the process of change.

These benefits include the following:

- Setting objectives in an organisation is a proactive act that provides a clear focus on outcomes that an organisation's activities are aiming to elicit. This is in contrast to many activities which are simply reactive to problems cropping up in situations recurrently that require crisis intervention from managers and outside consultants.

- Setting objectives for change may act as a preventive way of stopping problems occurring. Thus, research on the Aids virus can be as important as trying to care for and manage the victims of the virus whose increasing numbers stretch more and more scarce resources. Similarly in schools an objective such as 'each individual teacher is able to produce a clear learning programme for a child presenting learning difficulties', once attained, may well prevent many children not having their needs met by teachers unable to carry this out.

- Clear objectives allow for sensible planning about strategies and activities to attain them. Such clarity and detail can enhance the rationality behind activities being carried out in the given organisation, thus making efforts more efficient and effective. Clarity is also beneficial to outside consultants who can streamline their efforts into such activities as in-service training to transmit specific skills that are required for the achievement of the set objectives.

- Setting objectives enables both organisational managers and consultants to appraise and evaluate their own work. Thus, successful achievement of pre-set objectives produces clear feedback that individual activities are having definite pay-offs. Equally, if clearly attainable objectives are not achieved this may be important feedback information that leads to the change of strategy or activity. Precision in objectives enhances rigour in evaluation.

- Devising clear objectives can help schools to harness their expertise and experience of the learning process to their organisation (Garratt, 1987; Wilkinson and Cave, 1987).

- Setting objectives for change can empower people (Peters, 1988), creating success for each team member (Hastings et al., 1986).

- Setting objectives for change can help the organisation deal effectively with imposed change (Peters, 1988). This may involve particular clarity regarding medium term and core objectives. Acklaw (1990), for example, suggests that educational psychology services need to consider reducing the diversity of core objectives in order to enhance service quality at a time of imposed change and exposure to powerful market forces.

- Working towards objectives can help in learning about and formally researching school effectiveness (Beare et al., 1989). This can also help to create a positive, mutually supportive organisational culture not only within the school but shared with inspectors, advisers, educational psychologists and education officers.

- Working towards objectives can help promote interest in and knowledge of change techniques, which may be partly known to the school or relatively new to educational applications, such as quality circle techniques (Hutchins 1985; Fox 1989).

Thus, setting objectives for work in organisations can be a very powerful tool for use by consultants or organisation managers providing as it does a common direction, challenge, excitement, vehicle for planning, evaluation and appraisal, and an approach that encourages prevention, problem-solving and pro-activity.

We started our work with schools as consultants by setting out a menu of desirable and attainable objectives. We then, in consultation with school managers, generally headteachers, agreed specific objectives to be achieved within a set time scale.

Having agreed with schools the need to achieve key objectives independently and deriving plans and strategies from appropriate sources in psychology, we had to ensure that we regularly enquired about such changes; for, until we had a clear record system for skill dissemination, developments were not always brought to our attention. As we found ourselves asking about the attainment of school objectives, we were pleasantly surprised to find schools exercising skills often without bringing this to our attention. It became clear to us that we should be persistent, optimistic and consistent over a period of time, record precise skill acquisition, maintenance and independent use and provide encouragement and recognition for this process.

We wrote systematic spines or menus of objectives or organisational outcomes and found that a relatively small number of objectives were applicable to a large number of our schools. Examples included:

• staff can write and run individual learning programmes
• school involves parents in specific learning programmes on target children
• staff have specified counselling skills acquired in explicit training.

Although we planned the menu of objectives jointly, we adopted different strategies for working towards them and for negotiating the objectives with schools. However, the differences seemed not to matter; it seemed to be the precision and the agreement with the schools for joint action that led us forward.

The record formats we devised were also very simple, with record sheets for single school strategies being used sparingly and with key objectives for all or nearly all our schools entered on a single sheet with space too for recording progress. It was all very quick. The process of change lost much of its mystery and we became far less tentative about the degree of change that could be achieved.

Are objectives always appropriate?

It needs to be reiterated that thinking in objectives is only one approach to understanding and planning change in schools. Equally valid are approaches that do not focus on end points at all but are much more concerned with culture, processes or the circularity of all change processes. Morgan (1986) compares American approaches with Japanese in this respect:

> In the American view objectives should be hard and fast and clearly stated for all to see. In the Japanese view they emerge from a more fundamental process of exploring and understanding the values through which a firm is or should be operating. A knowledge of these values, the limits that are to guide action, defines a set of possible actions. An action chosen from this set may not be the very best, but it will satisfy parameters deemed crucial for success.

> (Morgan 1986: 93)

In Japanese systems and in cybernetics it is suggested that it can actually be systemically wiser to focus on defining and challenging constraints and limits rather than planning targets or ends. In this approach to strategy, instead of setting objectives for change the school should plan for what it wishes to avoid. This might include closure, exclusions of pupils, excessive reliance on the local authority and so on. The effect of this approach is then to define an evolving space for possible actions and action plans that satisfy critical viability limits.

Systemic approaches to families and organisations have been referred to. Most of these approaches emphasise that systems function in circular relationships. One process cannot change in isolation, for mutual causality is ongoing. From this perspective it may seem short-sighted to attempt to set objectives in a seemingly linear fashion. However, we believe there is still an important place for vision and for the setting of objectives as long as we are cognisant of possible circular effects occurring. Such effects are most obvious when objectives are imposed. Attendance objectives of an LEA may be met by a school simply learning new ways of recording statistics to show itself in a better light. In your own system it may be less clear what mutual causality circle is being completed when objectives are set.

CONCLUSION

We have looked at the positive effects of setting appropriate objectives for educational organisations and how basic principles in psychology made sense of this process for us, and made this not only feasible but enjoyable and stimulating. We have looked at alternative perspectives to objectives approaches and end this chapter by leaving you with the shared agenda of arriving at a vision which can be worked to passionately but realistically by everyone in education as a whole and your organisation or service in particular.

Perhaps in education today the waters have become a little muddy and our vision a touch blurred. The time is now right to take stock and reflect on what we really want to achieve for our children.

ACTION PLAN

Do you wish to adopt an objectives approach to planning school change?

- Clarify your own or your leadership's vision for your organisation.
- State this vision in a tangible way that can be understood and actively engaged with by all involved in the organisation.
- Share and discuss the vision and its achievement widely.
- Set out a small number of attainable targets with as much participation as possible for those likely to be involved in delivery.
- Set short-term targets, agree who will do what and when to achieve them. Ensure there is adequate discussion and involvement before these are finalised. Jettison targets that cannot be agreed. Ensure that the level at which they are set will ensure success.
- Monitor other effects of setting objectives particularly in relation to backwash and mutual causality. Is someone quietly setting you some counter-objectives?
- Discuss at various stages with trusted and skilled critical friends both within and outside the organisation. Keep testing your ideas for validity and for a good fit with reality.

Chapter 5

Consultation and negotiation

In this chapter we look at promoting change through participation in decision making, negotiation, consultation and making the best use of consultants. We emphasise the importance of these processes for the development of mutual support and cooperation.

PROMOTING CHANGE THROUGH PARTICIPATION

> The head is always, in law as well as in fact, responsible for the situations in his or her school. Successful heads have interpreted these considerable powers and duties wisely. They have not been authoritarian, consultative, or participative; they have been all three at different times as the conditions seemed to warrant, though most often participative. Their success has often come from choosing well, from knowing when to take the lead and when to confirm the leadership offered by their colleagues.
>
> (ILEA, 1985: Para. 3.25)

In reality of course there are many tensions between leadership and collegiality, management and participation, although aspiring towards their functional coexistence is both laudable and prudent. Constructive

Consultation and negotiation –
insiders and outsiders

participation is important for a decision-making group such as a school where the effectiveness of the decision is closely bound up with the willingness of staff to implement it. Collegiality has become a very popular notion. It has been advocated by different writers for different reasons and we are clearly interested in the idea of increased involvement of staff because of its relevance to whole-school development and change. There is an obvious logic to the idea of greater involvement leading to greater ownership and commitment to decision making, policy development and other change processes. Advocates from different backgrounds have encouraged collegiality for at least three reasons:

- increasing professional accountability (Campbell, 1985)
- increased participation in organisational development (Herzberg, 1966)
- as an alternative to the headteacher's concentration of power (Hargreaves, 1974).

Campbell (1985), describes the collegial school as having small working groups of teachers feeding back ideas for school-wide change to all the staff at staff meetings for decision making. These working groups would usually be led by leaders, co-ordinators or consultants who would also work alongside teacher colleagues. Such collaboration is usually supported by headteachers who have committed themselves to devolving responsibilities to the staff group and to supporting and servicing such activity. The key components of collegiality thus seem to be: consultation, communication, continuity, co-ordination and coherence. In the UK the ILEA, when it existed, and the DES fully supported moves towards collegiality, and in the United States and elsewhere there have been studies of outstanding schools which provide strong support for collaborative planning and decision making as well as collegial relationships (Beare et al.,1989). One strategy recommended in the United States for the development of school culture within the context of school-site management states:

> The staff of each school is given a considerable amount of responsibility and authority in determining the exact means by which they address the problem of increasing academic performance. This includes giving staffs more authority over curricular and instructional decisions and allocation of building resources.
>
> (Purkey and Smith, 1985: 358)

We have worked with schools that have devolved power and responsibilities in a variety of ways. A number of headteachers, including those of primary schools, have now delegated control of their budgets to other members of staff. Others have given the professional development and INSET responsibilities, special needs co-ordination, liaison with other schools and agencies to trusted staff empowered to carry out the job. Perhaps with the immense changes in responsibilities being devolved to schools in Britain and elsewhere in the world the move to broadening the participation and leadership density within a school is inevitable. Boyd, a leading educationalist from Scotland who has had substantial experience as a secondary school teacher, head and adviser, sets out his own view with regard to the development of whole-school policies:

> Participation is not easy. It makes demands on all concerned. I would argue that recent changes in school based curriculum development, in inter-disciplinary courses, in cooperative teaching, have all made school staffs more sophisticated and more willing to engage in consultation and participation. It may be a time consuming approach, and people may feel from time to time that it would be easier to have the head decide for them, but whole school policies will be an empty sham if those who are to be engaged in their implementation are not also to be involved in their formulation.
>
> (Boyd, 1985: 8)

Internationally it would seem clear that effective leadership and change require approaches that encourage and support high levels of collaboration not only with teachers but also with parents and pupils themselves. Evidence of the effectiveness of increased participation of staff in decision making and policy development is slowly emerging, but further research and the sharing of real experiences and case studies will be needed to go beyond the rhetoric into the practicalities of achieving the right balance between leadership and collegial relationships. This is an area that requires considerable reflection, discussion and enquiry, and schools moving in the direction of increased collegiality should not underestimate the impact of changing role expectations, power structures and established decision-making processes.

Before we leave this section it is worth reflecting on some very positive British evidence from Mortimore *et al.* (1988) who, having traced the work of 2,000 children over five years in 50 London primary schools, claimed to have identified the factors which influence the success of the primary school. At several points in the book the role of the headteacher is referred to. The most effective heads were found to involve their deputy and staff in decision making.

> The involvement of teachers in drawing up school guidelines was associated with exciting and stimulating teaching in the classrooms, and greater pupil involvement with work. Another aspect of involvement – the participation of teachers in decisions about the allocation of classes – was associated with greater amounts of teacher time communicating about work generally, and, more specifically, giving pupils feedback about work.
>
> (Mortimore *et al.*, 1988: 247)

Participation in the change process

The results of internal school reviews or organisational evaluation as described in chapter 2 provide many positive issues for school development. It may also be helpful to have a structured brainstorm about issues to which the staff may have to react over the period under consideration, such as the next academic year. These two processes will provide many, perhaps too many, areas of potentially positive and participative work.

Selection and prioritisation have to take place and some difficult decisions have to be made. It is at this stage that skills in consultation and negotiation will be most valuable. The process is to ensure that good ideas are identified, that potential difficulties are foreseen, that a manageable agenda for development is established and that these decisions contribute to the development and fulfilment of staff, individually and as a group.

When a number of suggestions have been made, they need to be clustered to avoid duplication and a count made of the number of times a particular issue has been raised. When this has been done, working groups can be set up to prevent reinventing the wheel, as well as to prevent duplication of effort. This can usefully involve a literature search, contact with advisers or other consultants, and contact with other schools and organisations. Such a search needs to be conducted quickly and efficiently. When this has been done, it becomes clearer how much work will be needed to reach objectives, and more will be known about the issues likely to be relevant and problems likely to occur.

This process also improves the involvement of all staff on practical and co-operative tasks. It helps to build up the school's network of contacts on positive issues, to identify sources of information and to reach other underused skills such as those of librarians. Time needs to be allocated and defended for these processes. Teachers can begin to evolve efficient house styles and conventions in written feedback and the use of skills in presentations to adults. This part of the process really begins to focus on practicalities and this degree of precision makes any differences of opinion specific and part of a much broader positive process. Much of the consultation comes in the recognition that giving staff practical, information-gathering tasks makes the change process one that is to be of benefit to the whole organisation. It also provides many opportunities for joint positive work and ideally, by giving all staff a role, can help to prevent the emergence of pecking orders.

This model of process-led, participative school development brings us full circle to the skills of consultation and negotiation that teachers apply to the classroom, rather than importing a model from other applications. This is important for a number of reasons. We have referred to the overall school ethos and core skills being applied to different aspects of the organisation, using an educational model of the change process throughout the school. In addition, there is a need to focus innovation on the core role of the school, on the children.

Consultation and decision making

Management literature gives excellent guidance about starting innovation in organisations. However, we are not aware of accounts that go into detail about the methods available for negotiation and consultation as part of the innovation process in schools and other educational organisations. This process needs considerable reflection, planning and critical analysis and evaluation, along organisational, psychological and political dimensions.

Consultation has historically been considered in relation to effective decision making and relates to the seeking of information or advice from others within or outside the organisation. As a result of considering and deliberating on information and advice gathered, decisions are usually, because of the constraints of time, made with less than complete information available. Most employees are able to recognise the extent of attempts by their managers to consult with them, and can probably evaluate how much impact and power they felt their own contribution to have.

When beginning to reflect on why, how much, when and how to consult with staff over decision making in a school organisation it is important to reflect on power, its use and misuse.

An ability to influence the outcomes of decision-making processes is a well recognised source of power, and one that has attracted considerable attention in the organization-theory literature. Since organizations are in large measure decision-making systems, an individual or group that can exert a major influence on decision processes can exert a great influence on the affairs of his or her organization.

(Morgan, 1986: 165)

Consideration of the parallels between human decision making and organisational decision making dates back to the 1940s and 1950s and the work of March and Simon (1958). They argued that decision making was the key activity of managers and that organisations can never be entirely rational because their members have limited information-processing abilities. Decisions in organisations are settled for as being 'good enough', being based on simple rule-of-thumb and limited search and information. This is similar to the use of scripts at a personal level referred to in chapter 1 to build decisions and practices on a set of information, ignoring and simplifying data, and identifying only very dissonant or ambiguous items for further examination. Since they wrote, there has been much research into considering organisations from an information-processing stance, often with the focus of how organisations deal with the complexity and uncertainty of the environment in which they exist. Galbraith (1977), for instance, found that the greater the uncertainty the more difficult it was for organisations to programme and routinise activity by preplanning a response. Uncertain tasks require greater amounts of information to be processed between decision makers engaged in performing tasks. Little wonder that schools have found it extremely difficult, with the intense levels of uncertainty, information and legislation overload, to produce realistic development plans over the last few years in Britain.

> Hierarchy provides an effective means for controlling situations that are fairly certain, but in uncertain situations can encounter information and decision overload.
>
> (Morgan, 1986: 82)

Less mechanistic and more organic organisations based on processes that are more flexible and ad hoc, with greater scope for discretion and judgement and generally looser properties, do better in times of greater uncertainty.

What Simon and March did not predict was the scale and speed of development of information systems in many organisations. The introduction of computers, databases, networks and interfaces have transformed modern organisations. Ever-increasing amounts of information are easily accessible and decision making and information gathering and reporting are increasingly automated. While schools have been slower to receive the full impact of technological developments, it is perhaps only a matter of time before they themselves will be seen as synonymous with their information systems, and the information system itself will drive organisation, consultation and decision making.

In an examination of organisations as political systems Morgan (1986) explores the kinds of power utilised in decision making and usefully distinguishes between three interrelated elements:

Decision premises Organisational constraints, assumptions, conscious manipulations, beliefs and practices about 'who we are' and how we do things round here.

Decision-making processes The ground rules that guide decision making. How should a decision be made and who should be involved? When will it be made? When should the decision be discussed? At what point on the agenda?

Issues and objectives These can be influenced and shaped by an individual's eloquence, command of the facts, emphasis, passionate commitment or sheer tenacity. The preparation of reports and involvement in the discussion will add to the power of individuals to influence decisions in which they are involved.

When reflecting on the way decisions are made in your own organisation it is worth thinking about these dimensions of power. How are decisions usually made? What usually happens? Why is it always done this way? Who is doing the most influencing? How, when and why?

Most educational managers would avoid the Clochemerle scenario described in the introduction to this book. They recognise that springing any innovation on the most easy-going group is usually a mistake. Yet pressures of time and other pressures seem to leave managers with unresolved dilemmas about the degree of consultation appropriate to a particular situation. Mortimore *et al.*(1988) argued that headteachers need a very clear view on leadership:

> They need to be able to divide the decisions they are required to make into two groups: those which it is quite properly their responsibility to take and for which any attempt at delegation to a staff decision would be seen as a dereliction of duty, and those which, equally properly, belong to the staff as a whole. In some cases it will be perfectly clear to which group a certain decision belongs; in others, it will be extremely difficult to decide. Mistakes will be made and the consequences . . . will have to be suffered. However if the head is perceptive and sensitive she or he will soon learn to distinguish which decisions are which.
>
> (Mortimore *et al.*, 1988: 281)

It is easy to recognise this point. Most of us are glad when trivial decisions are made by our managers, or actions taken that are clearly to our advantage, but there is a very wide range of other decisions where we would like to participate at some level and be listened to. Interestingly, the study by Handy (1984) of headteachers as managers showed that teachers and other staff came to the headteachers in primary schools for decisions so frequently that basic preventative management time was seriously squeezed. Yet the decisions on which advice was sought were largely trivial, and only a yes/no response was usually sought. In Clochemerle terms, this is much like the mayor's planning of the new pissoir being badly disrupted by every user of the old one asking for advice on how to deal most effectively with its barbarities on every occasion of use. Management can easily become reactive for much of the time with innovation being underplanned and underpiloted, and it is often the case that effective consultation is one of the first areas to be squeezed. This scenario also creates expectations of managers to engage in instant decision making. This can in turn lead to an emotional need to defend one's actions even if they were taken in the heat of the moment and may not have been well thought out. The need to save face comes from taking reactive actions instinctively, without having time or space to address the basic principles and procedures.

We see negotiation and consultation as much more valuable and fundamental processes that need to be protected and maintained by proactive leaders and managers at all times. In the previous chapter, we stressed the importance of setting objectives at three levels: short-term, medium-term and visionary. We indicated how identifying positive reasons for change would help to release creativity and suggested ways of doing this. We also looked at organisational evaluation as a positive exercise related to the change process, rather than looking at staff appraisal in a static, context-free manner (Manning, 1988). Effective consultation and negotiation are more likely to take place in situations where this kind of planned activity is occurring on regular cycles with maximal involvement of staff rather than in crisis-led or reactive situations.

So how might a headteacher work towards negotiating change with effective and efficient consultation? The question still remains: when do we need to consult with staff?

No one likes to be consulted and then feel not listened to when it comes to the final decision. Oppressed groups are no less suspicious of liberals than of more overtly dominant elements in society. This psychological and apparently universal truth may derive from a number of factors relating to membership of modern societies and organisations as well as from human psychology. We feel important and powerful if asked for our opinion or advice, as valuable to the other party. When we are consulted by our managers or superiors we are immediately put in touch with feelings of self-importance and omnipotence which are very sensitive to being thwarted, perhaps particularly in males in our society. At the time we may feel that what we have said has been properly listened to. However, if the final decision seemingly ignores our contribution we decide that the whole process was a sham. Our resultant feelings are then of irritation, resentment, anger and rebellion. Our behaviour may become petty or contrary or downright belligerent, since we have not got our own way! The Child may take over and a negative causal circle emerges that may be hard to change. Readers will no doubt recall such situations and their own reactions to what has probably felt like empty consultation or poor management.

What lessons can we learn from this?

- Consultation should not be equated with democracy;
- Individual expectations and feelings will be invoked by being involved in consultation;
- It is not worth consulting just for form's sake;
- It is necessary to make clear to those being consulted the limits and parameters of the decision being considered and how far their contribution is likely to affect the decision;
- Managers can expect to face negative feelings and behaviour at the end of any substantial consultation exercise. It is impossible to keep everyone happy.

While management by consensus might sound attractive it may be found to be the line of least resistance rather than the most appropriate, rationally determined path to follow. Consultation may be primarily for information and comment rather than to give away decision-making power and it is important to be clear and open about the purpose of consultation.

Specific consultation techniques

We refer on numerous occasions to methods of eliciting and applying to the organisation teacher skills, interests and beliefs. This emphasis will create many layers of dialogue and remove many sources of potential tension from a school. However a grasp of specific techniques of consultation is also required.

Quality circle techniques Piloted by Japanese industry, where attempts are made to use the traditional craft, high-quality ethos of Japanese workers to improve the quality of product and performance. It is also worth reflecting on many other aspects of Japanese management practice such as:

> the ritual of *ringi*, a collective decision making process in which a policy document passes from manager to manager for approval. The effect of this process is to explore the premises and values underlying the decision proposal. If a manager disagrees with what is being proposed he is typically free to amend the decision proposal and to allow the document to circulate again. In this way the decision process explores the decision domain until a proposal satisfies all critical parameters.
>
> (Morgan, 1986: 93)

While this can be very time-consuming, at the end the managers can be quite certain that most of the errors will have been detected and that all are committed to the final decision. There is a need to work on the policy, including details, in order to meet the commitment of consultation. In such an arrangement, negative or non-constructive thinking and feeling is less likely to be projected onto the workplace, in contrast to a single 'consultation' staff meeting, which is an open invitation to unhelpful criticism.

There is an extensive literature in this area not often familiar to schools. However, we urge greater use of consultation techniques derived from psychology and education, as well as from business. These might include the following.

Management by walking about (MBWA) Common in industry, and Peters and Austin (1985) cite many examples of its use. Many managers in schools may think they are doing this, but it should include both an involvement of the most senior management in problem solving at the most basic level, and the methods by which opportunities to identify and promote innovation are created. Headteachers walking about are not so much monitoring the school as enquiring into the school and listening to it. What happens on a walkabout is also a good indication of progress from a reactive mode of management to a more proactive one. Reactive managers dislike walkabouts; they simply are accosted with more so-called 'crises' to respond to. Proactive managers like walkabouts a lot; they learn so much about moving the organisation forward and using the skills of the people. How are we doing? What are we thinking? What do we need to be doing? Managing by walking about involves curiosity, the capacity to listen, and the ability to seek out challenges before they become problems that can ambush you (Nias, 1987).

Evaluation and feedback This is vital. There is merit in anonymous written evaluation of management performance by staff with specific requests for positive suggestions. These should be summarised and incorporated into an action plan devised by management to follow up the positive and negative points raised, especially the positive suggestions for improvement. A report back to staff must then be made in written as well as verbal form, otherwise the consultation exercise is clearly and rightly seen as superficial and cynical.

Some managers may find this a little daunting, but one of the authors did this with his school pupils throughout his time in teaching and found excellent suggestions coming forward. One example of this was the pupil who said that when the class of 14-year-old pupils came into the room quietly and calmly, the lesson always began with a very clear explanation of what was to be done. In contrast, when the class came into the lesson noisily and rowdily, the lesson began with the very briefest of explanations with the class being required to do a written task, no matter how brief, before explanation began in earnest. The pupil understood and approved of this as it meant that the class was always well settled within a short time. However, the pupil said that some children were a little nervous about this and all of them preferred the lesson starting with a clear introduction. She suggested that the lesson always started with the clear explanation, but with the class reciting back the key parts of the introduction. It might sound silly, it might sound old-fashioned when the teacher was running a liberal, activities-based classroom, but the suggestion was tried and it worked extremely well.

The use of creative thinking techniques Relatively unknown to schools. There are some good guides to this area such as Adams (1986). Perhaps the designation of the arts as the creative element of the school has reduced the responsibility of others to foster creativity? Common features of these techniques are the rules which exclude negative comments, ensure tight running of the groups and keeping the group on task rather than dispersing attention into irrelevance. They focus on the creativity that ordinary people have and which can be released by specific organisational methods, especially in groups, allowing and encouraging thinking out loud, rather than expecting developments to spring fully formed from a single source. These groups have specific rather than general issues to address and outcomes are sought where possible, although general discussion is regarded as helpful in beginning to explore fundamental or potentially difficult areas.

Consultation meetings for all staff Inefficient in terms of time – people hours – and need to have specific rationales to justify their existence. We do not feel that meetings, especially large meetings are effective or useful for consultation, with the exceptions referred to above. They can of course be used sparingly and valuably as rituals to highlight success.

Task-centred consultation Far more effective. Take an issue, prepare for the consultation exercise by summarising the literature or background, and have staff complete structured tasks such as examining the positive, negative and neutral possible effects of that issue on parents. The consultation in this instance involves extending knowledge of the area under consideration.

Having clear and well understood lines of decision making Vital. Consultation does not dilute the line of management and it is not a democratic process. It allows those who are specifically responsible for levels of decision making to ensure that all affected by the decisions have informed the decision. Well informed decisions can also be rapid, decisive and efficient if specific consultation processes are used rather than open-ended or unstructured methods.

Considering how the decision and the process will look to others An excellent personal or senior management team exercise. Devise a list of those likely to be influenced by a decision, and reflect on how they may see the decision and the process of decision making, both positively and negatively.

Acting devil's advocate Best done with clear agreement about the ultimate power of decision making, but can valuably inform that process. Identify options, then have a small group work intensively to find fault and negative outcomes. Then work to eradicate these from the preferred option or from all of them if the choice has yet to be made. McLean and Marshall (1988) describe two approaches to producing a critique of any strategy:

The Langford Model Each part of the strategy is presented by different team members and then criticised by three Devil's advocates. The first looks at how far the process for developing the strategy is in line with the organisation's values and vision. The second looks at the content and how far the strategy is taking the organisation towards or away from the vision. The third critic looks at how the strategy will be implemented.

The Brandenburg Concerto Team members adopt roles from which to listen to and respond to the strategy. Roles might include a main grade teacher, the headteacher, the local adviser, a parent, a governor, a pupil and so on.

We have discussed many facets of consultation. Perhaps the basic message is a simple one. Consultants may be found within the organisation as well as outside. Consultation processes facilitate study in depth of strategy and decision making options. In schools, where managers' time is under threat from the need to make many trivial but instant decisions, consultation is an underused resource. It is not to be confused with a democratic process although it does respect those at a junior level in the organisation and it does seek to explore the effects of strategies and decisions on all parties. Creating a democratic school may use similar methods but the two issues of consultation and democracy in decision making are separate.

Negotiation

Before embarking on any change programme it is crucial to map out all the interested parties likely to be affected by the change process and to consider how they can be brought on board (Hawkins and Shohet, 1989). Deliberating on this may well lead you to considerations of how best to negotiate with other parties involved. Garratt (1987) suggests three key questions that are relevant to maximising political support for any change effort within an organisation:

- Who knows? Who has accurate information about the problem?
- Who cares? Who has the emotional investment in bringing about change?
- Who can? Who has the power to reorder resources so that changes can occur? Who when faced with energy, commitment and facts can say 'Yes'?

Negotiation is often a key process in the mobilisation of change, particularly when the appropriate parties have been identified and the time is right for change. Outside consultants will be very helpful in these early processes of getting going and transcending tightly held assumptions and closed systems. A key area of management performance is the effectiveness of negotiation at the boundaries of the organisation. This seems especially important in education, where societies have seen schools as organisations in which the ideal society can be developed, preserved, legislated about or fought over. We do not see schools as major agents of social change and judge the evidence as suggesting that schools are relatively conservative systems within society, partly because of the weight of law applied to them and the funding sources:

> During the entire modern era in the United States, the school has been seen as a reinforcement of existing society rather than as a mechanism of social change.
>
> (Dalin and Rust, 1983: 10).

This is not a value judgement and not necessarily a desirable state of affairs. However, it suggests that negotiation skills are especially necessary in the implementation of ideas or projects which can be cast as 'radical'. We noted earlier that innovations in the area of equal opportunities need to be well thought out and objectives may need particularly well defined steps to be achieved.

Essential reading for any school innovator is *Getting to Yes* (Fisher and Ury, 1981). We applaud their definition of negotiation as a positive and ethical process. Negotiators should not start by seeing the process in adversarial terms; rather they should search for the principles each party to the negotiations wishes to uphold. When these have been drawn out, the negotiations begin as a joint endeavour to find the positions that will work to mutual advantage. In direct competition for resources, this will be difficult to achieve, but this kind of direct adversarial situation is the exception rather than the rule and building precedents and procedures for wise and reasoned division of resources should be the aim. Looking at resource allocation in special needs in schools and equal opportunities issues will need particular care and prominence in negotiations to reduce or to try to prevent 'resource drift' (Dessent, 1987). Ethical negotiation is particularly needed to defend and recognise the just demands and resource requirements of those who have least power in society as a whole and schools in particular.

Negotiators who try to compete immediately lock the process into a negative, uncreative loop, in which solutions of mutual benefit will not be identified or reached. Negative negotiators are often to be found when they are under pressures of 'credibility'. The losers in this process may be beaten but the defeat may build motivation for more conflict. As psychologists, we try to avoid taking sides. We can provide guidance, support, information, hypotheses or suggestions about cause or effect, but mainly we provide a framework in which positive solutions can be identified by problem owners. We find this strikes chords with teachers and we also find that teachers have some excellent if underused skills in this area, skills which they usually deploy to great effect with children, but less frequently with colleagues or parents. It seems that the application of these skills is often impeded by being set up with too close a brief and with too little security about credibility. This is not a set of arguments in favour of compromise as a substitute for policy. Rather it is the recognition that identifying basic needs and exploring the principles which the parties involved personify is necessary to optimise resource allocation and to devise creative solutions, thus reducing the likelihood of missing valuable items.

Conflict management

Conflict is an inevitable and integral part of everyone's life. We should not attempt to avoid it or suppress it even though it can be destructive as well as constructive. It can occur over resources, needs and values and there is a growing body of interest and research into conflict and the social skills and belief systems of assertiveness as contrasted with aggression (Priest and Higgins, 1991).

How might we begin to liberate teachers' negotiation and conflict management skills? Some action research could be valuable here. Identify a teacher in whose class the children seem to have few confrontations with each other and study how he or she avoids or deals with their conflict. Such a teacher will:

- set up the activities so that sharing is essential to success;
- provide strong urging to work together for success;
- talk of the benefits of co-operation;
- reward joint work;
- insist that group composition is fluid or is set by teacher;
- treat everyone as equally valuable;
- ask what everyone needs to do and wants to do, but is routinely directive;
- set a brisk pace in the classroom so that the work rate is high;
- have credibility with parents, who do not expect their children to act out adult conflicts on the school premises;
- ensure nobody is left out, but provide strong advice on social skills and practise what is preached, using these skills and the ethos at a number of levels;
- set up a strong class consciousness so that children are encouraged to see success as a whole-class affair.

If a child who comes into the school actively seeking conflict with other children begins to create problems, the teacher will:

- strengthen the teaching;
- provide a very tight agenda of tasks;
- give the child clear guidance about positive expectations and appropriate rewards and recognition for this;
- provide closer guidance to all about sharing and other situations in which conflict could occur;
- start to work with parents to eliminate the causes of confrontational behaviour;
- intervene before conflict escalates;

- give the child a range of types of acceptable behaviour if the child is feeling uptight;
- give the child fair treatment;
- consider the involvement of other agencies to establish and give advice on resolving the sources of the child's problem.

Putting these ideas into action is something that most teachers have done successfully with children, creating situations in which all children feel valued, but have limits imposed on their behaviour and learn the benefits of co-operation, and of tasks achieved efficiently. This does not involve inefficiency, reinventing the wheel. Having a range of friendships and not having enemies make for a pleasant and successful working routine. However, generalising from successful conflict management with children to that with adults is not always as straightforward as it might seem. Adults have more experience which can produce habits of conflict and can have more face to save or lose in negotiation and co-operation, which they may habit-ually 'save' through recourse to conflict. Negotiating progress often seems much harder than it reasonably ought to be: the Clochemerle scenario again.

In our society conflict is pervasive among individuals, groups, organisations and nations. Some would say this is inevitable, perhaps even natural considering the diversity of people's values, attitudes, beliefs, motives and goals. Teachers and others involved in schools constantly face the potential for real or perceived frustration of needs and concerns and this feeds the opportunities for conflict.

It is commonplace for the introduction of ideas which have been carefully designed for the common good to be resisted, and this can cause great unpleasantness. Processes of consultation prepare the quality of the innovation through the methods outlined above, but the move towards agreement is a skill area of its own. Headteachers we have spoken to often seem baffled by the Clochemerle scenario, but we find it obvious. People will resist positive innovation if to do so is their only or main influence over the system. If the manager says A, then the powerless will say Z, whatever the merits of A and Z and all schemes in between. If the manager is very authoritarian, the workforce will say A but do Z, a wrecking or sabotage response.

It is well worth reflecting on your own style and that of other significant individuals within the organisation, when faced with conflict. The two main dimensions are assertiveness and co-operativeness. Along these two dimensions, according to Thomas (1976), are to be found five distinct styles for dealing with conflict:

Competition Characterised by the desire to meet one's own needs and concerns at the expense of the other party, the most assertive and the least co-operative style.

Collaboration Characterised by maximum use of co-operation and assertion. Aims to satisfy the needs and concerns of both parties by: acknowledging that conflict exists; recognising each other's concerns, needs and goals; identifying alternative resolutions and their consequences for both parties; selecting the alternative that meets the needs and concerns and accomplishes the goals of both parties. It also involves the evaluation of the implemented alternative.

Avoidance Characterised by unco-operative and unassertive behaviour by both parties.

Accommodation Characterised by co-operative and unassertive behaviour. The other party's needs are placed above one's own.

Compromise Midway between competition and collaboration and avoidance and accommodation. Partial fulfilment of needs, concerns and goals of both parties.

To be effective at managing conflict you need to be able to use any of these styles and know when each style is appropriate. Most people develop one style and then tend to stick with it in most situations, thus neglecting potentially more effective styles. Having identified the appropriate style to adopt in a given situation it will be necessary to select an effective tactic. Research carried out by Priest and Higgins (1991) found the most commonly used tactics by teachers working with pupils included the following:

- to *inhibit* or smooth over
- to *ignore*
- to *adjudicate*, by applying a rule, usually in favour of the institution
- to *arbitrate* by moving towards a compromise (lose/lose) or to the selection of one position (win/lose)
- to *mediate* by looking at interests not positions, mutual problem-solving, regulating and improving communication, differentiating and integrating, adopting creative approaches using drama, puppets, roleplay, stories and role reversal.

As with the conflict management styles, tactics are more appropriate to some situations than others. The skill is knowing what the issues are, what style you will adopt and what tactics will work best in a given situation. It is interesting to reflect on some of the tactics pupils reported themselves also using in conflict resolution situations according to another part of the research carried out by Priest and Higgins (1991):

- selective forgetting
- humour
- apologising and shaking hands.

The replies to questionnaires seemed to indicate that staff only became involved in pupils' conflict resolution when the pupils were held 'captive', and virtually never because they wanted them to resolve their conflict with other pupils. Are teachers not perceived as helpful in these situations? Do pupils feel mostly in control? What about those who feel powerless to speak up? While consideration of pupils' conflict resolution may seem a long way from that of promoting school change it may indeed be very relevant when attempting to create an organisational culture that is seeking to learn and collaborate at every level. This will include pupils, parents, teachers, managers, advisers and administrators. Effective problem-solving, mediation and collaboration will need to pervade the successful school's ethos and be reflected in approaches to equal opportunities, human rights, personal and social development, decision making and development.

Basic negotiation in the school system

Of the above conflict management styles and tactics, effective negotiation probably most closely resembles collaboration and mediation. Fisher and Ury (1981) distinguish approaches to positional bargaining. They emphasise that participants are problem solvers with the shared goal of achieving a wise, mutually advantageous outcome reached efficiently and amicably. They emphasise the importance of separating the people from the problem alongside the suggestion that we should be soft on the people and hard on the problem. It is possible to proceed independent of trust, focusing on interests not positions. They encourage the invention of options for mutual gain, the creation of multiple options to choose from and the insistence on objective standards. Ultimately, they argue, we should all reason and be open to reason, yielding to principle not pressure. We think that it is important to view negotiation as a process:

- by which mutually beneficial outcomes can be identified;
- in which there are seldom winners or losers;
- in which macho, pressurised thinking has no place;
- which is creative, finding new solutions and new ideas and new ways of framing situations which are progress-oriented;
- with specified joint actions arising;
- which respects individuals' integrity;
- which involves the discussion of basic positive principles before the discussion of specifics;
- which involves preparation on the other participants' needs;
- which involves clarity and honesty about basic positions;
- which involves honesty and explicitness about beliefs and positions which are not negotiable and reliability about this;
- which seeks to divert resources towards joint progress.

Effective headteachers and leaders of organisations are usually recognised as being skilled negotiators. In one project an example of one of the four key skills of the effective head was their ability as negotiators:

> They met staff face-to-face . . . very frequently. They kept times between seeing staff to a minimum. Consequently, it did not take long to update one another, nor was there much time for difficulties to develop, let alone fester and infect other parts of the school. Simultaneously, if they suspected there was someone who was unhappy, discomforted or displeased their tours not only kept them in touch but also created opportunities for the 'problem' to be aired and shared, and provided a context whereby the two could resolve, say, some disagreement, on a one-to-one basis.
>
> (Nias, 1987: 97)

Negotiation would thus seem to be facilitated by close and regular proximity and contact, rather than avoidance or hiding.

Situation 5.1

Merlene, the Headteacher of Welcome Beck High School, has some difficult decisions to make. The school has a generally good reputation for caring and for the number of students who go on to higher/further education, but there are growing criticisms that examination results ought to be better.

Analysis of the results shows that there has indeed been a slight decline over the past few years, with particularly disappointing results in humanities subjects. Merlene would like to work out a strategy for improving examination results without making too much of this issue, as there are many positive points about the faculty mainly concerned. Merlene predicts that if she raises the issue of examination standards at a faculty meeting, defensive, negative, hurt attitudes will predominate and the defence will be that:

- the results are distorted by children with learning difficulties being guided towards these subjects because the staff are experienced and can cope with such children;
- the faculty membership always includes those who are not subject specialists, new teachers needing support and members of the senior management team;
- the faculty is poorly equipped because it has been constantly underfunded.

Merlene will find potentially difficult tasks like this easier to handle and the outcomes more positive if she has already established methods of effective consultation and negotiation.

However, whether this is the case or not, she will proceed effectively only if she starts by looking at some general positive principles.

The core objectives for the year will include examining and implementing strategies for increasing examination success. A two-year process of study and piloting will be set up which invites three faculties to participate in the first year in the production of a policy and practice guide for all subject areas in the following year. In that second year Merlene will hold a meeting with each faculty to discuss the principles for the enhancement of examination success. This will take place before examination results are known, so that the discussion is less likely to be seen as reactive or punitive. She will also negotiate targets for each faculty for the following year and resource positive projects accordingly. From the consultation, Merlene will write a paper for the whole school and community summarising the principles she has elicited from the consultation process.

Consultation and negotiation come more easily if a professional relationship has been established in the school, not as part of the management structure, but for the individual support of each member of staff. This will allow the teachers to deal directly and confidentially with the stresses and professional issues that might otherwise impede consultation and negotiation (Hawkins and Shohet, 1989). This is discussed in more detail in chapter 10.

Making the best use of consultants

The use of consultants is well explored in management and educational texts:

> Outsiders are independent, objective and impartial where internal politics are concerned. They will not be afraid to ask penetrating (even embarrassing) questions of anyone in the organisation – right up to the very top. Indeed, senior executives may willingly discuss with an external consultant sensitive issues they would not discuss with their own subordinate staff.
>
> (Bennett, 1990: 13)

In education, the definition of the role of advisers and inspectors has frequently touched on the relationship between appraisal, performance evaluation and regular consultancy. Many headteachers do not always make best use of visiting local authority professionals, such as school or educational psychologists, who might effectively be used as consultants for the change process they are engaged in. This group of professionals has been developing approaches to consultation in Britain and the United States for some years now and this has been particularly associated with their adoption of perspectives that encourage thinking about schools as whole systems, as opposed to the paradigm that focuses on individual children and their problems as has dominated traditionally.

Over the last 10 to 20 years, school-based consultation has emerged as one of the professional activities most preferred by school psychologists, frequently being ranked by practitioners as *the* most desired role . . . . Supporting the positive attitudes reflected in these and other publications has been a series of research reviews and meta-analyses indicating that school based consultation is, in fact, an effective means of service delivery.

(Gutkin and Curtis, 1990: 577)

Reynolds *et al.* (1984) see consultancy as a major professional function and outline three models of consultancy in educational psychology which we have found valuable in our own work. These three models are an ecological or problem-solving model, a mental health model and an organisational model. We will focus here on the first of these.

There are many variants of the problem-solving model. That cited by Reynolds has the following components:

- Define and clarify the problem
- Assess and diagnose the problem
- Brainstorm interventions
- Evaluate and choose among alternatives
- Specify consultee and consultant responsibilities
- Implement the chosen strategy
- Evaluate the effectiveness of the action and recycle if necessary.

Within our own work such a model is followed routinely at an organisational or individual child or group level with the educational psychologist acting as the consultant. This can occur through problem-solving activities relating to specific problems or to address areas of preventative work. The school, parent, child or fellow professional is, if necessary, guided through the early stages. However, effective consultancy takes the consultee through as many stages as possible as independently as possible in order to build generalisable problem-solving skills and confidence.

Caplan (1970) has provided what is generally considered the seminal theoretical work on consultation, giving details of a model which can be applied to a range of professions. Core elements of school-based consultation are well summarised by Gutkin and Curtis (1990) and include the following:

Indirect service delivery Consultants work with consultees about a client who may be a pupil, another teacher or the school system itself, rather than directly with the client.

Consultant–consultee relationship A meaningful relationship must be established with the consultee.

Co-ordinate power status Consultation must be a collaborative enterprise which places neither party in either a superordinate or subordinate role. Both must have equal authority in the decision-making process.

Consultee's right to reject consultant's suggestions Consultees cannot be forced to accept suggestions.

Involvement of the consultee in the consultation process Active involvement is crucial. Consultees must feel a sense of ownership of the problems.

Voluntary nature of consultation Ideally the consultee initiates the consultation. It cannot be forced on people.

Confidentiality This needs to be clear and ethical.

Effective consultancy can be achieved by the application of the above model, by the appropriate choice of consultant and by the negotiation of role with that consultant. Entry and acceptance of the consultant depends on the consultant's skills and attributes.

It is important to remember that you do not have to be a psychologist, adviser or an independent expert to be a consultant. Contemporary approaches to management are increasingly including reference to managers working as consultants in their own organisations (Day *et al.*, 1990; Schein, 1989).

> When should a manager be an expert, a doctor, or a process consultant? The formal authority of a manager makes it easy for him to fall into the expert or doctor role, especially when help is being sought by a subordinate. But if the goals of the manager are to teach the subordinate problem solving skills and to ensure that the solutions developed will be the right ones and will be implemented correctly, then being a consultant is by far the preferable way to begin to help.
>
> (Schein, 1989: 35)

Similarly, more junior members of staff could work together as consultant and consultee with appropriate support and preparation, with a focus on pupil, group or organisational problems or development. Either way anyone adopting the role of consultant faces the dilemma that Schein (1989: 18) identifies.

How can you be helpful in a situation in which there is a genuine choice between giving advice, telling others what to do, playing the role of expert, and helping 'clients' to figure out the solution for themselves, facilitating their own problem solving, even if that involves withholding what may seem to the consultant an obvious solution?

This is a common enough experience for all of us. We are asked for help and we automatically assume that we have some knowledge or skill that the asker is seeking. Yet when we give advice or attempt to get people to do what we think they should do, they resist. They suggest we have missed the point, tell us they have already tried it, or they invent reasons why it could not work. They may even give new information that makes the advice seem irrelevant or do something else to subvert what has been offered. They may appear to take our advice but then blame us when it does not work or they may keep coming back for more in an unhelpfully over-dependent way.

Schein (1989) argues that we have to be clear when it is appropriate to be the expert advice giver and when we should take the role of catalyst or facilitator. He goes on to explore three models of consultation and suggests what assumptions must be met for each to work effectively.

Purchase of information or expertise The client must have correctly diagnosed the problem, and correctly identified the consultant's capabilities to provide the expertise. The problem and the nature of the expertise or information to be purchased must be clearly communicated. The client must have thought through the implications of obtaining the information or service.

The doctor–patient model The diagnostic process itself must be seen as helpful. The client must be willing to run the risks of having a consultant observe, ask questions, study data and so on which may perturb the organisation. The client must have correctly interpreted the organisation's symptoms and have located the area that needs treatment. The person or group so defined must reveal relevant information to allow a valid diagnosis without hiding or exaggerating symptoms. The client must ultimately understand the diagnosis and implement whatever prescription is offered. The client will have to remain healthy after the consultant has left because the client will not have learned any problem-solving skills during this consultation, and the 'doctor' may have to be called back.

The process consultation model The client is hurting somewhere but does not know the source of the pain or what to do about it, does not know what kind of help might be available or which consultant might provide the help that is needed. The nature of the problem implies that the client would benefit from participation in the process of making a diagnosis. The client has constructive intent, being motivated by goals and values acceptable to the consultant and has the capacity to enter into a helping relationship. The client is ultimately the only one who knows what form of intervention will work in the situation and is capable of learning how to diagnose and solve his own organisational problems.

Schein argues that, to survive, modern organisations need staff who can learn how to learn and how to continue to solve their own problems. We support this approach to process consultation and encourage its existence at every level of working relationships within and outside schools. We have both been involved in INSET which promotes consultative and problem-solving approaches to working with parents, teachers and other professionals (Newton *et al.*, 1991). Clearly such approaches are crucial for the management and leadership of change.

> I believe it is essential for managers to become themselves effective process consultants vis-à-vis their subordinates, peers, and bosses. This use of the consulting process to pass on problem solving skills then becomes one of its most important developmental aspects, guaranteeing future problem-solving capacity.
>
> (Schein, 1989: 34)

Consultants can be most effective for consultee teachers in preventing feelings of burn-out, of being isolated and of having no one concerned for their wellbeing. Burn-out is a comparatively recent condition that it is important to address and prevent. Even in a school where innovation is deliberately planned to heighten feelings of achievement, stressed individuals can, in the early stages, project their emotional state on to the innovation and begin to block it. The change strategies we describe will be less likely to be blocked in this manner if positive consultancy characteristics are built in.

Problem-solving models have the merit of simplicity and of easy translation into objective terms, known as *operational definitions*. These models, in an organisation new to them, need to be applied sensitively and with some skill. Essentially, the acceptance of a problem-solving model and the role of the consultant in certain stages of it constitutes the acceptance of the world as it is and the rejection of unrealistic, miracle-cure thinking. It is then possible to move beyond a problem-solving model to a fully preventive model of operation with problem-solving used to address tactical problems. Learning that the most competent individuals and organisations have problems enables people to keep their problems in perspective.

Finally, we raise some issues about the acceptance of the role of the consultant in schools. We feel there are sensitivities about control, about levels of objectives and about the consultant's model of organisations. The consultant will need a contract of consultancy that fits the objectives of the school and makes appropriate use of the consultant's skills. Just as educational psychologists encourage schools away from deficit-model descriptions of children or groups of children, so they themselves must avoid such descriptions of schools or teachers and use the same objective-based approach. Finally, we suggest that teachers and schools experiencing problems may usefully be described in terms of how they view control. They may seek short-term control over events because of a perceived lack of more general control. An effective consultant will cover these points and the underlying issues in the negotiation process.

Situation 5.2

Merlene would like the involvement of a consultant in the raising of attainments in Welcome Beck High School. Initially, she simply has a feeling that the school will move forward more rapidly if fresh ideas are introduced and an outsider looks at the situation. However, when she prepares for this by attending a short course at the Regional Management Centre, she begins to understand that there are many issues that she has to address first: choice of consultant; the entry of the consultant to the organisation; goal setting and role negotiation; avoiding a negative focus; ensuring that her action will not be perceived as abdicating management responsibility for the problem and devaluing the ideas and contributions that could come from the school. It is interesting that these are presented in negative form which contrasts with Merlene's basic belief that she leads a good quality school. These points are best addressed by means of a series of questions which can be applied to other schools and organisations and related directly to the early stages of the problem-solving model.

- What, defined in general terms, is the problem?
- What perceptions of the problem exist within the school?
- Who might be involved in the problem-solving process within the school?
- What ideas have already been generated within the school?
- How might further ideas be generated?
- What might be the role of the management in problem-solving?
- How might the involvement of a consultant improve this process?

Merlene could discuss these issues at great length and could also produce a lengthy organisational plan. However she chooses at this stage to work at a simpler level. Her answers to the questions are brief but pertinent:

- Examination results are lower than they could be and management has deprived certain faculties of resources. (Definition)
- The children do not receive much backing at home; some teachers lack drive and commitment; examination results are not everything; only specialist teachers can produce outstanding examination results. (Perception)
- Initially a study group of teachers; later perhaps parents and students, and former students. (Involvement)
- Changes in timetabling; recruitment and staff development. (Ideas)
- By applying more structured methods of eliciting suggestions and the use of consultancy. (Further ideas)
- Merlene is not sure of the role of management in problem-solving. Perhaps this is the key area in the consultancy exercise? (Management)
- Might the consultant not help most effectively by clarifying the range of options generally and the role of management in particular? (Consultant)

Merlene now begins the process of deciding who is best placed to act as consultant. This is not as easy as it sounds. There is quite a range of possible consultants and her dilemma is that the choice might be seen to prejudge the definition of the problem and limit the range of strategies under consideration. Somebody from the Management Centre would probably focus on the role of management; somebody from the advisory service might well focus on a particular curriculum area; an administrator might have pronounced views about resource allocation. However, Merlene is a realist and accepts that there is no ideal consultant and devises the following specification for the consultant:

A *teacher* with a background of success and a knowledge of the examination processes; with knowledge of a range of schools and systems; with appropriate consultancy knowledge and skills.

A person unlikely to experience role confusion, who will be motivated to conduct the consultancy efficiently, who can allocate time to the consultancy and whose confidentiality will be respected.

Merlene identifies Andrew, a teacher who is on a full-time course in educational management following the closure of his school and whose programme includes a practical assignment. This choice is not ideal as he has no experience as a consultant and may have negative experiences arising from the closure of his own school. However, Merlene sees Andrew and they work out a consultancy agreement.

Andrew agrees an allocation of time to the project, he and Merlene agree the range of data collection and the method of reporting back. Consider the strategies below and decide how the consultant identified each possible strategy and with which member or members of staff each originated.

The strategy

- Five per cent of faculty budgeting is to be linked to examination results.
- Pupil attendance is identified as a key factor in achieving good examination results and strategies are to be implemented to improve this.
- A study is to be made of the range of examinations and syllabuses available and changes in the entry patterns are to be considered.
- A study skills course is to be devised for students in years 10 and 11. It is hoped that some former students may contribute.
- Careers advice is to be strengthened in the school.
- Parents' evenings for these years will in future emphasise the priority given by the school to achieving qualifications.
- Teaching materials are to be piloted by another volunteer faculty.
- Teacher attendance records will in future be a factor in assigning teachers to examination classes.
- Where possible class sizes will be reduced for these classes.

- Examination entries in mother tongue languages are to be increased and teaching of mother tongue is strengthened in partnership with the community.
- Children with basic skill difficulties are to be given access to adult literacy and numeracy materials.

This is not intended to be an ideal or generalisable list. Its purpose is to demonstrate how the involvement of the consultant resulted in the school devising strategies which are much more imaginative and positive than the initial formulations or discussions of the issue. This was in spite of the exercise being top-down and relatively superficial. It did not address any basic issues about the school, its organisation, its ethos. The exercise was functional, quick, management-led yet valuable.

It may seem strange that we, as external consultants, portray successful innovation as internally led. However, the discussion above began with detailed consideration of the starting point, stimulated by an education management course run by consultants. Consultants can be used at different points in the process. What is not likely to work, as has been often recognised, is the use of one-off consultancy bringing an action plan to an organisation. The process we have outlined is a creative one into which other input can be made at any stage; yet it remains a process at the core of which is staff creativity. In this creative, mutually supportive atmosphere, the role of the consultant can be especially valuable. We find that the application of psychology to stages of school development is one of the best received of our functions, especially in giving advice on the positive, creative links between the organisation's development and the teachers' skills in fostering children's development.

> External consultants can also help organizations . . . to unfreeze the closed systems, the tightly held assumptions and the unwritten rules, and to create a window of opportunity through heightened awareness and through expanding the realm of possibilities. By being an outsider the consultant can avoid being trapped in the limiting assumptions that constrain the horizons of possibility within an organisation.
>
> (Hawkins and Shohet, 1989: 146–7)

Promoting mutual support and co-operation

We are interested in helping schools to look at the skills and experience they have in promoting co-operation between children and applying them to the organisation. Unusually for this book we also want to offer some suggestions as to why this may not come naturally to schools.

Teachers' salary scales in almost all European countries tend to promote competition rather than co-operation. A project will be seen by one teacher as a way of moving towards promotion and by others as that teacher's attempt to take the work of a number of staff and pass it off as an independent project. Salary increments in schools usually relate to specific roles, especially in large primary and all secondary schools. Every occurrence can be categorised as an individual's problem or task.

Teaching is a stressful occupation. Stressed people will often attribute stress on to others or to situations. A teacher's difficulty with a particular task or group of children soon becomes a management failure.

Teaching is an occupation whose practitioners are relatively isolated from other adults. The time teachers have available to work co-operatively together is limited and in many schools teachers may be socially and professionally isolated. Teachers do not have much time to spend on joint activities, and such time as is available is often after school or rushed, with little time to respect interpersonal niceties. It is also a fact that political conflict about teaching may promote conflict between teachers, who may be influenced by the stereotypes presented by the media.

Managers can set out to improve these conditions but teachers can also do this on their own initiative. It is much more pleasant to work with people with whom relationships are good, to share ideas and suggestions, to sympathise about problems and to share the workload of joint or overlapping tasks. Teachers often make lifelong friends at work, even marry those they met at work, but there are still those schools where the staff head for home as soon as possible and the staffroom is deserted and run down.

Perhaps a more common situation is one where the staff appears to have a good level of mutual support and friendliness, but where teachers from minority groups feel left out or professionally isolated or where teachers with strong religious beliefs or those who have no interest in sport or alcohol feel excluded or marginalised.

In the same way that teachers prevent conflict between children and between themselves and children through a positive work agenda and early intervention, schools can promote a mutually supportive planned agenda of co-operation. The process of exploring and applying specific techniques to make the most of positive attitudes is helpful, especially in providing initial momentum.

Our message then, is for leaders, managers and consultants to start by helping to promote mutual support and mixing among staff, including themselves. All staff need to be involved in activities, both social and work-related, which involve mixing positively, by making such activities pleasurable or satisfying professionally.

ACTION PLAN

- Reflect upon and analyse the level of participation in school management and decision making that is occurring within your school at present.
- Plan for ways of increasing the collaborative and collegial nature of

relationships that exist, while clarifying the decisions and actions that will characterise effective leadership in this situation. Are there areas for you or others where professional development or changes in operating practices need to occur? What developments already exist that you can build on?

- Update your knowledge of consultation and negotiation processes further if this chapter has interested or challenged you by reading the texts mentioned. Remember that the way these processes are engaged in is critically important for school development and mistakes can be costly to levels of trust and respect within an organisation.
- Plan to be clear and precise when consulting and negotiating.
- Reflect on your style and tactics of conflict management and negotiation. Are you caught in one fixed mode? Try alternative styles and tactics in different situations until you are more tuned in to the appropriate times to use each.
- Try out some of the negotiation and consultation skills discussed to increase your repertoire. Try these out with staff, pupils, parents and pupils. Keep challenging yourself about the level of mutual problem-solving that is occurring in your professional relationships.
- Consider what else you might do to facilitate mutual support and co-operation occurring at every level in the school. What example do you provide for others? Can you change?

Chapter 6

Policy development, objectives and INSET

So you know where you want to get to and you have perhaps involved outside consultants, but still you are left with the decision: how are we going to get there?

Later chapters look in detail at some of the techniques of change in organisations, and especially their application to schools. In this chapter we look at how policies are devised and implemented and at the role of professional development activities in the context of organisational objectives. We explore the potentially circular relationship between organisational objectives, professional and policy development: successful synthesis of policy and practice should always revolve around professional development activities. We look at the links with policy in a desire to encourage the existence of policy documents that are living entities, driven by real-world concerns and objectives and fuelled in their delivery by effective professional development.

OBJECTIVES AND POLICY DEVELOPMENT

In chapter 4 we proposed that objectives be devised and worked towards on three levels: short-term, intermediate and visionary. We do not find it easy to

Policy and practice

see how policy can be meaningful and informative to practise without the levels of objectives of clear intention giving reality to policy statements.

When policy is being devised, the interaction becomes complex, with more types of people with potentially varied backgrounds and capabilities needing to contribute. In particular, policy making is an important element in a school's relationship with the community it serves.

Let us consider reasons why working out a policy might be seen as desirable and to highlight the more positive reasons which are likely to offer most to the developing school. Initially, reflect on the following questions:

- who is concerned that a policy needs to be devised?
- is the policy a new one or is the proposal to devise a policy in line with a particular need or innovation elsewhere?
- how detailed is the policy intended to be?
- who is the policy meant to guide?
- who is seen as having a legitimate input into the policy?
- how will the policy be evaluated?
- when will the policy be reviewed?
- how will the policy be put into practice?

It is important that these and other issues be looked at. Articulating policies that have little impact on practice leads to cynicism. There may be strong opportunistic reasons for policy statements. They can give the illusion that something is happening, that somebody is in charge. They can reflect external pressures, may be tied to resource provision, or may express a management hope that something will happen if it is put in a policy.

The final arbiters of school policies are usually political although there have been attempts over the years to make school management non partisan. However, the boundary between political direction and operational control is one at which tension can regularly occur. Politicians can be voted out of office and can feel with justice that their survival depends on the implementation of certain educational policies. Professionals may feel that policies imposed from a political power base can be divisive and that schools which do not reflect a consensus will risk alienating important groups among the parents, children and broader community. These are negative reflections on policy making but even these can have outcomes of reappraisal and a commitment to change on a set time scale.

More positively, policy making can also lead to a decisiveness about action so that developments can be built on and sustained into long-term development. Examples might be a commitment to fund preschool places for all in the community whatever other calls on the budget there might be, or to provide every child with the opportunity to go on school study trips annually. Wholly positive reasons for policy statements, policy working parties, policy-related professional development, policy review are easy to find, when articulated in objectives-based language. Policies can:

- define management decisions
- define the time at which decisions are made
- give a rationale for objectives
- give precise guidance about what is clearly defined and what is left to discretion
- commit management, the community, the educational administration, and others to common action
- define and explain positions which may not be obvious at first sight
- provide a succinct briefing for those new to the school, visitors and others
- give vigour and effect to legal and administrative requirements
- provide whole-school consistency and commitment
- set and disseminate minimum standards and encourage outstanding performance
- summarise effective resource allocation decisions
- focus on key areas
- provide practical guidelines for action in a given area.

Effective policies for change can bring together these features, and are especially valuable in outlining practices which are not obvious without the close analysis of an issue through the preparation and discussion. It is in this respect that policy is related closely to professional development.

OBJECTIVES AND INSET

Supposing you decide that professional development, in-service training or some other form of training or learning activity is what you need to change attitudes, provide skills and achieve your objectives. What will you do? Will you set up an INSET day? Will this really achieve your purpose? Or will you simply engage your staff and yourself in a time-consuming, perhaps interesting but more likely a rather transitory one-off event that leads nowhere despite good intentions?

Much in-service training in Britain and elsewhere is open to criticism. Of relevance to our concerns in changing school systems effectively and efficiently it is worth recalling that INSET has no guaranteed lasting impact on participants' attitudes, skills or behaviour, especially when:

- it occurs as a one-off event
- the credibility of the course provider is in doubt or is let down by poor performance during the course
- participants' motivation for attendance conflicts with the course content
- participants have no specific link with the policy
- attendance is compulsory for all staff, even if it is not relevant to them
- course materials and content are seen as irrelevant or too unrealistic for practical application

- it deals with policies that have not been discussed thoroughly or piloted adequately
- it deals with policies that are imposed and not supported by examples of effective practice.

The impact of INSET is weakened further when participants are not actively involved as learners in the process but are instead left as passive recipients of information. We argue in this chapter that INSET will continue to be a poor means of promoting school change if it is not linked to explicit developments in policy or practice. In some situations the lack of a clear contract between INSET providers and school managers can sound the death knell of effective professional development or organisational change.

The reluctance on the part of most headteachers to develop a comprehensive and systematic staff development policy together with the failure of many LEAs to link INSET funding to contractually agreed and evaluated outcomes forms a powerful combination militating against the sort of coherent structural change envisaged by both the Warnock Committee and the Fish Report.

(Barton, 1988: 70)

Equally, training must not exist in isolation from the real world of schools. Take management training for instance:

Thinking about management development, in both the public and private sectors, has changed markedly in recent years . . . . The main shift has been from a view that training is the sole source of knowledge and skills acquisition towards a recognition that experience, advice, support and encouragement must be made regularly available in everyday working conditions and relationships. A good system of management development aims to accentuate and enhance positive experiences, and it demonstrates a concern for the development not only of people but also of the management structure as a whole.

(DES, School Management Task Force, 1990: 7)

The positive aspects relate to the synthesis referred to earlier, in which professional development moves policy and practice forward to a more effective combination of school and community working together.

In this context, training can be an extremely powerful vehicle for achieving change if the process is carried out effectively and successfully, taking account of the real world and we will explore in detail exactly how this can be accomplished in our next chapter.

We argue here that to be successful as a change agent you will need to work in collaboration with powerful and influential colleagues inside your school system as well as with those on the outside. If you are intending to use INSET as one method of change then what you need is to agree with your colleagues exactly where and how this fits in with the achievement of your vision, objectives or policy development. You may need to create a successful fusion between a number of differing elements if progress and development are to be possible.

National governments are well aware of the power of linking training and policy implementation. In Britain, for instance, training monies in the form of Education Support Grants (ESG) have been targeted on policy development areas that have been identified as a national priority. Each school is required to have an annually reviewed school development plan and five professional development days and directed time have been introduced to ensure that all teachers are involved in training in relation to new policies and initiatives.

Providing learning opportunities

One way of thinking about training is to construe it as a means for providing learning opportunities for staff as well as for children. This broad view of professional development encapsulates the richness of adult learning as it can occur in a range of situations including the following, with examples:

- self-initiated: reading a book or writing an article
- informal discussion: in a staffroom discussion
- semi-informal: in discussion with a visiting adviser
- formal: at an organised INSET event.

Clearly the closer the learning can be to the self-initiated end of the continuum the more powerful and effective the learning. The skilful change agent or manager encourages and promotes individual learning opportunities with appropriate levels of support and challenge. While you may not always be in the position of initiating the innovation, a key management task is to plan, support and monitor the change process. Schon (1983) argues that the headteacher needs to provide environments that minimise constraints on learning, in which a variety of personal experiences can be reflected upon, talked about and assimilated or accommodated. In other words reflection on as well as in practice is actively promoted. Individuals and groups need regular practice to reflect on and share practice, to identify issues for change and to generate alternative strategies.

This encouragement of improved problem solving and reflectiveness amongst teachers fits well with models of healthy psychological adaptiveness and flexibility, essential for dealing with change.

Legislation and litigation

The first stage before embarking on policy development or INSET strategy is arguably to look at the requirements of legislation. Internationally, there seems to have been a resort to legislation to seek to ensure that schools perform certain functions. This has certainly been the case, not just for schools but for many agencies concerned with education and with the wider needs of children, in the UK in recent years and in the USA, where for example 'the legal regulation of school psychology has increased geometrically during the past decade', (Reynolds *et al.*, 1984). Perhaps this reflects a scepticism that legal control schools will go their own way, and that political input into what actually happens to schools will be limited.

For schools, a basic need is to ensure that legal requirements are known and reviewed regularly, at the very least to ensure that the school is not involved in costly and time-consuming litigation in areas like child protection and welfare, attendance records, health and safety matters, curriculum and use of punishments. We find worrying gaps in schools' awareness of their responsibilities in vital areas such as child protection. It does not appear that these areas are always dealt with in detail during initial teacher training. There are usually guidelines somewhere in the school but they have not always become a living part of the school's expertise. In the UK it is likely that there may in the future be far more litigation surrounding the rights of children than in the past, as more consideration is taken of pupils' legal rights and not merely their special needs, and in the light of the 1989 Children Act.

Local decisions cannot be disseminated without a strengthening of the policy aspect of INSET. In the UK, local public educational policy is currently made through local council committees and minutes of these meetings are readily available; yet it is still difficult to keep in touch, and the production of a summary of decisions and details of points raised about important decisions would be of value. If schools work to develop an awareness of national and local issues then perhaps heavy-handed legislation is less likely. On the issues on which there is legislation, schools need to know their obligations. Similarly with national and local policies, maintaining a system of information flow is important so that schools know the key decisions. In the last section of this book we look at how a school, in spite of imposed change, can strengthen its individual character without too great an overloading of the staff. We note here that it is for the headteacher in particular to be able to disseminate effectively the news from outside, the details of legislation, the decisions of elected members and how they will be interpreted. It is part of the process of building leadership to ensure that the relationship between what those in the school do and the situation outside the school is as smooth as possible and hence that accounts of legislation and imposed policy are accurate, that the implications for the school are looked at coolly and that this can be relied upon.

POLICIES

Policies often outline a framework of law, and state how an organisation will discharge legal responsibilities. They can be legalistic in tone and devised at a management or political level. Many policies provide clear guidance on how best to implement the policy, giving precision and detail. Some of them have a legalistic presentation, others are more user-friendly. They all expect and require certain key actions to be undertaken, levels of awareness and knowledge to exist, and responsibilities to be undertaken. Yet, as texts cited in chapter 4 show, there is worldwide scepticism on whether educational organisations can reach objectives for change and it is frequently asserted that educational organisations are rigid. Does this mean that policy writing becomes a paper exercise? Equal opportunities policies, for example, are often paper exercises, open to criticism for creating the impression that something is being done while at a day-to-day level no action change is evident. INSET relating to equal opportunities policies may even be merely a cosmetic exercise. Ineffective management can excuse failure at worker level by citing policy documents but we do not find this kind of explanation justifiable. The increasing level of litigation on special needs casework in the USA and on a smaller scale elsewhere suggests that legalistic frameworks for policy are not easy to implement and do not always fit the educational world. Essentially, a legal framework can escalate and define conflict whereas successful policy implementation can and should reduce conflict, to focus energy and resources on the effective education of children and young people. In our field of work especially, there are concerns that legal work can take up too much time and is ultimately concerned with the allocation of resources rather than any effective application of psychology. However, developing a knowledge of legislation and recent national and local policy and relating INSET to this is potentially a powerful and rewarding activity. We take an optimistic line on this as on other aspects of innovation and change in education. However, to be successful requires a link between attitudes and behaviour.

Policies can best be construed in simple forms as expressing the mission statement relating to a particular area, and outlining the levels at which objectives can be addressed in terms of attitude and behaviour. Successful policy making and expression provides a synthesis of these levels.

Successful policy in the making

We feel that a valuable and successful policy will both reflect and challenge existing thinking and that the positive way to address the devising and implementation of policy is to see it in terms of challenging thought and action to create a successful synthesis, a harmonious framework for action.

This means that policies have to go well beyond obvious thinking, beyond the scripts that allow us to coast along. Devising a positive policy on child protection involves looking at the rights of children, at all adults' actions as well as obvious abuse, at the treatment of children historically, at the child's contribution to positive policies and actions. Equal opportunities and special needs policies need to address features of societies; they represent attempts to turn back the negative momentum of the overall society to marginalise and victimise, and apply to the devisers as well as to others.

Perspectives on policy

The process of formulating policy and setting goals to put policy into practice is well worth examining in detail. Policy can originate at a number of levels or from a variety of sources: from central government, local or regional government, from administrators, from teachers, headteachers, parents and, rarely, from children. Policy may apply to a wide variety of activities: school improvement, equal opportunities, reading, computing, class grouping, types of teaching, healthy lifestyles, pastoral care. The word policy can be and is used to cover both grand designs and small steps. The term is often used to grant or add legitimacy and sometimes to avoid justifying actions: we have to do this because it is government policy. Specifying and articulating policy can be an exciting way forward. Implementing policy has to start at the top and policies have to be delivered by the work force which is vulnerable to criticism for failing to reach objectives. Leadership studies celebrate the willingness and the ability to set policy and practice at optimal levels and then to work successfully on implementation, to have the vision but also the realism and the drive. In addition, leadership involves the synthesis of consultation and direction (Southworth, 1990; Mortimore *et al.*, 1988).

Successful policy making and implementation is dealt with throughout this book. However, more specifically, policy making in its early stages involves identification of a general area, analysis, goal setting, deciding implementation paths, exploring wider administrative, political and community dimensions, negotiation and consultation, and final formulation and presentation of the policy (Van Velzen *et al.*, 1985). Effective policy making is the cohesion and acceptance of objectives at all levels to improve the chances of the organisation reaching the objectives and not waste energy in conflict.

How can policy making be a positive process?

Policy makers at whatever level in the education system need to make their policies 'implementation friendly'. This means among other things to provide clarity on the nature of the change, link it to local needs, provide training and support, and to provide sufficient time for the innovation to succeed.

(Hopkins, 1990: 192)

The process of identifying an area for policy formation is especially important and in our final chapters we urge the devising of policy for and by the school, for educational reasons, and only in response to external pressures which are adapted to the context of the school and its needs. This does not mean that external factors should be ignored; insensitivity to the wider context is dangerous and can be seen as arrogant. When policy is specified at a national or regional level, no school can afford to be unaware of this.

To be positive, policy making and implementation are best seen as an ongoing process, an opportunity to do some creative group thinking. The policy represents the culmination of the processes of change which we have outlined in this book, the formal adoption by the organisation of layers of objectives for the whole organisation. If policy is seen as an instant or single event, the chances of conflict are greatly increased because the school will have missed out on the positive events and processes we describe and incompatible surface arguments will be articulated to express a basic sense of powerlessness in the organisation. Successful policy making will move everyone forward.

Ideally, all the staff members will be part of the policy-making team. People who feel that they have been an integral part of a policy decision then have the vested interest in seeing that it succeeds. The teacher who is merely told of a change via a written memo is likely to become disgruntled and feel left out.

(Day *et al.*, 1990: 82–3)

Writing a policy document is often the ritual first thought of. We are in favour of written documents giving clear and precise policies and objectives. The problem lies in written policies being seen as top-down and devised after inadequate consultation. This does not mean that policy making is blocked, rather that the effectiveness of policy implementation will be increased by the involvement of those working and those with interests in what will take place.

As noted above, policies can cover a wide range of topics in schools. We find that policy devising and implementation on particular issues worked well where schools set up steering committees, at best of five people or so. These committees work well as action forums, and may meet relatively infrequently. The purpose of the meetings is to chase progress towards objectives and to create a motivation, skill and experience network. Much of the work is done by those who are not part of the committees, which report to staff meetings but whose work is informed and enriched by the committee's expertise.

Such a structure is not the only organisational structure that works efficiently, but it has the advantage that it is not bureaucratic and is action-based. It may well look at actions based on the implementation of an outline policy initially derived from outside and developed in the light of the practical experience gained, using easily attainable objectives and ultimately focusing on issues of curriculum access. By starting with the actioning of a pre-existing draft, it can find an easy route into issues so complex as to precipitate endless discussion without action and perhaps provoke splits within the school. Joint work on attainable objectives is less likely to do this. Ultimately the discussion within a school may prove to be at a sophisticated and informed level. Other positives are that a school is likely to focus on its own actions, rather than go outwards to find solutions to societal problems, and less likely to create friction with its ranks.

There are some good examples of written policies and their implementation covering a broad range of areas. It is important for schools and other educational organisations to obtain these, so that effort is not duplicated, that the perspective is not too local, and to check that nothing important is omitted and ensure that the final product is as good as possible. For an individual school it may be very valuable to bring together a number of policy documents from elsewhere; but the final policy must belong to the school, and the process of devising it is as important as the product. Ultimately the aim of written policies is to change behaviour and copying a document is not a very effective change mechanism.

As mentioned above, arranging working parties with certain prerequisites about composition can provide an effective method of devising policy documents. If a policy document should provide information and guidance that is not obvious, then bringing together expertise and perspectives from within the school is required. The other constraints are that such groups cannot substitute for the powers and responsibilities of others and that setting procedures for groups with no representation is likely to be ineffective or counterproductive.

Producing policy documents benefits from the active involvement of the management. This ensures that policies developed within the school will mesh with the situation outside the school and reduces the likelihood of boundary disputes, and will be implemented with the appropriate priority for resources and organisational arrangements.

Policy formulation and implementation requires consideration of how to deal with existing structures, practices and opinions which seem from the outset to be outmoded. Almost any new policy initiative will be seen as a threat by someone and there may well be vested interests with a great deal at stake. We have tried to promote the belief that a dynamic, developing school with a clearly defined set of beliefs will be a positive place to be part of and hence few direct conflicts will result. However, in policy making certain conflicts may become clear and may be highlighted by the process of policy formation.

> Before policy makers can produce 'implementation friendly policy' and heads and teachers construct development plans to achieve 'cultural' as well as curriculum goals, the necessary synthesis between school improvement and effective schools knowledge has to occur . . . This synthesis still presents a formidable challenge.
>
> (Hopkins, 1990: 193)

Making the links in practice: is a synthesis possible?

Let us look at a real-life situation.

Situation 6.1

Jane was the head of a large semi-rural primary school in the south-east of England. In her second year of headship she began to receive visits from a new educational psychologist (EP) committed to a whole-school approach to meeting special educational needs and with some clear ideas regarding effective classroom practice in this area. This EP was to work with the school as a consultant. Together they took the school through the following process:

1 Shared objectives were agreed and clarified with regard to future school development. Objectives included:
   • all staff able to use curriculum-based assessment checklists to assess pupils identified as having special educational needs
   • all staff able to complete and carry out individual learning programmes
   • all staff to work together using problem-solving methods to devise strategies on finding difficulties teaching certain pupils.
2 An INSET programme was embarked upon to develop staff attitudes and skills in relation to above explicitly stated objectives and in the broader context of special educational needs. This involves all staff, is school-based and is largely run by the EP. The programme is a rolling one lasting over three years, involving termly sessions and active learning methods.
3 The headteacher incorporated a special educational needs consultant role as part of the job description of the language post holder.
4 A special needs project was set up in school during a period of industrial action. As a result, all staff were involved in small discussion groups but output of these groups was summarised and refined into a special educational needs policy document.

5 The headteacher actively monitored completion of assessment checklists and each half term inspected learning programmes planned and carried out on targeted pupils.

6 The headteacher and EP met termly to review progress towards objectives and to agree new objectives for the year ahead. Agreement was then reached as to how INSET will facilitate the achievement of these and to how policy statements will evolve from this process.

As can be seen in this example the process of carrying out INSET within the school context was not an event in its own right or even loosely affiliated to what have come to be known as school development plans. Instead the INSET was ongoing and integral to the process of meeting agreed objectives and facilitative to the process of policy development. In this situation there was the additional benefit of keeping those most involved with the objective setting actively immersed in the carrying out of the INSET.

This argument is supported within current literature and research on management and change. For instance, the work of Bollington and Hopkins (1989) describes a very similar process in relation to the introduction of appraisal within an LEA. They recommend the following process:

• Relate change to teacher needs.
• Models/documents/procedures need to be clear and well presented.
• Presenters are well briefed and respected advocates at LEA/school level who can convince of worth and gain support through:
• Ongoing INSET allowing time to reflect and discuss implications of change.
• Planning and managing the process by providing a mixture of encouragement, training, support and pressure.

The overlaps between the two processes described are clear and provide us with some practical unpacking of the theoretically attractive notion of achieving a synthesis between policy development, objectives and INSET.

Now let us compare this approach to that in another school which faced the same need to develop a policy:

Situation 6.2

Douglas decides to release his special needs co-ordinator for a full week with supply teacher cover to work on drafting a whole-school policy on meeting special needs.

1 The co-ordinator liaises with relevant professionals, including the educational psychologist, and spends time reading anything she can lay her hands on that may be relevant including legal documents, government publications, LEA publications, published and unpublished

resources and so forth. At the end of the week she drafts a discussion paper which looks very much like a finished policy.

2 An INSET day is arranged for all the staff and school governors.
3 The day begins with input from the headteacher and the local psychologist setting the scene and explaining the national and local expectations of this policy. All are then involved in a sequence of activities designed to promote active involvement with the document and opportunities for discussion, amendments and development.
4 Finally the draft is redrafted as a policy and is circulated for final written feedback and approval.

The next year is then spent ensuring that practice matches the principles outlined in the policy.

Very interesting comparisons can be made between situations 6.1 and 6.2, which shared the same objective but were managed in very different ways. Let us consider some questions which emerge:

- Were both approaches equally valid?
- What were the strengths and weaknesses of the management of change in these two accounts?
- How important were the individual coordinators in the process? What skills did they need in relation to synthesising ideas, carrying out INSET making the best use of professionals and so on?
- How involved were the whole staff in the two models?
- Which model for change will be most enduring and why?
- How crucial was INSET to the successful completion of the policy?
- Do you think the policy will be implemented in both the schools to the same degree? What are the critical variables at work?

Clearly there are many ways of synthesising policy objectives, policy development and INSET and you will need to find your own way forward taking care to maintain a sensitive balance. It is apparent that some form of synthesis can and must exist to some extent if change is to be most effective and robust enough to survive and be meaningful.

Objectives provide direction and express intention, policy development engenders commitment and involvement, and INSET helps to provide the skills, knowledge, confidence and levels of objectivity needed for successful delivery of the policy and thereby the objectives.

Celebrating policies: rituals and ceremonies

It is at the policy level that many rituals can be performed. Frequently policies are outlined in documents and we will deal with these in more detail later. Documents need to be launched and the ritual of launching these is a well known one but one that can be effective and enjoyable.

Rituals and ceremonies can build *esprit de corps* and pride of association, but they can similarly manipulate and distort, confuse ends with means, and serve less public agenda. Where rituals are coupled with high ideals and a philosophy of educational excellence and social justice, they are powerful tools for education . . . . Every organisation needs formal enactments of its culture, and some pageantry reinforces the impact. (Beare *et al.*, 1989: 196)

The people who planned the piloting of the policy initiative can be celebrated, those who implemented it with particular success can receive recognition, the team approach can be highlighted and those who do not usually receive recognition are easily made part of this. Publicity and perhaps even ceremony can be attached to the rituals, both for internal and external consumption. Effective publicity requires keynote events, interviews, photographs, films, documents, visits and other visible manifestations. They involve those who have a contribution to make to the policy process in celebrating the success, the outcomes of their interest. The policy and process have to be expressed in a usually brief set of impressions, images and phrases. The formulation of visionary objectives and their expression in short and medium time scales helps to focus on the kind of rituals which will do the process and product justice and seize the public imagination.

These rituals can help an organisation to say a great deal more about its ethos, priorities and plans. Rituals can bring together everyone concerned with an organisation and give policies enhanced meaning for a whole school.

What kind of rituals have we seen in this role?

The 'expert consultant' speaks during a special visit to study the policy or practice.

Somebody from outside the organisation is brought in, to discuss, to give the results of a completed study that is going on or to be briefed on it and to make internal or media comments on it, praising the policy and how it has been put into practice. Where possible, this person will be of substantial status not necessarily in education. However, we feel that these rituals are good opportunities for schools to promote links with researchers. On occasions they will tell the organisation what it already knows and does, but this kind of ritual can be valuable in building credibility for the project or for the school generally, building an intangible asset for the future and providing the right kind of publicity. This kind of consultancy involves high status, high profile presentations and documents. Sometimes the expert is less aware of the practical side of the issue, and learns from the visit often finding it genuinely interesting, especially if it is thoroughly arranged.

The researcher visits

Being visited to be involved in research about an innovation can enhance the policy and how it has been put into effect. Here there is a lower but different public profile, with the important function of informing the school about dimensions which would not otherwise be accessible. It also provides opportunities for media pieces and other publications and the active involvement of the staff in the research.

The dignitary visits

Somebody in authority or somebody famous comes to visit and is shown something which expresses the policy.

The award

The equivalent of an Oscar is given for distinguished contributions. Awards give an opportunity for ceremony, and individuals often are captivated by this; the drawbacks are that they can make others feel left out or second best; and showing someone as the star performer or demonstrating the ultimate way of doing things is to invite criticism. This year's Oscar star is next year's has-been.

The social

Having social events with some element which links them to the policy and practice can be fine, so long as care is taken that everyone is included and catered for.

The special occasion

The school equivalent of National No Smoking Week, of national or religious events. The school rituals we attended as children were poor imitations of events celebrated elsewhere, tending to celebrate the achievements of the select few. However, many schools have special expertise which can be applied to the rituals of school development. An excellent class teacher will have rituals built into the annual programme: not too many, not too predictable, but essential parts of the process of the partnership of learners and teachers. Teachers can sometimes be stressed by having to spend time on organising these events as well as the teaching, so it is best to limit them and link them closely with policies and practices within the school and to areas the teachers generally feel confident with.

ACTION PLAN

- Don't jump into one-off INSET events.
- Agree objectives and link INSET to the achievement of these.
- Involve well briefed and respected advocates at LEA and school level in change process and INSET.
- Involve consultants in the planning and implementation stages and use their technical expertise for support.
- Relate changes to teacher needs and allow staff time to reflect and discuss implications of change.
- Plan, manage and monitor change, policy development and progress towards objectives in consultation with those who hold influence, knowledge, power and who offer support both within and outside your school.
- Find out about existing draft policies as starting points.
- Decide how to organise to achieve targets.
- Examine the school rituals to reflect and celebrate policy and practice. Rituals need to be rewarding; enjoyment needs to be part of the range of rituals.

Chapter 7

Successful in-service training

It was the best of times, it was the worst of times

We have just seen the importance of the links between INSET, policy and organisational development. In this chapter we take a closer look at in-service training as a form of professional development. We look in some detail at what it is and at whom it is aimed, explore the models of INSET that exist and examine in detail how training can be most successfully planned and delivered.

BACKGROUND

In England and Wales, as elsewhere in the world, it has long been believed that teachers should regularly update their skills. However, while teachers had been attending courses and updating their skills from the beginnings of state education, it was only in 1972 that the need to regularise and invest in INSET was highlighted in the seminal James report (DES, 1972). James recommended that all teachers should follow their initial training with a period of induction to their professional work and, periodically, with spells of INSET.

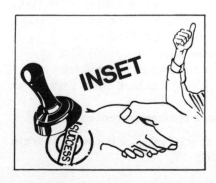

Successful INSET

Since that time the pace and scope of educational change has made INSET even more crucial as a means of updating and refreshing teachers and enabling them to reflect on the quality of their practice. In England and Wales there has been considerable variation in the amount, quality, efficiency and efficacy of the INSET that has been provided (Mortimer and Mortimer, 1989). What has also become clear over the years in many countries including the UK and the United States is that schools are complex organisations which are not amenable to crude attempts to engineer change:

> Those in-service education policies which focus exclusively on the provision of courses, operating on the assumption that all is required is for teachers themselves to be schooled, fail to allow for this complexity and hence may have little direct influence upon school practices.
>
> (Bailey and Braithwaite, 1980: 211)

Thus this chapter must be seen in the context of the rest of the book, INSET being only one part, albeit a significant part, of any change process.

WHAT IS INSET AND WHAT MAKES IT WORK?

Potentially effective in-service training is one of the most useful ways of moving an organisation forward towards an agreed vision or to specific objectives. It may provide the vehicle whereby the deliverers of the vision learn what they need to do to be effective in the classroom or wherever else they are operating. It can provide opportunities to develop as well as to celebrate skills. Successful INSET can provide the best opportunity for schools to apply their teaching skills to their own organisation. It can allow members of the organisation to come together to explore ideas and ways forward as well as to mix socially with daily practical barriers removed.

In-service training is the development of the skills, confidence, knowledge, performance and attitudes of existing practitioners. Although the day-to-day experiences of the work can lead to fluency in task performance, INSET refers to the formal occasions when training takes place. The range of activities that INSET covers includes:

- Sabbatical leave to conduct research or study as epitomised in the 1980s in Pittsburgh, Pennsylvania where every high school teacher in the system was given an eight week 'mini-sabbatical' (Hovey, 1986)
- Day release arrangements to conduct research or study
- Attendance at evening, weekend or holiday courses or activities
- Attendance at courses or activities during teaching time with cover provided for classes
- Whole-school sessions in the school or at conference venues.

Professional development activities that may be relevant but which we are not considering in relation to INSET include:

evening courses
correspondence courses
study groups
reading and research
job shadowing
role rotation
discussion
training and experience in the community.

The traditional INSET model in the UK used to consist of either lengthy courses, such as spending a year in a higher education institution requiring a full- or part-time secondment, or voluntary short courses. The short courses were usually offered at teacher centres or school venues and were provided 'on an ad hoc basis and attended by enthusiastic, professionally minded and ambitious personnel' (Crossley *et al.*, 1985: 120). Both long and short courses tended to be provided away from the 'coal face' of the classroom, by experts not necessarily aware of the needs of teachers or schools or of the importance of matching provision to needs.

> Even where INSET was perceived as valuable by the teachers who had received it, once back in their schools it was frequently hard to apply what had been learned or to persuade colleagues to modify their practice. Finally, and bluntly, those teachers most in need of INSET tended not to go on voluntary courses
>
> (Mortimer and Mortimer, 1989: 134)

Out of frustration with the ineffectiveness of such INSET, school-focused INSET was developed to provide staff development to meet individual needs within the context of agreed whole-school policies. These are most often school-based and at best illuminate the effectiveness of promoting change from within and of fostering commitment and ownership (Dalin and Rust, 1983). The validity and importance of planning change, curriculum development and related INSET together have been increasingly recognised by a wide range of practitioners, and fit well with models of school-focused development and improved effectiveness.

School-focused INSET was also encouraged by developments in the UK in relation to the funding of professional development. From 1986, with the introduction of Grant Related In-Service Training (GRIST) and its significant change to the funding of INSET in the UK, there has been a decrease in attendance at long courses and an increase in school-focused INSET. The latter is now more linked to perceived needs of the whole school and more often management-initiated to enable staff to acquire skills and training essential for the delivery of school development objectives.

The focus of staff development programmes has moved from meeting individual teachers' needs to meeting those of the organisations and education systems in which they function.

(Allsop *et al.*, 1989: 29)

Still more recently there appear to be moves within school-focused INSET to shift away from the more formalised input of visiting speakers or outside 'experts' towards more collaborative action research, drawing on the services of research consultants to work alongside staff (Oldroyd and Tiller, 1987). Such ideas link well with international views on professional development that place the learner as central and crucial to meaningful learning. It is interesting to note these comments on an Australian project on educational leadership:

An initial assumption was that professionals would want to take primary responsibility for their own learning, and in-service education. This meant that the content and processes of in-service education had to be sensitive and responsive to learners' perceptions of needs. It also implied that in-service activities had to be seen as opportunities for real growth along intellectual, emotional, social, educational, aesthetic, skills and career dimensions.

(Duignan and MacPherson, 1989: 13).

In the Netherlands Tulder *et al.* (1988) attempted to identify the critical characteristics that INSET focused on educational innovations should contain. They sought their data from recognised experts in the field of INSET in the Netherlands and ended up with a list of statements. Discussing these they comment:

Although the participants consider it very important that in-service education should be school-focused where possible, the relatively low appropriate assessment scores for this statement might indicate the fact that the panel finds subject oriented, individually focused in-service education also important. Finally, the experts have the opinion that skills must be emphasised, but that objectives regarding knowledge, insight and attitudes must not be neglected.

(Tulder *et al.*, 1988: 219)

Our experience is that looking at INSET within a broader context of professional development and examining the skills and qualifications that exist within an organisation is extremely valuable. We believe that schools need well considered, coherent staff development policies that provide realistic and differentiated staff development, building on existing personal and professional strengths.

We find that schools have many skills and qualifications which are not widely known or recognised, not even within the institution. We frequently begin INSET sessions for whole staffs by going round and asking everyone about their interests, skills, experience and formal qualifications relevant to the topic of the day and are pleasantly surprised by the response. We find, for example, that teachers with overseas qualifications or experience have training in areas where a major contribution can be made. We find many who have been following evening classes to degree level and above and others who have followed courses relevant to school in other settings such as counselling courses run by church and other voluntary organisations. Much of this work is of a good standard and not always known or valued by the school in which they work.

Thus, we offer a broader answer to the question 'What is INSET?': *INSET is the process of identifying existing relevant skills, qualifications, experience and interest in the organisation and building upon and adding to them.*

WHO IS INSET FOR?

Traditionally, INSET took up little of a school's attention. Teachers might go on secondment or retrain in shortage subjects and courses and teachers applied or not in accordance with their interests, motivation and time available. It was not regarded as a core activity nor was it closely targeted on organisational objectives.

Currently, INSET is available in many countries not only for teachers, but increasingly for others working in schools or elsewhere in education. Those involved include school governors, non-teaching staff, class teachers, school managers, advisers, psychologists, administrators and others concerned with schools. INSET, then, can be for a wide-ranging audience and delivering INSET coherently across such a range can become complicated. Rapid changes in education have been introduced over recent years necessitating staff INSET which has to be devised and delivered as a matter of some urgency. Examples in the UK include training in information technology, new financial procedures, financial administration, new examination syllabuses and the National Curriculum. In a school, a starting point is to consider all those who have direct contact with the children and to consider how matters of ethos, purpose and vision are understood and interpreted.

How do adults learn best?

Any educational change, such as the introduction of a new teaching strategy, is dependent on individuals changing. Changing people implies the use of a learning process that depends heavily on each individual's capacity and willingness to reflect on practice and to experiment with new ways of thinking and acting.

(Duignan and MacPherson, 1989: 18)

Frequently in this book we urge that the skills of teachers be applied or adapted to the development of the organisation and its culture. Later in this chapter we look at the implications of this for the delivery of INSET. At this stage, it is worth noting that adults may come with many preconceptions, habits, rationalisations for their habits, as well as sets of tensions, enthusiasms and expectations. These can be positive or negative or irrelevant, but INSET planners do well to predict or survey these before finalising INSET. Even if this cannot be done in advance it is always worth while to try to find out as much as possible about any group at the beginning of any INSET event, however familiar they may be to the trainer. We feel that adults learn best as children learn best, with positive, clear, meaningful, relevant, well-prepared sessions, with practical, engaging activities and follow-up. Perhaps the precision of delivery, practicalities and follow up are particularly relevant to adults as learners. 'People learn best when they are actively engaged in their own learning.' (Duignan and Macpherson, 1989: 19)

Tough (1979) following a series of studies found that self-directed learning is an all-pervasive activity in the general population. Almost everyone engages in at least one or two major learning efforts each year. The average was eight, with some individuals undertaking fifteen or twenty. Typical projects occupy 100 hours and are usually associated with a person's job, home, family or hobbies. The most common motivation for engaging in such activity was the anticipated application of the resulting knowledge or skill acquired. In 70 per cent of these cases it was the learners themselves who took the responsibility for planning, controlling and supervising the whole process. Frederickson (1988) uses this and subsequent evidence to assert the powerfulness of self-directed learning and its role in continuing professional development.

> Tough's and related studies indicate a previously unrecognised degree of pervasiveness and sophistication . . . . This would imply the adoption of a learner-centred perspective in short course provision: viewing the course as one episode in a broader self directed learning project and seeking to maximise the extent to which individual participants' personal learning objectives can be accommodated.The positive facilitation of self directed learning represents a further area for positive attention.
>
> (Frederickson, 1988: 123–4)

Situation 7.1

The charming village of Ditchmuddling has a school with a falling roll, even though the population of the village is increasing with middle-class commuters moving into new housing. The school has been identified by the

LEA advisers as having a number of problems and the priority has been to raise the attainments of the pupils. The school has six teachers, including the headteacher, and two of them are thinking of retiring. The head teaches a class for half of the week. The headteacher and the staff feel that they are being criticised unfairly by the advisers and that the school has been underfunded for many years.

This is not the easiest situation for INSET, which might be perceived by staff as endorsing the implied criticism and placing the responsibility for problems on the staff. However, successful progress is made through the following series of measures:

- Ditchmuddling School is agreed to have done well in music, with excellent involvement by pupils and the wider community. Key teachers in the school are asked to advise and contribute to the area's INSET programme on music. This begins to recognise and value the school's strengths, ensures that teacher/adviser divisions diminish with joint work and that INSET quality is a shared target.
- Science initiatives are required of all schools, and this is chosen as the priority area for Ditchmuddling. The INSET is for all staff, including the headteacher.
- The adviser chairs a session asking all the staff about their initial teacher training, the courses they have attended relevant to science, and relevant experience. This is done in an informal atmosphere and the adviser notes areas of particular strength.
- The second session takes all staff through the design, running and evaluation of a practical science activity, to be run by the teachers with the pupils during the week. The headteacher will team-teach these lessons.
- The third session involves feedback about this, and then has staff working in smaller groups to design activities for the next few weeks. These are shared, run and evaluated.
- In the fourth session the adviser gives a formal presentation on the key principles of science education and relevant theory. This is scripted and has some brief exercises.
- The fifth and final session is shared among the schools in the area with each one contributing the materials and practical outlines they have been working on and drawing them all together so they can all use them.
- Ditchmuddling School is given additional funds for science equipment two months after the INSET, following recommendations from the adviser to the local authority, to devise and pilot a further series of science activities for the area. They are given a temporary increase in support from an advisory teacher to aid further developments.
- The staff then discuss with the headteacher and adviser the next set of priorities for school development.

What models of INSET delivery exist?

Having agreed that INSET will feature as a part of your change process you will need to decide whether staff will attend existing INSET courses, whether you will be involved in planning school-based development activities and INSET or whether you will be attempting to have the best of both. What will influence your decisions regarding INSET? The following are typical of INSET arrangements currently available in the UK and elsewhere:

- courses at teacher centres either with open access or for particular groups such as special needs co-ordinators or headteachers
- school-based INSET for all staff or targeted groups
- INSET for all or selected staff from families or clusters of schools
- individual staff attending national, regional or local courses and possibly providing feedback to other staff
- advisers, psychologists or inspectors working in collaboration to provide INSET in or out of school
- individual staff trained in specific skills or knowledge who then cascade their learning to other staff in their own or other schools

Mortimer and Mortimer (1989), researching INSET in England and Wales, found no particular preferences from twenty-two LEAs for any particular type of INSET:

> Rather, the range of INSET consciously chosen by LEAs was made evident. One-third of respondents specifically used the word 'variety' or 'balance' in their responses. Provision ranged from one-day, in-school courses, to weekend residentials, to longer term, full time secondments (although these were increasingly rare and in some cases abandoned all together).
>
> (Mortimer and Mortimer, 1989: 137)

We have already looked at some of the problems and inefficiencies of short voluntary courses, particularly when they are run at centres away from schools, and also at the financial problems and limited school development impact of individuals attending longer courses. We continue to highlight the value of collaborative INSET enterprises with individual and families or clusters of schools.

A popular version of one type of INSET delivery has come to be known as the cascade. In the UK an example of this would be the Coventry LEA's Special Needs Action Programme (SNAP) as directed by Ainscow and Muncey (1984). In this kind of structure, a basic course is written and produced with scripts for trainees and trainers, a validation and certification arrangement and a steering committee. It is targeted on practical skills at a classroom level. The cascade is the delivery system. The first stage is to train trainers. The first group of trainees become the trainers, under supervision, for the second group of trainees. Certification arrangements and supervision ensure that the quality of the training remains adequate. Such a structure has a number of advantages:

- precision in the planning and delivery of INSET
- skills spread through a system quickly with controls on standards
- trainers are also practitioners for much of the cascade
- second-level courses can be devised to reach higher standards for smaller numbers
- simplicity in planning administratively.

However there are some potential disadvantages in this kind of system. Changing the content of courses which have been set up in this kind of structure is relatively difficult and they can become left behind with new developments. Without a tightly organised validation and supervision system trainers who have completed the course themselves may not feel or be sufficiently confident or competent to train others. The cascade structure assumes that a script and mastery of the skills in the course equate with being a competent trainer; perhaps the success of INSET can be maximised by maximising trainer competence. This structure can exclude or devalue experience and skills and other INSET if they are not recognised in a particular system of validation. This is inefficient and can add to resentment and inter-professional rivalries. It is not a structure that takes account of the school as organisation, the differences between schools or what the staff already have to offer. Finally, this structure needs resource allocation of time and money to make it work effectively. However, these reservations should not obscure the basic worth of courses like these which have a precision and practicality which are especially valuable.

One way forward for cascade-style delivery arrangements might be to continue to promote closer links with colleges to build on the modular approaches of the Open University, for example. It might also be important to make INSET validation and design part of the process of increasing qualifications and overall professional development while retaining the facility to target INSET on practical and topical issues. This would also have the benefit of uniting the efforts of a wide range of INSET providers and reducing some of the tensions in the processes.

Can arrangements other than cascades be effective? We feel that they can be effective if the lessons learned from chapter 6 are borne in mind. Effective INSET can be valuably delivered if linked closely to the achievement of specified school objectives. For this there must be a common framework for the devising of policy, funding and other resource allocation, and a good grasp of the practical skills required.

Well organised LEA 'flagship' courses devised to fit the needs of school development and LEA initiatives will readily be seen by a significant number of teachers as fundamental to their professional practice, and periodic repeat courses as refresher exercises, much as is done with important skills such as flying and other refresher courses for pilots to renew their licences. Repeat courses are more likely to be undertaken if they are updated and reviewed. Within an education system, planning and running such courses takes a great deal of effort and negotiation, but they can be particularly effective.

Some clear structure must be adopted, perhaps the combination of an element of cascading and the linking of a clear school and LEA professional development plan with specified 'flagship' courses. There are two main reasons for this assertion, one positive, one less so. The more positive reason is that staff who master such courses are likely to seek and find promotion out of a school or organisation which then finds that it has lost key skills which, without a system for replacement, can be hard to regain. The less positive reason is that we can all lose skills under day-to-day pressures and reduce our scope to a limited subset of well rehearsed, safe activities. Such deskilling is a risk that is consequent on being busy, but a system of skill maintenance and enhancement can make an organisation less deskilled than it might otherwise be. Ideally this needs to take the form of ongoing support and supervision structures within the school as well as outside, and may have links to formalised appraisal schemes.

How is INSET planned and delivered?

Funding arrangements have given some degree of precision to this process in the UK but the lead times on this can be long and the new role of advisors means that, although they still have responsibility for identifying INSET needs and working out funding arrangements, they will be running less INSET themselves. INSET planners are therefore not necessarily INSET providers and are part of a separate INSET system. They may not have a system for identifying potential INSET providers and may limit the range of providers as a result, missing important skills and contributions. This can lead to some tension and inefficiency in seeking to create coherent and effective LEA-run INSET programmes. It is worth considering what issues can be addressed to improve INSET planning and delivery. What makes a successful course? Mortimer and Mortimer, describing their survey of English and Welsh LEAs, report that:

> Courses were deemed successful if staff were able to feel some ownership towards them (for example, by being involved in the selection of the topic and the course planning or presentation) or if the courses were seen as relevant and related to the needs of the whole school. Courses which were well planned and executed and in which participants were active rather than passive were also deemed successful.
>
> (Mortimer and Mortimer, 1989: 137)

Effective planning is thus essential and must involve those insiders who are part of the change process and also outsiders, or *critical friends*, as they are often known. Rigour is required for the identification of exactly what curriculum of skills and knowledge is required. It is also worth reflecting on the levels of objectivity and confidence that are to be encouraged among participants. This is likely to require a considerable time allocation and agreement on detailed principles. In a book aimed at taking a professional development approach to managing primary schools in the 1990s, Day *et al.*,(1990) argue that, whatever the starting point for change, the headteacher needs to pose a number of questions:

- What challenge and support do individuals need from me? Can this be made available?
- What help and support does the teacher/group of teachers need from inside and outside the school? Can this be made available?
- What are the priorities for action?
- Is this activity practical in terms of time, energy and resources?
- What will the teachers gain from the activity? Sceptics will want to know what is in it for them and for their pupils and what the cost will be.

These questions are highly appropriate for anyone about to plan any kind of INSET event and are supported by comments made by the DES in 1990:

> If training were planned on the basis of a corporate response to individual initiative, it would place greater emphasis on flexible open learning structures designed to be readily accessible at the time of need for individual and group use.
>
> (DES, School Management Task Force, 1990: 25)

We list below some principles of effective INSET and suggest schools and educational organisations begin by trying to produce their own list of effective INSET and analysing the reasons why they consider it effective.

Basic arrangements can help the effective planning and delivery of INSET. INSET planners will do well to look at basic arrangements to simplify matters for the trainees, help the day or session to run smoothly and allow them to concentrate on the INSET. If parking is a problem at an INSET venue, tell them in advance so that their journeys can be timed appropriately. Providing childcare arrangements will increase the attendance and the punctuality of trainees and will show that the INSET is properly planned and that their involvement is important and valued. Lunch arrangements can be the making or the breaking of INSET that lasts whole days. Sorting out prior reading and course materials is essential. When there is more than one presenter, it is vital that there is a check at the planning stage on who is doing and saying what. It is also essential to maintain vigilance to prevent gaps, overlaps or contradictions. The leader must never interrupt a co-presenter or seek to clarify a point being made; this is patronising. Demarcations must be sorted out well in advance. Presenters should be present for all sessions, both to ensure coherence, to build on the mood of the INSET and also to give the message that all parts of the INSET are of equal importance. For the same reason, senior staff in schools should not only be present throughout but should be involved in all the activities and the follow-up.

Principles of effective INSET

The history of INSET has not always been a smooth one and, while there may be a number of reasons for this, it is more important to find ways of ensuring that INSET is effective and successful than to dwell on these. The principles of effective INSET are, we believe: theory; practice; preparation; interaction; presentation; collaboration; evaluation; implementation; support; follow-up.

It is worth considering the following questions when embarking upon any INSET exercise:

- What use of theory is the INSET making?
- How will the INSET change practice?
- Will these changes link to school development objectives?
- How much preparation has gone into the INSET?
- Are the sessions lecture, activity or interactive, and how much of each is included?
- How much care has gone into the presentation? What materials have been produced and what is their quality?
- What level of interpersonal skills has been sought by the presenters?
- Has the INSET come fully finished from consultants, or has it been finalised after discussion within the school?
- How is the INSET to be evaluated and by whom?
- What arrangements have been made to ensure the INSET is not a single session, forgotten soon afterwards? What follow up will be done?

Let us examine each question in some detail in the light of the principles listed above:

What use of theory does the INSET make?

Repeatedly in this book it is emphasised that use of theory is valuable, and that schools can refresh the theoretical knowledge they have by practical applications to the daily work with children and to the organisation. In INSET there is the opportunity to link theory to practice, and current research with future practice. Models, theories and areas of research of many kinds can all be relevant to the school as an organisation. These can include information-processing models, sociological theories and many others from many academic disciplines.

These also constitute a wider range of theory than we covered in chapter 3 and can provide a range and richness of perspectives to move an organisation forward. The list might look daunting for the average school, but can be brought in gradually. The place to start the introduction of theory and the use of research findings is with the formal training of the staff, the areas they studied as student teachers and the research relevant to the changes planned.

What are the practical outcomes of the INSET?

Successful INSET will often give very detailed guidance and sets of understandings that can be implemented directly. It will draw on real examples and will be at the highest level of detail in the examples that it gives. We all know the experience of trying to work out how an appliance works from a handbook, and extra detail and precision is always welcomed. Demonstration and supervised practice would be welcome if it came with the handbook for the appliance. We urge that INSET is directed at practicalities. This does not entail a worm's eye view of the world. It simply means that theory is translated into practice as an integral part of the INSET. In a review of over two hundred research studies of the effectiveness of INSET Joyce and Showers (1980) identified four components of training as necessary for effectiveness:

1 Presentation of a theory or description of skill
2 Modelling or demonstration of skills or model of teaching
3 Practice in simulated and classroom settings, with structured feedback
4 Coaching for application.

Practical outcomes should fit in with the school's development plan, vision or specific objectives if they are to have maximum effect on an organisation, especially where all are involved.

We advise would-be INSET leaders to rehearse their practical advice before the session to see if it really makes sense to someone who does not have the background of the INSET leader. Assisted rehearsal of practical skills as part of INSET and video rehearsal combined with positive feedback from this where possible can help.

It is worth planning to end INSET sessions with or to incorporate in them a section called *Where do we go from here?* or *Agenda for action*. This section should lead to the production of a clear action plan with dates, time allocated and clear objectives, which may be limited provided they represent real change.

How much preparation has gone into the INSET?

The INSET that works best has had a lot of work input at some stage. A good rule of thumb is that successful INSET will usually take three or more times as much preparation time as running time. For key INSET, it is as well to plan for much more time in preparation than can seem possible. This points to INSET preparation for wide applicability, for quality and thoroughness. This time is ideally spent:

- checking that the needs of the school have been accurately identified and that others besides the headteacher have been involved in this
- conducting a computer literature search to produce a summary of recent work in the area that is genuinely up to date and state of the art, writing a verbatim or near-verbatim script of the INSET and producing a high quality booklet for future reference
- checking that guest presenters share a basic understanding of the objectives of the INSET and how their input will relate to those of others
- checking that the arrangements are tight
- trying out the activities
- ensuring that the practical skills really are practical
- preparing advance material.

What interaction is built into the INSET?

What are the participants being asked to do? We advise considerable precision in this, at the preparation stage running through exactly what activities will be done, how long they will take, what the participants' perception of them might be and so forth. What will be the interaction among the participants, between the participants and the presenters? Will the presenters take part in the activities? What will be the balance between the amount of listening by each person, presenter or participant, and the amount of talking, individually or in groups? How can we ensure that everyone feels happy about contributing and has a fair share of time to contribute, so that activities are not dominated by the presenters or a few participants? How do we ensure that participants or presenters do not become limited in their interactions to a single small circle?

It is important that INSET encourages reflection, problem-solving and active engagement:

A supportive social climate was considered crucial to participants' willingness to experiment freely, to learn from each other, to give and accept constructive criticism in a non-threatening manner, and to reappraise deeply embedded assumptions about their professional self, actions and values.

(Duignan and MacPherson, 1989: 16)

We find that focused, specific, practical small-group tasks and a balance of quite brief ones in the early stages of the INSET with more extended ones later on works well. A progression from individual activities to work in pairs then increasingly larger groups can be a good way of opening up interaction and maximising participation. We also find it preferable to have precisely defined tasks rather than wide-ranging discussions, at least in the early sessions of the INSET.

What is the quality of the presentation?

We have already argued that written materials and other media must be of high quality, and stressed the effectiveness of thoroughness rather than glossiness. A good range of techniques and visual aids will help a presentation: mixing overhead transparencies with flipchart, tape recorder, video and live drama. Try to make use of pictures 'worth a thousand words', cartoons, simple diagrams and humour. One of the authors was recently impressed at a local special school by a teacher whose whole presentation on effective support for mainstream teachers was embellished by a series of overhead transparencies of apposite cartoons contributed by an art teacher. No words were used on these transparencies but the communication was both humorous and powerful. This is an excellent example of INSET that will be remembered for years to come.

A straightforward presentational style, avoiding jargon and excessive lecturing is generally advisable. There is nothing wrong with a more extended lecture if a script has been prepared and distributed. Alternate between presenters for different sections of the session and punctuate the presentation with practical activities, including coffee breaks.

It is at this stage that the skills of teachers are most usefully applied to the organisation of professional learning experiences. The quality of presentation to teachers and others in INSET should be at least as good as the best lessons or classroom presentations. If the presenters struggle with this at the preparation stage, then seeking advice from teachers about presentation is the obvious thing to do. The use of humour is an effective tool for communication, as are quotations, particularly at the start and close of sessions. We like using Chinese proverbs or radical statements. Quotations can seize the attention and help to round off sessions, rather than allowing them to peter out. Timing of sessions is also essential. Forty minutes is the maximum for a lecture, twenty minutes for a presentation which is part of a longer session. It is worth remembering that participants' concentration rapidly begins to wane after the first forty seconds, and declines further after the first three minutes. The rest can be downhill unless the session is kept active and interactive!

Paying attention to the non-verbal aspects of communication is also important in relation to presentation. How are you standing? Are you making eye contact or burying your head in your notes? Are you standing still or wandering around, emphasising that the audience cannot wander but you can? Do you look excited, interested, or tired and tense? Are you speaking slowly and clearly enough or are you speaking too slowly and need to speed up? Unconsciously you will convey a wealth of unintentional information. Practice, rehearsal and honest, constructive feedback are hard to take but vital.

To what extent is the INSET a collaborative event?

As we have been stressing the need for presenters to do some very detailed preparation, collaboration may seem hard to build in. However, if the INSET is to have practical application, piloting within the school with one or two teachers is the ideal way of making the INSET collaborative. Even if the INSET has participants from a number of schools or organisations, piloting in one or two will ensure a collaborative edge to the INSET. This may simply mean that examples of the practical work are up to date, produced by those present and of reasonable rather than exemplary quality. It is often very worthwhile to involve a range of outsiders in the planning and delivery of INSET, including psychologists, inspectors, advisers, teachers, consultants, non-educationists. This needs careful preparation and commitment as noted above.

Kennedy (1987), in an examination of teacher development and innovation, examines three types of strategy that a change agent might consider, as put forward by Bennis, Benne *et al.* (1969):

power-coercive
rational-empirical
normative-reeducative.

He argues in favour of the third strategy, as its implementation necessitates a collaborative, problem-solving approach that involves all those affected by the change process. This strategy places the responsibility for the degree of change and acceptance or rejection of its various aspects on the teacher. He demonstrates how this strategy was used in a project relating to English language teaching at the University of Tunisia, and concludes that it is particularly appropriate in situations of small-scale behavioural changes where both insiders and outsiders are present.

How is the INSET to be evaluated and by whom?

INSET evaluation involves both general and specific feedback, and is frequently done by questionnaire at the time. General feedback is motivating for the presenters and always seems to throw up some interesting and unexpected points. At its simplest, evaluation should include a listing by participants of positives, negatives and improvement suggestions regarding the initiative. Specific, general and open feedback is valuably sought at any level of detail.

If there is a need to evaluate in more detail the reader will probably find it useful to refer to chapter 2 with particular reference to allowing a balance between qualitative and quantitative information. It seems useful to have four foci when evaluating INSET:

context
input
process
product.

Under each heading the would-be evaluator faces some difficult questions, particularly over what are appropriate criteria for each area, who is sponsoring the evaluation, what political relationship exists between the evaluator and the target group and how far future funding may be tied into the results of the evaluation. The evaluator will be attempting to discern what skills and knowledge have been learned but will also be interested in the more elusive areas of confidence, attitude change and levels of objective reflection achieved. However, perhaps the evaluation that really evaluates is the checking of the extent of practical change in the school or organisation at the follow-up stage. INSET should be changing what the organisation does and this should be observable six months and even a year afterwards. While this sounds a reasonable enough assertion it can be very difficult to establish the nature and extent of the impact of INSET on teacher behaviour. Evaluations of teacher behaviour in response to INSET have been studied in a range of ways including the following:

• Questionnaires and interviews
• Simulated teacher performance in a laboratory setting
• Real classroom settings, using informal observation schedules or self-report instruments
• Systematic observation in real settings.

An evaluation once carried out will need to be written up and disseminated.

Any would-be evaluator is faced by a number of important decisions: about his political relationship with the sponsoring body and the target group; about research design, criteria and methodology; about control of access to data; about personalisation of data; about adopting a descriptive or judgemental role; and about the style and form of the dissemination.

(Bolam, 1979: 9)

How is the INSET to be followed up, supported and the skills learned implemented in school?

INSET is likely to be effective if it is spaced out, fortnightly, for example, with the time in between to be used to practise the areas being covered in the sessions. Five or six sessions with practical work provide good short-term follow-up. This is likely to be effective if the original INSET has a favourable presenter ratio, to allow detailed planning of the practical follow-up for each course member back in their classroom. Producing the follow-up action plan is another method, mentioned above. This is usually covered as part of the INSET and the processes of organisational change need to be clearly stated or available to supplement INSET.

In some effective organisations, funding levels are linked to maintenance of skills and practices from INSET and specific performance indicators are devised. Detailed and resource-linked follow-up is likely to be most useful when the innovation the INSET facilitates is either difficult, or moves against the prevailing ethos of the organisation or society. This engenders specific measures to try to ensure behaviour change. Equal opportunities INSET is sometimes supported by contract compliance measures, which mean that continued funding is contingent on reaching and maintaining targets. Business contracts can also be made contingent on meeting targets, in employment for example. For the employment of those registered as disabled, these targets are seldom reached, even if backed by legislation. With special educational needs, the concept of 'resource drift' is now well established. This means that society generally gives such a low priority to children with difficulties that, without tight control, even the resources earmarked for them can be eroded. Where INSET relates to these areas, follow-up is particularly important and linkage to funding and tight performance indicators necessary. LEAs in the UK are increasingly likely to try to contract with schools over the use of INSET in return for specific developments such as in the area of equal opportunities. Follow-up will also provide research information for future planning and implementation of innovations.

Follow-up also involves a rolling programme of INSET rather than one-off presentations. This has the advantage, too, of being able to become increasingly collaborative at a number of levels. Ongoing support, supervision and networking are also potentially very effective means of maintaining INSET impact, and ongoing implementation. Allsop *et al.*, (1989), describing the results of a collaborative INSET programme, include, among others, these comments by headteachers at the final phase of the project:

> Follow-up support is essential after the course has finished to maintain the professional empathy it has engendered. Support networks should be established. Present and subsequent members could meet causing further development to take place. We should meet again as a group, as well as with enquiry partners. Networks for MPGs [Main Professional Grade teachers] must be established, since they will find it difficult to maintain contact. Headteachers may support MPGs undertaking difficult tasks, by giving opportunities for essential work to take place. Support should continue after course completion. Special support could be needed for

those who panic. MPGs must be aware of whom to contact if problems arise.

(Allsop *et al.*, 1989: 29)

Validation and accreditation

Validation and recognition of INSET skills can make the impact of such professional development activity even more powerful. Some courses in special needs areas have been worked out in partnership with college authorities or are certificated by the LEA. This is popular with teachers, leads to precision in curriculum design and delivery, to trainer consistency and to assessment of practical skill attainment. It can promote good links between colleges and schools and between theory and practice. It can help to promote a professional standard of preparation of INSET. With this degree of detail in the validation process, one expects that the INSET will have effects on the organisation that are robust across differing circumstances. One volume of papers edited by Farrell (1985), about evaluation of the effects of the EDY (Education of the Developmentally Young) course (MacBrien and Foxen 1981), its delivery and follow-up, looked in some detail at how different arrangements were used to deliver the basic scripted course. The contributors were confident about the basic strength of the course and had delivered it to good effect in a wide variety of situations, including intensive input rather than the usual spaced sessions.

Relationships

Relationships can be built up during INSET sessions to an extremely high degree. As educational psychologists, INSET provides us with opportunities to build relationships in circumstances of generally lower stress than in casework, and we welcome these opportunities. The relationships are social as well as professional, but the professional relationships between presenter and trainees, and among those attending are important and often longstanding. The implications of this are:

- to devote sufficient time to activities to permit full exploration of issues
- to provide precision in activities so that routine answers are not sufficient and some change and challenge takes place;

and to ensure:

- that the more formal presentations are thoroughly prepared and delivered with effective social skills
- that issues are returned to on more than one occasion
- that theory and research are important parts of INSET
- that follow-up practical activities are discussed thoroughly in sessions

- that specific techniques are called upon to open up group creativity and collaboration
- that practical follow-up work leads to the creation of shared records and resources
- that social time is adequate but not excessive.

The relationships formed during high quality INSET may not be precisely those formed in teaching with and among children but a number of similarities may be seen. In particular, positive learning experiences create and are fostered by high quality relationships that can contribute to professional personal realisation, referred to in chapter 1. This is an area for discussion and action research in schools to follow up quality INSET.

Training provision

In the education service as a whole, there are pressing problems of scale and access to training. It is necessary to increase the relevance, scale and accessibility of training at realistic unit costs. Time should be made available to teachers to undertake training, but programmes must be organised to create minimum disruption to the work of the school. This will require a radical review of the general balance of provision.

(DES, School Management Task Force, 1990: 20)

The DES in 1990 recommended a number of shifts in emphasis in training. They suggested a move away from tutor-directed courses to support for self-directed study by individuals, school teams and peer groups. They proposed that there should be less off-site training and more in-school or near-to-the-school training. Training should occur not at predetermined times but as ongoing flexi-study. Distance learning materials, information packs and projects may take the place of oral presentations, while school-determined agenda would take over from provider-determined syllabus. Finally, redirected emphasis would in future be placed on performance enhancement rather than knowledge acquisition.

THE FUTURE: INSET IN THE TWENTY-FIRST CENTURY

Following the lead of Beare *et al.* (1989) in their book *Creating an Excellent School*, we offer a vision of INSET in the middle of the twenty-first century. What does the future hold for INSET in the context of managing change in schools?

Without doubt the trend towards effective school-focused INSET will continue. Methods of school-based needs analysis will become commonplace and increasingly sophisticated. Schools will increasingly make more use of their own expertise in INSET-style activities as well as in related action research and collaborative problem-solving.

The impact of Information Technology may finally start to get a real grip on schools in the twenty-first century. Information access will become essential to all individual and corporate development, and will in fact drive development in many ways. Teachers will all have access to classroom terminals and laptop computers, and will be linked to main-frame local authority computer systems at school and at home. Up-to-date information that will reflect state of the art teaching methods, content and processes will be available from a vast international database. Links will be made possible not only between schools in this country but also across the globe. Such improved communication, led by increased information access, will accelerate professional innovation and development. A new fascination with knowing exactly what is the most recent understanding of any given learning situation will become a preoccupation of teachers. The regular use of interactive video for specific learning purposes and data-packed disks or access to a mainframe network will allow unlimited access to information and learning opportunity.

Accountabilities will be harsher for schools and teachers but this will be balanced by more fluidity in the teaching day and week with more job-sharing and part-time work allowing for longer working days and a longer working week, with more learning occurring at home in a computer-assisted mode for pupils as well as staff.

Teachers will become increasingly proficient and challenged to work closer to parents in and out of school situations and this will become a much more critical aspect of professional development than in the past. This will be fed by a welter of research even further illuminating the learning benefits to be accrued from teachers and parents working together. Teacher and parent support groups will be emerging in a number of countries. Teachers' development will extend to meet the increasing needs of pupils presenting a whole range of disabilities, who will all attend ordinary schools by right.

Teams of INSET providers and INSET consultants will abound and will work with schools to extremely tight objectives and contracts, but will face increasingly challenging areas such as family therapy, sexual abuse, accelerated learning projects and so forth. All teachers will be involved in regular supervision groups and will be appraised regularly and will be feeling much more supported and challenged. Salary and conditions of service may become much more closely linked to appraisal schemes. School and individual staff members are likely to be rewarded with monies for demonstrable developments in terms of understandings, skills and change (Manning, 1988). Sabbaticals would be a regular feature of professional development along with teacher exchanges.

Evaluation and research and development activity will tend to involve more staff, in management systems with more lateral structures and loose/tight properties. Small working groups or units will be operating flexibly and creatively in the majority of larger schools. Research and evaluation consultants are likely to be bought in to support such activities.

Finally teachers will find themselves fully involved in the education not only of children but also of adults from cradle to grave on a daily basis. Ultimately professional development will be equated with professional survival and the pace will be even faster than in the twentieth century. We can perhaps look forward to completely new innovative approaches to self directed professional development and INSET delivery than have been considered to date.

ACTION PLAN

- Be clear why INSET is being undertaken. Does it fit in with the organisational objectives of the school, LEA or government? Will it enrich the work and development of the individual staff member? What and whose needs are being met by the INSET? Are these needs clearly identified?
- At whom is the INSET aimed? Will it meet their needs? Always try to involve participants in identification of needs and if possible in the planning of the INSET.
- Choose a model of INSET delivery which is most suitable to the process of change which is being engaged in, and which fits well the professional development goals it is aimed at.
- Clarify the level and type of involvement of participants particularly regarding:
    needs identification and clarification
    INSET planning
    INSET delivery
    INSET evaluation.
- When providing INSET ensure that close attention and planning is given to: theory, practice, preparation, interaction, presentation, collaboration, implementation, support and follow-up.
- Review, monitor and evaluate the effectiveness of all INSET activities engaged in by school staff, and use this as the basis for further planning and for decisions regarding future INSET.

Chapter 8

Research and development

R&D refers to research and development activity both quantitative and qualitative. It is a powerful change process in its own right which pervades much of our endeavour in the educational world.

There is now a belief that some of the large-scale educational change initiatives of the 1960s and 1970s were less effective than they could have been and less efficient in their use of resources, partly because of an assumption that research findings could easily be transferred into classroom practice. This is no doubt a simplification, but is a useful issue on which to start in considering a model of research and development to apply in school.

Certain types of basic research that would be potentially useful can be hard to carry out in school conditions. Research on the causes and social interactions of violent behaviour, for example, is limited by three main factors (Marsh and Campbell, 1982): society's near obsession with violence and the accompanying media fuss around research in this area, the difficulty of studying violence as a neutral observer and the problem of academic compartmentalisation in the varied fields of anthropology, genetics, physiology, psychology, sociology and criminology. Our view is that the research literature on violence gives too much prominence to violence without the context, e.g. of racism and sexism (Schostak, 1986) and too little

Research and Development

to the problem more frequently experienced by teachers, verbal aggression, as part of the circular interactions we refer to earlier in chapter 3.

An alternative model is to use researchers as field workers in supporting school-initiated developments. There are many interesting accounts of innovation projects arising from school initiatives (Bassett, 1970; Phi Delta Kappa, 1980; Reynolds *et al.*, 1984). It is not always clear from these whether a research element was important in the innovation. To give another example, Mulford's (1987) account of indicators of school effectiveness in Australia is perhaps typical in omitting a research link although it is easy to see how research could have been involved. Mulford's key factors were:

- sense of mission
- great expectations
- academic focus
- feedback on academic performance
- positive motivational strategies
- conscious attention to climate (a positive, safe, ordered school community)
- leadership
- other aspects:
  teachers take responsibility
  parental involvement
  system support.

Any of these areas could be exciting areas of action research, but in this as in many other accounts of school improvement and effectiveness, no strong research and development aspect is evident. In this chapter we look at ways of bringing these elements together, to foster school-initiated developments that are informed and improved by research.

We have also referred (in Chapter 4) to a scepticism that innovation in schools was easy, leading to a governmental tendency to think in terms of quite dramatic methods of promoting change, allowing some institutions to wither through lack of funding while setting up new ones. This seems to have some aspects of the R&D model about it once again, the assumption being that there is a clearly defined model for successful schooling which can be put into practice, an assumption that implies universality. We feel that an examination of how research can help the change process in schools is needed and the application of research methods in schools may be no less valuable than the application of research findings to schools. We are interested in the links between research and development and the growing role of action research.

ACTION RESEARCH

One potentially powerful means of informing policy development and influencing practices, from the level of national government through to what happens in local schools, is research and development activity. This can be carried out in a variety of contexts and for different purposes. School-based R&D is often referred to as action research.

Clark (1972) gives a useful outline of action research. He describes it as oriented to practical problems with theoretical relevance, involving practitioners and scientists. It can be disseminated in journals or reported to a sponsor or both. Thus it lies at a mid-point between pure research that has little if any practical or immediate relevance, and applied research which may be limited by reporting back to a specific sponsor with no incentive to disseminate the findings or to link it to theory.

All of us in our daily lives are regularly influenced directly or indirectly by the work of those engaged in R&D. The packaging, marketing and advertising of the products we are constantly invited to buy are based on carefully designed research activity followed up by development work: breakfast cereals, drinks, clothes, holidays, furniture, foodstuffs and cars provide daily examples. The researchers who look at these matters may well be interested in pure research, but their research is directed at sales targets, at a positive return for the expenditure on the advertising budget. The questions looked at may have some longer-term perspectives, looking to build awareness, recognition and image, but usually have an overriding relevance to the here and now, the coming sales season.

Political parties have become increasingly practised in countries such as America and Britain in their research into what the voters want. They follow up their research by increasingly sophisticated presentations and marketing plus policy developments to ensure the closest possible fit between voters' desires and party intentions.

Health education is an interesting area of action research; as new medical knowledge comes from basic research, applied research looks at how people can change their habits to benefit from the discoveries, in particular in the field of prevention. For instance, will the improvement in GPs' communication skills be correlated with reduction in tranquilliser prescriptions?

R&D affects our thinking and actions in many other ways and there is a great interest in what research can offer to our day-to-day lives. Educational and child psychologists are, like teachers, often wary of admitting to their profession on social occasions because of the many questions about children that follow:

How much sleep do children need?
How should children be disciplined?
What is the best type of school for my child?
Are schools doing a good job?
How far should parents be involved in their children's education?

How do children learn to read?
How valid or reliable are intelligence tests?
How often does child abuse really occur?

Your own answers, to some of these questions at least, are bound to be influenced by information you have been exposed to that is based either on opinion or research and ideas that have emerged or been developed as a consequence.

In education we should be especially interested in learning, in finding out, not just about matters far removed from our daily experience, but about that daily experience. If it is important, it is worthy of attention and study and the more systematic the study the more useful it is likely to be. The processes and techniques of study should be of particular interest to educationists too.

Our culture and the whole education process is built upon constructs, ideas, available information, theories and skills. Much of this has been handed down or has evolved over generations but significant amounts have emerged from systematic efforts to research and develop. Workers involved with the education of children and young people have engaged in such activity and it is their legacy and ongoing theoretical and practical work which influence us all in our daily work.

A physical education teacher was heard to remark how pleased she was to hear of some research that indicated, in contradiction to some earlier research, that though children may be less active today they are not less fit than in the past. She was also pleased that the research was rigorously carried out and felt confident with the findings and also with the credibility of the researcher. It was not that she was waiting for her prejudices or casual observations to receive corroboration – a closed approach to research. Rather, she was using her own observations to question the *status quo* in existing research findings, and had within herself the research hypothesis that the professional researchers went on to explore.

One of us taught a number of pupils who originated in Bangladesh at a time when the research claim was that Asian children did well in British schools, a claim that was in no way supported by what was happening to these Bangladeshi children. Later research led to a much more discerning analysis of pupil attainments and to concern at a national level about pupils of Bangladeshi origin or family. Questions about widely held assumptions are at the heart of valid and unprejudiced research.

The power of research

We each draw out our own construction of what we believe and understand of the world in which we live and work, but this is fundamentally affected by the information and ideas we are exposed to. Research and data collection will help our constructions of reality, our scripts for operation, stay close to reality, and allow for more development and innovation.

Governments at both national and local level are well aware of the importance of research and will often repress or express the virtues of research as it reflects on their aims and intentions. Government groups commission research and development activities. In Britain this has usually taken the form of Royal Commissions, think-tanks or task groups looking into such areas as meeting special educational needs (Warnock Report), exploring care in the community (Griffiths Report), or examining national assessment arrangements in all schools (TGAT Report). Responses to publicity or concerns expressed publicly are often related to research, either revealing previously confidential reports or commissioning further investigation. The research and suggested developments of such groups has often been acted upon selectively and politically, usually in the form of legislation. Thus it is that research and development proposals seldom, if ever, survive in their initial pure form. Research findings can form or contribute to important rituals in education.

What happens at a macro-level also occurs at a micro-level in other organisations including schools and even families. At all levels research and development activity is central to decision making, change, policy development and implementation. In particular, R&D is a powerful medium for changing school systems.

INITIATIVES IN EDUCATIONAL RESEARCH

GRIDS (Guidelines for Review and Internal Development in Schools (McMahon *et al.*, 1984)), PADS (Preventive Approaches to Disruption) and other school improvement projects have demonstrated the integral link of research activities with the improvement process. They combine school-based learning activities with the results of earlier research, to give specific information and skills, and to open up an agenda for further change. Reid *et al.* (1987), for example, list the following factors for school change:

- improvement of both teaching and learning
- development of the school as a learning institution
- humanisation of schooling
- involvement of staff – collegiality
- research/INSET.

However, it is worth noting at this stage that few teachers in any country have been made aware of educational action research in their initial training. They may well have done projects or dissertations which have involved observation, interviews, questionnaires or other research tools, but seldom if ever as part of an overall module on research skills and applications. We need a way forward to equip and empower schools to conduct applied research using the skills and experience they have, and also to build additional research skills.

In particular, the skill of asking the most appropriate questions for research to address is valuable. Research in a school can involve a wide range of activities, and research activities can be very time consuming, especially if hypothesis testing is to be part of the process, or if the sample size needs to be large. Teachers have limited time, as the main focus of their time and energy is and must be on teaching. Research within and by a school, must be uncomplicated, convenient and useful. Data collection is best left until a late stage of research, and best done initially as part of a pilot exercise with a small sample. Research which starts with a large data collection activity is unlikely to be effective in terms of its costs and benefits. It is worth recalling at this stage that purposeless frantic activity is a sign of stress, not of progress.

Precision about the purpose of the research is vital and will ensure a good outcome from a limited time allocation. Action research needs to have most of the time and energy going into the action, with the research being precisely designed and convenient, rather than elaborate and encroaching on the performance of core school activities.

A starting point for a school is to ask questions which have implications for future action. Some examples of questions are given below. These questions relate to a particular school, not to establishing fundamental truths about education; even full-time researchers balk at that. They also relate to how to move forward collaboratively, on positive paths. It is not motivating to have staff compared or competitively evaluated. If the evaluation is negative, those who have put a lot of work into a project or activity may feel that they have failed the test and either become demoralised or will question the design of the research and/or the motivation of the researcher. Research questions are best aimed at the process of exploring new objectives and how to reach them.

This is distinct from the process of appraisal (Poster and Poster, 1991). Concepts of appraisal, evaluation research, management activities and supervision information need to be kept distinct with different uses of data.

Simple research principles that can be used by schools include:

- exploration to suggest possible hypotheses
- basic statistical application and analysis
- questionnaire design and analysis
- pilot studies
- structured interviews
- literature searching
- observation and video
- miscue analysis
- hypothesis formulation

- replication
- control groups
- sampling
- prediction/analysis of trends.

It is not the purpose of this chapter to give detailed guidance about these and other research techniques. For those interested there are a number of useful texts, for example, Hegarty and Evans (1985). However, it may be wiser to look at the audit of assets referred to in chapter 6 and to see what skills already exist within the school, and how the agencies and others who work with the school can contribute skills. For example, the UK National Curriculum includes within design and technology the requirement of a working knowledge of problem-solving models. Students gain from applying classroom skills to real-life situations as well as to the formal curriculum. The staff who teach this and the students who learn and practise this can contribute to the devising of hypotheses in operational terms. Those with qualifications in statistics, psychology, chemistry and other sciences, mathematics and other areas will have had some experience in these techniques, even though their skills may be rusty. It is useful preparation for managerial posts to gain some expertise and experience in looking at the school as an organisation and a valuable way of promoting co-operative work among staff.

The main focus of our current advice is on the ethics and practicalities of school-based research and the need to link it with the attainment of school development objectives. We noted earlier in this chapter that investigation of basic educational processes is not likely to be of great benefit to the school and can be left to full-time professionals. Given limited time, linking research to specific school objectives will be of most value, as will a precisely defined time allocation and report-back date. The best research is often that with the simplest design.

We would also stress that the rituals of research need consideration. Research can trigger the 'expert' specialist role which is not particularly helpful in promoting the progress of the whole school. An objective for school development might be for each faculty or pastoral group in the organisation to complete some action research in a school year. This could be timetabled to allow for the necessary INSET and consultation on content and coherence across the school. Ultimately, every teacher would gain from the skills of action research in the classroom, applied with rigour to the progress of individual children (White and Haring, 1980). Specific strategies to disseminate skills and confidence in this area can be included in the professional development section of the school development plan.

Ethical considerations can be addressed after considering model guidelines from organisations such as the American Psychological Association, the British Psychological Society or other groups such as the

Society for Responsibility in Science. Schools can also develop their own policies, procedures and guidelines in addition to these.

> The methodological developments required for effective field research (including increased flexibility and participation) may require more explicit reference to ethical behaviour. This may also be the case for the more traditional 'academic' sector.

(Gray and Lindsay, 1991: 79)

It is appropriate to aim not only to meet basic ethical requirements but to seek to attain very high standards as part of the school ethos. In such discussions, the question of the ownership of the research will be salient, as will openness and clarity about methods used to allow the detection of bias (Gray and Lindsay, 1991).

Specific institution-based R. & D. can have a profound effect on the development of a school over a short-term period such as a year, or over a much longer-term period can become a permanent feature of the school culture. At its most basic, research and development is a permanent feature of school life. Questions are always being raised and answers sought:

• What are the reading results in the fourth grade this year?
• How many children of which age groups receive free school meals?
• How many parents are involved in helping within classrooms this year?
• How effective are our equal opportunities policies and practices?
• What do we know about the school's neighbourhood?
• What methods do parents use when reading with their children at home?
• What is the school's reputation in the community?
• Are attendance patterns seasonal or curriculum-related?
• Is pupil behaviour improving?

Many schools go much further than this in the more systematic use of R&D, engaging, for instance, in a systemic self-appraisal, using the GRIDS approach, or SSI (System Supplied Information (Myers, 1985). One headteacher in Britain carried out a detailed survey to assess the level of parental involvement in her school. Her methods included interviews with parents and teachers, interview schedules, and discussion groups. In another school, a special school for children with behavioural and emotional problems, the research issue was the extent of violent behaviour.

Situation 8.1

There was concern and some uncertainty as to the actual level of violent behaviour in this special school. There is frequently rough behaviour, verbal aggression, talk of violence in the community setting and so on. Staff are often uncertain about the true level of aggressive behaviour: is it taking place away from their supervision or covered up by aggressor, victim and witnesses colluding to report nothing? (Casdagli and Gobey, 1990).

With the help of a consultant in a one-off discussion, the staff decided to construct an operational definition: a closely worked out formula of words which would ensure the reliability of the data collection and hence of the conclusions. The plan was to record, first, incidents of violence towards adults which resulted in visible marks two days later or medical treatment off site, and, secondly, similar incidents between children. There proved to be very few recorded instances of either type of violence. The staff concluded that their perception of what had been happening was unduly pessimistic and that much of what occurred was ritualised aggression without any physical consequences. Their conclusions for action were:

- to ask for a literature search to investigate verbal aggression and to suggest strategies to reduce this
- to look in more detail at the behaviour of one child where regular aggression did seem to take place
- to begin to discuss as a staff group how the children's apparently aggressive, challenging behaviour aroused feelings of aggression among themselves, which were disturbing, undermined their confidence and created a negative agenda.

The time taken by staff on this exercise was not recorded but was not regarded as a problem.

Situation 8.2

In a discussion and development planning group in a nursery unit the issue was raised of the interruptions through phone calls to proactive, planned work. One team member's post required that messages were taken from the caller; the others were able to answer most calls themselves. In the data collection period there were sixty-eight messages that had to be taken on behalf of the first team member. The number of calls made to the others were not a matter of concern. What was of concern was that some of the calls were very time-consuming. Many were about the availability of places in the nursery, and there were separate arrangements for giving information about this which the callers were bypassing. There was a feeling that the calls were a poor use of time, and time spent on the telephone was unproductive for staff and to callers alike.

It was said that the habit in the neighbourhood was to make extensive use of the phone. As some people were nervous about their personal safety when travelling to visit their friends on the estate, they had developed the habit of phoning instead, and having lengthy and wide-ranging calls. Some staff admitted that they too enjoyed talking on the phone and did so at length at home. Perhaps the phone calls were socially valuable for staff and callers, but seemed to have few tangible positive outcomes.

A series of strategies were considered and implemented to reduce the time taken on the phone. The simple recording of the messages received was encouraged as part of the recognition by staff and callers alike of the fact that time spent on phone calls was disruptive to the work with children.

These are two examples of research investigations of different levels of complexity. They both related directly to specific aspects of effectiveness at work and had quite different but substantial outcomes, some of them easy to quantify, others less easy but held to be valuable by the teachers/nursery workers.

USING THE RESEARCH AND DEVELOPMENT WORK OF OTHERS

Internationally and locally there will always be in education a constant flow of R&D activity. The question often facing the in-school change agent is how best to access this and effectively use it to guide and inform the change process. We would suggest the following guidelines if you wish to use the work of others to influence developments in your own school:

- Plan your regular reading and allow time for some random, stimulating reading. You will need to be in touch with the broader world of education as well as more specifically with the area(s) you are most concerned with.
- Analyse critically research and development work from which you are drawing. What are its shortcomings? What were the design/ methodological flaws?
- Log down the key points you are drawing from the R&D.
- Analyse the links between the R&D and your own situation. What are the similarities and what are the differences? What could you usefully replicate?
- Begin by sounding out the key movers in your change situation the proposals you are likely to be making. Explore likely pitfalls/obstacles and consider ways around those that involve yourself and others as far as possible.
- Set out your proposals to the senior management group or other decision-making or policy-developing body in your school, taking care to state them as options to be considered and not firm conclusions. Ideally, spell out the positives and negatives of each proposal.
- Follow up discussion of the proposals with something in writing to all those involved outlining what you understood was agreed.

There is much impressive international R&D work, some of it particularly appropriate to the change process itself: for instance the management model research carried out in Australia (Beare *et al.*, 1989). You may also find useful

R&D activities being carried out in your local area. A number of LEAs in Britain have been using their educational psychologists extensively for R&D. For instance, in one area between 1989 and 1991 the LEA commissioned work on the following:

- What happens to pupils with emotional and behavioural needs in this county?
- What are we doing for under-fives with special educational needs in this LEA? Do we need integrated nurseries? What would they be like? How can we build on existing neighbourhood support to help children remain in their local communities? (Newton *et al.*, 1991)
- How could we set up a database on all pupils with special educational needs?
- How can we fund schools on the basis of indicators of special educational needs? What are these indicators and what formula could we use? (McConville, 1991)
- What should we be doing for children with speech and language difficulties?
- What happens to pupils with moderate learning difficulties in this LEA?

Whatever sources of research you tap into maintain a critical perspective as the quality of research varies enormously, even though this may have little relevance to its actual impact.

> As to the argument that the impact of research depends on its quality, I find this very implausible. We can all think of examples of poor research that has made a big impact, or good research which has made very little.
> (Tizard, 1991: 11)

CARRYING OUT YOUR OWN R&D

A detailed account of how to engage in R&D is beyond the scope of this book. We would, however, recommend that you consider the following before engaging in R&D activity:

- Be clear of the objectives of your R&D.
- Be clear on the questions you are setting out to answer.
- Be clear on the scope of your project. Don't be overambitious!
- Be clear on your timescale. If one is not set out for you, set one for yourselves. Like many activities R&D will fit into whatever size pot of time you provide!
- Be clear on team roles. Who is co-ordinating? Who is reporting back? Who is recording/writing up?
- Be clear on your task specifications. If they do not exist draw up your own.
- Use outside expertise where relevant, including that of visiting advisors,

psychologists, local universities, colleges and others who you may not have realised have a research training component in their background.

• Consider and discuss in your working group some of the interpersonal dimensions to working together. These aspects can floor R&D teams so are worth a regular discussion/airing however stressful this may sound.

• Be aware of the context of your work but try to avoid political pressures undermining the objectivity of your work.

• When reporting back go through similar stages as those outlined above with regard to using the R&D of others.

Getting started

We have noted how research can be seen in user-friendly terms. Children are required to conduct research and enquiry in the early school years and not only can they be very good at it but it can be among their most enjoyable experiences. It is well worth asking how children are guided into successful early research within each school.

A good starting point for a school wanting to build its self-research skills is to recognise that the very best research is that which shows that the right question was asked, that the right hypothesis was selected and that the rigour came from clear thinking. The starting point for research is to work out general areas within which the research will be useful and interesting and then to consider whether to be more specific and, if so, how.

Research and statistics

One valuable area of research is in eliciting information within an area of interest. Gathering impressions, opinions and information should not be ruled out as lacking rigour. Gathering information must ensure that no aspect is omitted, that consultation occurs on the scope and importance of specific items and that information and skill that already exist are not overlooked or duplicated. If more specific research is to be undertaken, then the less focused information-gathering may produce interesting possible hypotheses for detailed investigation.

There is no reason to try to introduce unduly complicated research methods or detailed statistics or to duplicate the work of full-time educational researchers, although it is well worth while cultivating a relationship with people or organisations who have high level research skills.

Situation 8.3

One of us with a colleague (Bayley and Tarrant, 1990) looked at work done on children's perceptions of race. Gaine (1988) had presented data suggesting caution in assuming a positive effect from anti-racist teaching. He presented data from analysing children's writing on the essay title *Black People in Britain* which suggested that the first half of such essays would contain more positive statements because the children perceived that this was the kind of comment expected by the teacher. More negative comments would occur in the second half and these would represent the real views of the children on race.

By replicating this and having children also write essays on *Women in Britain* the researchers found that analysing the essays provided some very thought-provoking issues and suggestions for further work, despite the fact that the level of analysis at this stage was simplistic. The children's comments suggested, for example, that:

- Positive comments about black people often contained stereotypes about athleticism and entertainment.
- Positive comments about black people often related to specific individual contact with black people.
- Positive comments about career opportunities for women seldom related to specific and individual goals or opportunities.
- Few of the comments reflected individual responsibility or actions; equal opportunities was something that other people provided through laws or information on TV.

The teachers involved in this research found the analysis of the comments valuable; and the action research of this group of teachers with a full teaching load, who had attended a course of a mere three days' duration, was of good enough quality for production in a house journal.

Asking questions

Asking questions is at the heart of all research. Asking those questions which have implications for action is at the heart of action research and the link between research and development. Situation 8.3 refers to the details of how teachers might achieve equal opportunities objectives and the implications for action are considerable, both for teaching and highlighting the need to evaluate the teaching.

Thus the whole area of research and development is extremely rich for the educator and change agent. Its role in creating a school culture in which enquiry, reflection and change are ongoing and integral processes at every level are obvious. Finally, for research to have any real impact on school development it will be crucial to build what Tizard metaphorically refers to as 'gateways' at school, local authority, national, and international levels.

For every area of social policy, there are crucial gateways through which research findings must go if they are to become known to policy makers and practitioners. In the case of educational practice, for example, the crucial gateways are the contents of initial and in-service training and higher degree courses for teachers. For central and local authority policy makers, the education supplements, but more importantly the quality press and the media generally, are probably the main gateways. The researcher whose ideas do not pass through these gateways has little chance of making an impact.

(Tizard, 1991: 11)

In schools the gateways may not be so dissimilar and will include management group briefings, in-service training, the use of school newsletter and so forth. Ultimately, as Tizard argues, the critical gateways need identifying and the findings and ideas pushed through.

ACTION PLAN

- Clarify in discussion with others what you understand by research and how this links to school development. Follow up unanswered questions with further enquiry and reading, perhaps linking with a colleague or visitor to the school.
- Find out what research is ongoing in your school and the local area. Reflect on the value and merits of what is happening and look for links with your own ideas for change.
- Who is and who could be engaged in research in your school? What can you do to promote some action research within the school? What would be a good place to start? Would this link well to objectives for change and other professional development activities already planned or would it be completely new? Whose agreement would you need?
- What access does the school have and what use does it make of information about ongoing research nationally and internationally? What journals and books regularly or periodically come into school? Who looks at these? Could others be ordered that would facilitate access to such information? Is the school computer linked to any source of information on up-to-date educational research?
- Plan your own research project and clarify team roles and objectives.
- Carry out research to set time scales and work out the best ways of reporting back to the rest of the staff to maximise impact and their sense of participation. Be careful in your choice of communication gateways to maximise impact.
- Critically evaluate your research and with others look at the implications for practice. What needs to be changed? What can be changed easily? What will the next steps have to be?

Chapter 9

Evaluating and monitoring change

In this chapter we look back on what you have achieved while going through the change process. This is a crucial stage, but one often left out, not only by overworked managers adopting a largely reactive unplanned approach to change, but also by enthusiastic professionals keen to press on with the next strategy for change. Looking back on what has been achieved often reveals that our day-to-day perceptions underestimate the amount of change that has occurred, because it often takes place in small stages. In the same way as checklists or records of achievement help to record and focus on positives in the development of children and need to be updated and discussed regularly, organisations benefit from a positive process of looking back on change before moving on to the next cycle.

It is also helpful to see change as cyclical, and occasionally to allow time for evaluation rather than change, for reflection and consolidation rather than innovative action. The quality of what we think and do will be better for the variation; where stresses have occurred there will be time and space for healing, for emphasis on progress rather than on problems and for mutual support and discussion. Thinking about core beliefs and objectives will take precedence over details. Stepping back from the day-to-day routine helps in the development of strategic thinking.

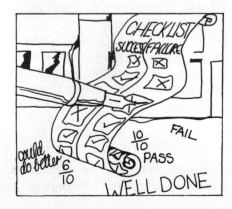

Evaluating your organisation

Looking at what has been achieved puts our daily concerns and anxieties into perspective. Core beliefs can be realised and reflection on these will be a fundamental part of the maturing and strengthening of the school. It is rare indeed to achieve all targets. If that occurs, then perhaps those targets were unambitious.

It is helpful to adopt an objective perspective on what has been happening over a period of time: to take a step back to see more clearly may make your next actions more effective. A number of references have already been made to economics, in which prediction and data analysis are closely linked. For management, the questions will also be about the allocation of resources to support innovation, about the realisation of policies into practice and to consider why, when and where the school was pushed off course. There will be a need to consider how effective the record-keeping was, and how it might be developed to save time and still yield the most valuable evaluation information in the most accessible form. Management can also consider how best to consolidate achievements within the organisation so that they become part of it and a strength for the future, and less tied to the charisma and commitment of an individual or small group.

> We emphasize that planning and evaluation activities are related integrally to management and decision-making processes in human service organizations. Information gleaned from these activities is useful to the extent that it is used to inform decision-makers and thereby improve decisions.
>
> (Illback *et al.*, 1990: 799)

It is also worth reflecting that, although the focus of this book has been on an objectives-based, action-led approach, human beings need the opportunity to relax on occasions. By adopting a change cycle, a school can give itself a time of relative ease, of less focused discussion. In a change cycle of three years, this might be a period of three months. Starting up again might lead to the problem of overcoming the inertia that could build up even in this brief time; but there needs to be the recognition that, while humans generally thrive on successful hard work, they also become stale and more likely to be alienated if the targets are always being increased.

Ultimately, children are likely to benefit from attending a school in which hard work is tempered with reflection and recuperation, in which staff work hard, but not simply for the sake of doing so. Recuperation, revival and renewal, important three Rs in schools today, are virtually never referred to or dealt with seriously by staff or their leadership.

CYCLES OF CHANGE

As with many developmental processes, change can be usefully understood as occurring in cycles. All processes may be seen to have a beginning, a middle and an end. Rather as the snowball rolling down the hill gathers more snow, so change may begin in very small movements and gather momentum at a speed dependent on a multitude of factors. To continue the analogy, the initial cycle may be initiated from within; the snowball may crack apart and start to roll as a consequence of internal changes or outside forces. It may even be kicked off course by a passing rambler. This use of a simple analogy does not imply that change need be uneven, crude or jerky or that only one cycle can be operating at a time or over the same time scale.

What is clear is that change cannot be seen simply in terms of mechanical cause and effect. Some kind of model which allows for interactive effects is needed. In psychology, routine analysis involves a number of originating factors, described as independent variables and their interactions. In economic models too, a large range of variables are routinely included. Models of mutual causality, where A and B are both involved in circular or dialectical relations, attempt to present more sophisticated, albeit more complex, ways of understanding change.

What is important is that members of organisations identify new ways of thinking about the circular and other forms of relations in which they are involved and begin to consider how these are formed and transformed as well as how these are mutually determining and determined. Thinking in loops or in opposites and exploring the way in which systems maintain the homeostasis or create imbalances will be important in your understanding of change cycles. Creating *rich pictures* and conceptual models of school systems is one approach to problem-solving and planning described by Checkland (1981) and developed further by Frederickson (1990) and others in an approach referred to as Soft Systems Methodology:

Towards the next cycle

In relating evaluation to planned change it is helpful to view schools from a systems perspective. Applying this viewpoint, schools are seen within the context of larger systems or the suprasystem (e.g. they are part of a community and of the state educational agency) as well as various subsystems working within the school (e.g. administration, school psychological services, special education programs, English department). Each of these systems and subsystems is interrelated and interdependent on the others.

(Illback *et al.*, 1990: 812)

The literature on school change regularly indicates that systems factors such as administrative support, school environment and staff opportunities for participation in the change process are crucial to success.

Stable and unstable cycles

Organisations do well to plan to thrive in chaotic environments (Peters, 1988). Equally, well presented plans may promote an unwarranted sense of order in the world which can be close to complacency. The relationship between orderly and uneven progress merits examination, and economic cautions about boom leading to bust and the search for policies that will promote sustainable progress give valuable starting points in this area.

The concept of a closed feedback loop is one that can be applied to success as well as failure, to growth and recession. It has been argued and supported by good evidence that change processes characterised by positive feedback where more leads to more and less to less can be unstable if not balanced by negative feedback where changes in one variable lead to changes in the opposite direction. Exponential change brought on by loops of positive feedback cannot be maintained in the long term if not balanced by stabilising loops. The Club of Rome project, which looked at the predicament of mankind and pioneered the idea that we should understnd world economics as a system of loops, found this true internationally in terms of world population, pollution, food production and resource depletion (Morgan 1986).

It is crucial that we make every attempt to evaluate effectively what is happening in our changing organisation and not be content even if evident progress is being made. The same messages and methods which were applied with fine judgement and with excellent outcomes can be applied insensitively or unthinkingly if not reappraised. In certain instances this can lead to trauma for the organisation or for individuals within it. An important aspect of evaluating change in order to move to the next cycle is to look not only at the success, but also at the price of that success. Can the success be sustained and the cost in human terms reduced? The change cycles of evaluation and innovation we advise will make such risks and extremes less likely.

EVALUATING CHANGE

Evaluation is the process of systematically gathering information for the purposes of making judgements or decisions. We argue that evaluation is crucial to effective change cycles for the following reasons:

- it helps us to understand what is happening within our organisation
- it provides effective feedback to influence decision making and action planning in relation to future change
- the process confirms or otherwise the course of action that has been engaged in over a given period
- the process fits a holistic model of school development already referred to and is an important way of maintaining impetus
- evaluation will highlight and lead to the recognition of successful actions and individuals as well as problems which need to be addressed
- information will be gleaned on more and less visible aspects of change including feelings, stress, value judgements alongside hard data on such areas as improvements in performance and attendance
- evaluating change helps to involve the whole organisation more in the planning as well as the outcome, allowing a range of contributions and a less personally dependent debate.

Before starting on any evaluation of change it is important to be specific about the objectives of your evaluation, the questions you wish to address and the scope of your endeavour. Caldwell and Spinks (1986) differentiate minor evaluations carried out annually and more major evaluations carried out every three or five years. They also emphasise the need to adopt a manageable and practical approach to evaluating specific projects or programmes, rather than try to review everything that has been going on throughout the whole school year.

It is essential to be precise about who the client is in the evaluation: who will see the outcome, who will act on it and what is the scope and circulation of the information gained. The objectives of an evaluation might be framed as in the following example:

- to appraise the effectiveness of the whole school policy on spelling adopted last September
- to highlight factors which have contributed to improved attendance this year
- to clarify strengths and weaknesses of the school's new strategy for parental involvement in pupil's learning
- to look at ways of recognising positives in the probationer induction

scheme and to consider developments in this to be put into practice the following year.

As we have emphasised in earlier chapters, the more specific and explicit you can be when setting objectives, the more likelihood there is of their attainment. Such objectives are, with few exceptions, intended to be shared and made public and this reduces risks to the organisation and individuals.

It is helpful to keep the number of your objectives to the minimum necessary to inform the decision-making process or to answer the essential questions of the evaluation. Questions relating to updating an action plan need to take two forms. The first relate to reframing areas of activity: to include new areas, to drop others and to take a fresh look at some basic issues. The other relate to specifics of how much progress has been made towards objectives already set. This process is not to be seen in terms of personal success and failure and should not be addressed in any competitive sense, but as a process to use the skills of all to move forward as effectively as possible. Questions might be framed as follows:

• Shall we continue to develop our whole school policy on spelling?
• What is it that we are doing right in relation to promoting school attendance? Can any of these ideas be developed further?
• Are we getting the choice of books for home school reading right in relation to our parental involvement strategy?
• What are the areas in which our probationers are most effective?

It is useful to spend time clarifying which questions will provide the most valuable insights. You will be most interested in questions which yield unambiguous data or clearly expressed views that can be easily applied to future practice and decisions.

Areas in which the questions either seem hard to devise or in which decision making seems difficult can occur. These can either be reconsidered to see if they really need to be included, as they may prove to be excessively time-consuming. Or, if there are areas that cannot easily be dropped but seem difficult, setting up a pilot programme is recommended. This should take up less time and other resources and yield almost as much information about ways forward.

The methods of evaluation you select once again involve the quantitative and qualitative activities referred to earlier and may include the following:

• interviews with teachers, parents, pupils, governors and others
• questionnaires: open/closed questions and other written contributions
• video analysis
• pupil observation
• analysis of written records and existing statistical data
• assessments of pupil/teacher performance

- discussion groups, especially structured group activities such as brainstorming
- consultancy
- personal supervision.

The most obvious and usually the most vital method if you have been setting objectives for change in specific areas at the beginning of a cycle, will be seeing whether or not these have been achieved. You may be simply checking off whether or not you have met your criteria for success, your desired outcomes, your planned objectives.

This can also help to give the organisation a sense of continuity. On a cycle of three years or more there will be personnel changes, both functionally within the school and through people leaving and arriving. The children will have changed too. It is always valuable to spend a generous allocation of time going through this process as this will provide information and an effective additional briefing for those who arrived after the initial planning. It will also break ice in the planning group before the planning of the next cycle begins, so that even those new to the school will contribute. An example of checking objectives is given in table 9.1.

Table 9.1   Checking objectives

Objectives	*Level of success*
Each teacher in the school completes an individualised learning programme for a pupil with learning difficulties.	100%
Whole school policy document on anti-racism to be produced.	Complete
Attendance to be increased to 92.5% this year.	Not achieved

This method can be very straightforward but does rely on effective and clear objective setting at the beginning of the period of time (e.g. over a year). It is also important for the level of success to be assessed using valid and reliable methodology and not to rely too heavily on subjective impressions. To use computer parlance, the better your input the better your output or 'Rubbish in, rubbish out'. The more thorough your evaluation methods the better your results are likely to be. But however you choose to carry out the evaluation it does not have to be too complex or excessively time-consuming to yield excellent results.

Whatever form of evaluation you engage in, you should take particular account of the less visible aspects of change. In particular, you should focus on the human aspects and impact of change, particularly in the way it produces strong feelings and stress levels. These may not always be to the benefit of the change process and can be extremely unhealthy for individuals as well as organisations.

In times of stress it is sometimes easy to keep one's head down, to get on with it and not take time to reflect. Organisations, teams and individuals can collude with this attitude for a variety of reasons, including external pressures and internal fears of exposing one's own inadequacies (Hawkins and Shohet, 1989). One common characterisation of teacher stress is purposeless, feverish activity. The greater the pressures, the more essential it is to step back and reflect to ensure that the effort being made is being used to maximum effect.

Habitual, obsessive activity is not helpful to the school and is a poor model for the students. The process of addressing the renewal of the review and development cycle is not easy in these circumstances, so precise, achievable objectives are especially helpful here. Where stress is a major issue, this will help to focus attention on real strategies and positive actions at a time when less positive responses might otherwise take over. Specifics and steps towards progress will lessen the risk that stress is projected on to others, within the school or outside, or that blame dominates the agenda rather than problem-solving and positive discussion.

Stress and personal feelings need to be on the agenda for the review and planning of the next change cycle. Chapter 10 deals with stress and change in some detail, so we deal with it here only with reference to planning and reviewing for the next cycle. Stress levels need to be monitored in an ongoing way when an organisation is undergoing significant change, but should also be considered as part of any major evaluation using explicit measures or by giving participants opportunities to share subjective experiences. Undischarged stress staying within the body can emerge in physical, functional, mental or emotional symptoms. These less visible aspects may not be your primary evaluation focus but are overlooked at an organisation's peril! The dilemma is usually that these issues need to be raised in organisations but the organisation needs to have the strategies ready to resolve them. This is addressed in the chapter which follows. At this point, what matters is to note that there is a real need for consideration of the renewal of the change cycle as an area for objectives and development and this in itself is helpful, usually much more helpful than a free discussion and simple sharing of problems.

Core beliefs

Pulling together the results of the evaluation should be a time for a critical re-examination of core beliefs. Have we been understanding what has been going on appropriately or accurately?

Many British teachers initially found it hard to accept the high degree of interest in their child's education on the part of parents, including and especially parents who do not have much contact with schools and who live in areas of serious social disadvantage. Research in areas of London clearly indicated that very high percentages of parents were very interested in being involved in their children's education even though for a variety of reasons they felt uncomfortable about approaching the local school direct. Topping (1986) describes this and other evidence that has been gathered in a number of international studies about the importance and value of parental involvement in education. The practical implications of this and other research is extremely well set out by McConkey (1986).

In one local piece of evaluation work carried out in 1989, a headteacher found that her PTA committee was impeding greater parental involvement as it was perceived by other parents as a powerful clique. This kind of finding challenges core beliefs and usually needs good quality data, research and piloting. Examples we have personally encountered in addition to the above are:

- The move from segregated special provision to integration offers challenges to the belief that special facilities for children with special educational needs/exceptional children are the best forms of educational placement.
- Quicke's (1982) portrayal of the profession of educational psychology in the UK as conservative and traditional in operation in contrast to many progressive statements made by that profession.
- The reconsideration of racism awareness training (Katz, 1978) when it was realised that it could be making white participants more complacent, feeling they had done something, at the expense of black participants who relived distressing experiences as part of the workshops.

Such challenges to core beliefs are necessary to keep an organisation vital and up-to-date, but can be difficult unless the reasons for change in an organisation are addressed from the start and in much more detail than is customary in our experience.

Evaluation information is required in any challenge to core beliefs and helps us towards critical self evaluation for teams, individuals or the whole organisation. Evaluation may lead to us reframing our ideas and restructuring our outlook on change and development. Our localised evaluation efforts may have to take account of broader developments in the world outside our organisation, including new research and developments, new legislation, changes in administration arrangements, the political climate and so forth.

MONITORING CHANGE

We tend usually to think of evaluation as occurring at the end of the activity; yet it can often be more effective if carried out as a series of ongoing exercises pulled together at some final point. A series of such evaluation exercises over a period of time is one way of understanding what we mean by monitoring.

Monitoring is essentially a process of keeping an eye on a situation as it continues, develops or changes over a period of time. The presence or absence of monitoring in an organisation may indicate a motivation to look for or not to look for change occurring. Clearly not every variable can be closely watched, but often in the busy world of school only crises and end-of-year results are monitored and this only at an intuitive or unconscious level. By focusing on specific areas consciously and explicitly with a clear recording system, fluctuations and developments or regressions can be observed and responded to appropriately long before a crisis or failure situation has arisen.

Methods of monitoring are varied and tend to overlap with evaluation methods but typically might include the following:

Dipstick approaches These resemble one-off evaluations carried out in series over random or preplanned time intervals.
Review meetings Involved participants meet to discuss what has occurred, what is going well, problems that need tackling and future planning.
Ongoing records maintained graphically Participants keep regular records which are pulled together by a co-ordinator who plots on a graph the progress or otherwise.
Informal consultation Periodically those involved in the change process are asked about how they see and feel things are going and results are recorded.
Performance indicators Progress is compared regularly with a set of stated objectives or performance indicators that are agreed in advance to be indicative of success.

Who to involve?

Like evaluation, monitoring will involve those within and those outside your organisation. Insiders will include teachers, parents, governors and pupils themselves, and wherever possible they should be encouraged to be active in the monitoring and recording processes. Concerns about losing control over the process usually arise from a lack of structure; if the purpose of monitoring is to help the organisation move forward and the focus is on specifics, then this openness is valuable. Evaluation at the end of a change cycle should give substantial weighting to processes and outcomes involving children, the fundamental clients of schools. Ultimately all innovation should be judged by how children are influenced by it. Pupils can usefully be involved in monitoring aspects of their own performance using self-monitoring techniques which are now well established in Britain and America in relation to applied behavioural psychology (Gardner and Cole, 1988). Alternatively, the system of Records of Achievement which is now being developed extensively in British schools is useful for the ongoing monitoring of various aspects of the curriculum, learning and other areas of school life. Where the openness of the planning and evaluation process is especially valuable is in identifying efficient ways of drawing on these resources of information, especially in reducing bureaucracy and checking how much time really is required to produce a particular outcome.

Outsiders may include consultants, inspectors, advisers, psychologists, administrators and other school visitors. They can be involved in explicit evaluation or monitoring activities or can simply be approached periodically and interviewed or just sounded out in relation to their perceptions of the school changes.

PREDICTING CHANGE

What can we do that will definitely work? Can one learn to predict the future? Are outcomes matching our predictions? Prediction is always an attractive concept when considering change in the complex and ever-changing world of school organisation. While it may seem attractive to put on a fortune-teller's costume and appear to speak with authority, there are more down-to-earth methods which can self-monitor for accuracy. In addition, our rather arbitrary cycle of three years allows for full reconsideration in the light of unforeseen circumstances such as new legislation. Prediction is particularly important for effective monitoring and future planning. But how can we predict? Clearly there are many cautionary tales of apparently well planned organisations failing because of unforeseen circumstances. However, we feel that a more accurate picture is that of organisations failing because they did not look in a particular direction.

The discipline of applied economics is instructive. Considerable time and energy have been spent planning to improve the economic standing of our individual nations. The work of economists and politicians in this area reveals just how difficult accurate prediction is, even with a lot of time, money and brainpower committed to the activity. However, economics provides us with some basic methodology for predicting outcomes and trends over a period of time. Essentially the approach involves making and monitoring projections about the future in the organisation in relation to chosen variables, which for a school might be attendance figures, parental contact, reading assessment results, the number of programmes being run.

Similarly, with individual educational programmes, detailed logs chart the

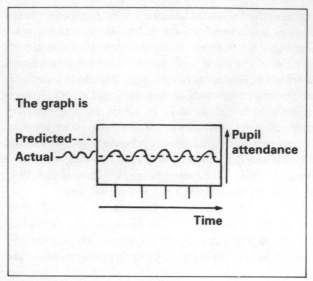

The graph is

Predicted- - - -

Actual

Pupil attendance

Time

Figure 9.1 Predicting progress

progress of the child towards a target (Haring *et al.*, 1978; Engelmann and Carnine, 1982). Something is always lost with the expression of a situation in quantitative terms but an increase in the use of basic statistics will be valuable and the techniques of data analysis are usually to be found in a school but seldom applied fully to the organisation. Basic visual presentation by graph or chart is within everyone's domain and this is how to start reviewing progress. Expected outcomes are projected with a line or are written down along a time scale laying out a critical path, most easily done graphically. These expectations can then be checked against actual outcomes as part of the ongoing monitoring process. The match or mismatch between the projections and the outcomes give direct feedback on the strength of the predictions. Where predictions are close to outcomes, it is possible effectively to use these predictions again in the future as they have clearly worked well. If they were wildly out, then the predictions need reconsideration next time.

The level of analysis can be very sophisticated and there is plenty of room for development but the principle to follow is to give weight to those elements of a large prediction at the early stages of review which have proven to be the best predictors. In a school situation, if the first two predictions of the attendance rate by the team responsible for 13-year-olds have been accurate to within a half percentage point while the predictions of the team responsible for 14-year-olds have been accurate only to within two percentage points then overall predictions of school attendance should rely more on the former team than the latter. As the sequence progresses through each review stage then the future predictions are adjusted according to accuracy so far. Of course, they can also be adjusted in many other ways. Essentially, the skills for the techniques for the regulation of the elements in a prediction will be found in certain members of staff, either in the maths/business/economics faculties or in the programme design and monitoring expertise of teachers of special educational needs. Such mapping of predictions and outcomes works especially well and gives good visual impact over extended periods with data easily updated termly or half-termly.

You can still use objectives or performance indicators in the stronger form of expected outcomes. These predictions, if linked in to a time scale, will again be useful for checking out the feasibility of re-using predictions. The more proactive the school, the more likely it will be that prediction will be easier.

Reporting

At some stage you will need to report the findings of your evaluation and monitoring activity. This has already been discussed in some detail in earlier chapters in relation to reporting research and development and evaluations of your organisation as it stands. When reporting evaluations of change the following are important considerations:

- Exactly who needs to know about what has been found out?
- How will this review information improve performance?
- Who is going to get to know about the evaluation?
- What will they be expected to do with this information?
- How will the findings be presented?
- How can you make sure that the implications of the report are followed up?

It is important to provide feedback to those involved during the course of the change cycle and to find the right form of gateway to do this effectively (Tizard, 1991).

> The content, manner and form in which evaluation results are disseminated are crucial factors that influence utilization. Throughout the evaluation process open two-way lines of communication should be maintained and a participative style of interaction established.
>
> (Illback, *et al.*, 1990: 814)

Positive feedback regarding specifics and outcomes during change cycles reduces the stress of keeping existing systems going without too many crises while setting up new systems by giving information about progress. In our work we often see children's attitudes transformed in the first few weeks of a learning programme and we try to set up feedback for ourselves.

Care may be needed in setting the scene prior to a presentation so that good or bad news is not necessarily received cold, which would blot ou' other important aspects of the evaluation. Earlier comments about setting the scene and choosing the appropriate gateway for communication will help here.

A written report may be considered important as a record of what has happened and to support any presentation. Generally it is recommended that this is kept as short as possible. Caldwell and Spinks (1986) suggest that major evaluations should take up two pages and minor ones one page. This degree of succinctness, while highly desirable in terms of communication, is not always easy to achieve but is worth striving towards. Written reports should attempt to stimulate visual pictures or images in the reader's mind for most effective impact.

Situation 9.1

In describing a major piece of evaluation work looking at one LEA's response to preschool children, one of us used the image of taking the reader on a journey: methods were described as a vehicle, the planned evaluation as a road map, problems located as bumps in the road, performance indicators as signposts and so on. This kind of metaphor is helpful not only for the audience, but also to depersonalise the success and failure and to make the enterprise a shared one.

A written report delivered in a presentation about an evaluation needs to be as straightforward and clear as possible essentially covering the following areas:

• What was done and why?
• What has been found out?
• What are the implications?
• What are our options for the future?
• How will we know we are getting there?
• What are the costs/benefits, especially in terms of time and money?

A presentation should not last longer than forty minutes and ideally the thrust of what needs to be said should be communicated in ten. It may take considerable analysis and reflection to reach the stage where this is possible, but what you will have by this point will be extremely valuable. The aim is not to speak discursively to a captive audience but to provide review data and move the change process forward optimally.

Presentations should make use of all the relevant audio/visual aids available as a means of communicating to the target group. Communicating feedback about the details of the change process is one of the most important functions required for sustained effective change and needs to be done expertly. Numeric data, percentages and so forth are best displayed in simple graph form. More qualitative information such as themes, patterns, feelings, constructs may require you to be more creative. Words placed in different type faces and sizes will help. If these are placed along dimensions, in boxes, in grids, even around concentric circles, this will all help the audience to tune in to the message. When presenting qualitative data it is extremely powerful in presentations and written reports to use as many actual quotes to support your points as possible. It is also effective and appropriate to include comments from children: innovation in a school that has no impact on children that they can perceive is by implication marginal.

Situation 9.2

In a recent evaluation of a series of INSET events (Newton and Taylor, 1991) one of our colleagues divided up responses into four key areas and used quotations to support the occurrence of each as follows:

Knowledge

'I feel I now understand some of the reasons why parents do not get involved more in schools.'

Confidence

'I am much more relaxed when speaking to parents about problems they are facing with their children.'

Skills

'The problem-solving approach works extremely well and I have used it on two occasions now with positive effect.'

Objectivity

'I'm not the only teacher who finds these issues difficult. I can see things more clearly now and see how my reactions sometimes get in the way of doing the best job.'

The quotes say much more than could possibly be communicated in reported speech and will be better remembered. Any leader of a presentation or collator of written feedback needs to present points that will be remembered in the months and years ahead in order to inform the change process.

Finally, in relation to reporting it is extremely important to be aware of the political context of the evaluation. It is worth being sensitive to the likely reactions of those who will be exposed to the evaluation. Where are they coming from? What are their priorities and agendas? Is this good news for them or what?

Reporting and celebrating

These two have to go together. Most of us tend to move from one moment of success to the next problem. Yet, if we are serious about achieving a culture of positive change, then we need to dwell more often on successful change and, symbolically but very definitely, celebrate with those who have been involved. We need also to link the celebration with precisely defined events and the milestones in the review process.

Beare *et al.* (1989) emphasise the importance of visionary leaders who communicate their vision through their use of actions, rewards, words and symbolic activity. They also emphasise that when enhancing a school's culture it is important to consider ceremonies, rituals, rewards, organisational stories, organisational heroes, metaphor and analogies. It is the timing of these actions that really defines the effective leader, adding to the security of the staff that, when something good is done, it is noticed and appreciated. A manager or colleague who celebrates, but lacks a precise knowledge of the organisation to know the right time for celebration, will be advertising a lack of grip.

IMPLICATIONS OF EVALUATION: WHAT NEXT?

The evaluation is done, the report written and presentation made. What next? It is at this stage that those involved in the evaluation may feel their work is at its most vulnerable.

Ideally there will be serious reflection on the results of the evaluation by those who designed or commissioned it. The evaluation should have confirmed, maintained and helped in the recognition of successful activities. It may also have shed light on misplaced plans, objectives and strategies which need to be replaced or altered in the next cycle of change. Modifications may include less ambitious objectives, more creative strategies, innovations or closer monitoring. Thus, negative and positive feedback loops should be set up by the evaluation process providing for successful change with stability in the organisation.

What should we drop?

The literature referred to in chapter 4 notes the belief that change in education is hard to achieve. We take a more optimistic view, but organisations need to address the issue of which initiatives, departments, structures or practices are to be terminated and how.

This question cannot be avoided. It does nobody any good to collude in maintaining an outmoded organisation, section or working practice, or to keep accumulating functions, some of which are best done elsewhere. Ultimately the pain is greater, with more redundancies, more criticism, more feelings of failure.

Perhaps 10 per cent of what an organisation is and 10 per cent of what it does has to be changed annually to avoid storing up catastrophe for the future. Such quantification is arbitrary but useful as a guide to review and goal-setting. If objectives are set at a visionary level, an intermediate level and a short-term level, then these must reflect new initiatives, the maintenance of practices at a high level of professionalism and the termination of aspects of the organisation's structure and practices.

This can be distressing. It can also become personalised and unpleasant. It is less likely to have these effects or for them to be so severe if termination is built into the organisation's discussions of objectives, practices and evaluation. It is all too easy to go along with existing routines which are still of some benefit; but this is to be avoided because, without selection, the main human resources of the school can be dissipated. Questions for discussion at review might be:

- How do we terminate a third of meetings currently held?
- By what date do we plan to end these meetings?
- What date is the obsolescence date of these materials? When do we throw them away?
- When do we review and change job descriptions?
- At what intervals do we consider changes in the faculty structure?
- When are policies replaced?

The trap is that schools become conservative in many ways because of pressure which creates and imposes change: staff turnover, legislative changes. The solution is not an easy one, but it is to have genuine replacement and review dates built in to the organisation. A school that has built staff skills, confidence and openly discusses the *end-by* question will have fewer problems in this difficult area. Staff will have skills, will be less set in routines, more amenable to change, of more use to the organisation and to other organisations.

Leaders in education need to practise this too. They can lose their effectiveness, expect the organisation's effectiveness to continue, fail to delegate to those who are ready for more responsibility. In our experience, few schools have fallen to pieces while their headteacher has been away on a course or for some other reason. This is not to say that the role of the headteacher is not the most important one by far, but rather to say that a successful period of leadership will permit a change of role, possibly to one that allows more time for strategic thinking or more direct contact with children. To be successful, to stay in post but to keep to the same routines, is doubtless necessary in some aspects of the school, but we are sceptical whether these are the most important ones. If the objective is to create a school that is comfortable with change in a changing world, then the headteacher needs to be engaged in a changing range of activities. A regular and defined change cycle helps ensure that this occurs.

The next cycle

The next cycle of change may involve a fresh start with brand new objectives and strategies, or may be a modification of the earlier cycle in the light of the evaluation. In either case it is worth planning at the outset the form of monitoring and evaluation which you intend to carry out. In terms of attitude, the use of the cycle can be linked to the core belief that the school will be a significantly changed place at the end of the next cycle.

ACTION PLAN

- Clarify your organisation's position and context in relation to cycles of change.
- Set out your evaluation questions and objectives.
- Decide on the most appropriate methodology.
- Agree monitoring methods and make predictions.
- Carry out monitoring and/or ongoing evaluation.
- Carry out evaluation.
- Present results.
- Celebrate.
- Agree next steps and move into next change cycle.

Chapter 10

The human factor of change

Other professionals get tired; teachers become exhausted.

(Hargreaves, 1978)

Humans perform best when they have some stress: to be underloaded is as unattractive and uncomfortable as being overloaded. Humans need work: some even feel that hard work is good for them, both physically and mentally. We need to find a middle course between dying of boredom and working ourselves to death.

This can make management difficult. Having a workforce that will thrive on hard work and challenge, but also cave in and give up if faced with too much hard work and too much challenge can make the management of innovation problematic. Much of the literature on change processes in industry and business covers the sociology of organisations and the structures to be found in organisations that are either more or less inert. In large, ordered organisations, hierarchical and bureaucratic structures are common. Bureaucracy is not necessarily a term of opprobrium. In bureaucratic organisations, roles have been defined, procedures worked out and the individual fulfils a role which is not usually specific to that individual. Some of the organisations that historically have shown the

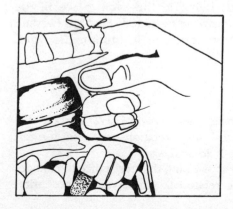

Asserting your philosophy amid imposed change

greatest ability to survive have been bureaucratic to some extent: the Chinese Mandarin system, the administration of the Roman Empire, the Catholic Church (Morgan, 1986). These survived periods of leadership so poor as to put into perspective our occasional complaints about our own leadership. They employed relatively few layers of management, had local control on many issues and common standards for the organisation.

Within such organisations, individuals were expected, indeed required, to transfer to other regions, and their individual stability came from standard procedures: the basic structure was dictatorial, the implementation and administration regulated. In other looser forms of organisation, roles may be less clear and regulated, and freedom of choice over action greater. While this may bring flexibility it can bring its own anxieties. For any organisation we need to ask where the expectation of change will come from and how it will be maintained, how the individual stability within change will be addressed and how the change process will be monitored. Sources of advice on the change processes in business urge that we should learn to like change, to find it pleasurable and interesting.

Human habits have provided an early and continuing field of study for psychologists. Over-rigid habits are strikingly incompatible with the routines of life that most people pass through uneventfully. Those people sometimes referred to as obsessive compulsives have routines of such rigidity that they function in society with great difficulty and suffer severe problems if their routines are disrupted. Some people become anxious about any change to their precisely defined routine, even though they perceive their life as so set as to be predictable, dull and boring. In severe cases where individuals respond well to intervention it is often because they have made a decision that change must occur, that they and their families cannot continue to miss out on so much that life has to offer. Achieving change may cause much anxiety but at least accepting change, indeed wanting it to happen, is no longer an issue or a barrier.

Yet we all suffer anxiety and bad temper if our routines are disrupted. Then we find out just how little tolerance of change we have allowed for: we rely on set journey times, on goods being in the same place in the supermarket and so on. Conversely, humans in restricted situations become bored and in very restricted situations become institutionalised and sometimes self-destructive.

Resistance

'Every force creates its equal and opposite force.' Lewin (1952) adapted this statement from physics and related it to human relations. He went further, developing the useful concept of force-field analysis.

At a basic level we urge a rather obvious point: that resistance to change, set habits, defeatism and inertia are related to anxiety and insecurity, however these may be presented. Resistance is as natural a phenomenon as change itself, but it is crucial constantly to remind ourselves of the factors that feed it. Plant (1987) outlines a number of factors that can fuel resistance and unwillingness to change which include the following:

fear of the unknown
lack of information
threat to core skills and competence
threat to power base
fear of failure
reluctance to experiment
reluctance to let go.

At some stage in our lives we all recognise these factors at work, and there will doubtless be items in this list that have a bearing on your own functioning right now. Resistance often focuses itself on or transfers itself to areas that are not necessarily the major source of change. In one special school in which major changes were taking place to the role and function of all the staff in the school, a riot nearly took place simply because all the seats had been moved out of the staffroom so that it could be decorated. Rumours were rife as to the impending permanent loss of this room, in exchange for a much less attractive room.

Individuals may find it difficult to cope with externally imposed change. They may be frustrated in their ambitions, unhappy in their final school posts or unlikely to gain further promotion. Some will become apathetic or resentful (Day *et al.*, 1990).

In a book such as this, intended to be optimistic about school change, there must be occasional reminders of a more difficult reality. Some schools have gone on for years with a headteacher who has lost any sense of positive leadership and staff who have become invincibly cynical, locked in a circular negative relationship with management. One such school is described now.

Situation 10.1

School X is in the heart of a British city with high levels of social disadvantage, reflected in child abuse, emotional and behavioural problems and learning difficulties. The staff welcomed their new but redeployed headteacher. Some ten years later the school was locked into crisis management; non-attendance and exclusions had never been so high, and dealing with externally imposed innovation and legislation was chaotic. The headteacher, despite the efforts of his deputies and a series of school inspectors and psychologists, seemed to have lost the ability to steer his school or give any sense of clear direction. The deputies were thrown into reactive stances in every crisis situation and these were a daily occurrence as they attempted to keep the school going.

Expectations in relation to achievement, attendance and positive parental contact slipped to an all-time low, and the police were regular visitors, following up an increasing incidence of juvenile crime in the district. Staff morale was low and stress extremely high and attitudes were becoming increasingly embittered and cynical. Most of the school's most valued staff went for other jobs, especially as the school roll began to fall, adding to the downward cycle in which the school seemed locked. The special needs of at least 40 per cent of the pupils were not being met and most were underachieving. A significant number of staff were off on long-term sickness leave following mental breakdown or stress related illnesses, and staff absenteeism was high.

Ultimately, as concerns increased among LEA staff, a long overdue full inspection took place leading to some fundamental recommendations for change. The headteacher, now approaching his mid-sixties, was encouraged to stand down and eventually reluctantly agreed. An inspector and educational psychologist worked particularly hard with the school at this time. A deputy covered the headteacher post for a term and the appointment of some new key members of staff soon led to a dramatic change in school culture which was to be followed up and further developed by a new headteacher with a very clear vision. Attitudes and old negative cliques amongst the staff began to break down and new fresh ideas began to take root as the process of renewal began. Sometimes it seems innovation in a positive direction cannot begin without some fundamental changes taking place. The sad part of such a story is when this takes as long as five to ten years.

MANAGING CHANGE AND PEOPLE EFFECTIVELY

Exploring how much change we can stand can be begun in a number of ways. We suggest a learning model with three phases: exploration, competence, mastery. This is an adaptation of a model of learning used for children (Haring *et al.*, 1978).

We are often asked by headteachers and others how to deal with the problems which arise from an individual teacher not reaching a basic level of competence. We respond by urging that the development from competence to mastery be given more attention and support. The strategies to help people who have anxieties or over-rigid habits usually involve desensitisation: agreeing and insisting on very small but progressive steps forward, but with a great deal of praise for progress and warm personal support throughout. The agenda is for change, but the relationship is strongly positive. Some of the community psychiatric nurses we have met embody these two aspects admirably: determined but pleasant. This seems a good model for the skills to bring change in education.

For workers who are highly stressed, responses can be on the same continuum as for those who have the tightly circumscribed habits referred to earlier. They are not logical arguments, but defences against threats to a position taken up because of fears of or actual failure to cope. Such positions can generate considerable power within a group.

In the work situation, the headteacher can pursue a number of strategies which can be applied in combination. These strategies are both positive and negative:

- Avoid becoming the focus of projected stress. This can be done by refusing to spend time hearing lengthy accounts of problems where there is no commitment to and no evidence of action. Talking problems through is fine so long as this is a problem-solving activity. If not, then becoming the audience for this is a stressful experience in itself, can give undue attention to strategies which perpetuate rather than solve or manage problems, and can lead to collusion in second-rate or inadequate job performance.
- Attempt to agree some problem-solving actions.
- Insist on specified changes, no matter how small. Insist on a method of recording change, defining it unambiguously. Be very firm about these points otherwise habits can become very fixed and much harder to shift, so do not collude in any way with the avoidance of change or shy away from the need to insist on change. If this is not done, abdication of responsibility will have taken place and the situation will deteriorate.
- Allocate most change to those areas in which change is easiest and initially most profitable, especially moving from competence to mastery.
- Promote an ethos of determination to change coupled with an ethos of personal regard for staff. 'Be hard on problems and soft on people.' Look after your staff and many problems will find their own solutions. The general situation will ease as energy goes into outcomes and is not lost in conflict and misunderstanding. As noted earlier, people are assets.
- Relate changes to visionary goals. Linking small steps to workplace fulfilment is a key skill.

Why might people prefer change at work?

Although we have referred to some clinical examples of why a minority of the population find change very hard to deal with, and we all find change in some of our routines somewhat worrying, most people most of the time like change. We use change to cheer ourself up when things look bleak. We redecorate a room, buy new clothes, have a different hairstyle. Every season there is a new fashion, new opportunities for leisure and enjoyment. One of the features of institutionalisation is the absence or rarity of such opportunities. The work environment can be seen in the same way. Few feel enthused about doing the same things for forty years until they retire. The low fliers can be more interested in the job when change is seen as an integral part of the school, the high fliers will have more to put on their CVs and the school will be seen as a place from which and in which to progress.

Taking care of ourselves and others

Why do we take on too much? Why do we make obvious and avoidable lapses? It is easy to advise others that effective time management and saying no are good ways of avoiding overload. Why do we still make the same mistakes for ourselves and need constant support and reminders to stop us reverting back to old unassertive habits? Why do we agree to do things which we cannot do and which will not be done properly if at all? The only products of this are likely to be stress and reduced credibility, yet we still do it. Some of the reasons might be:

- finding it difficult to be assertive
- feelings of guilt
- wanting to be helpful or not wishing to be unhelpful
- pressure from peers, parents, children and others
- being unable to delegate.

What does taking care involve? In the world of work, looking after someone can be seen as an anomalous concept. People are paid to work, are presumably mature and independent and it would be patronising to think otherwise. Furthermore, have we really the time to sort out everybody's problems?

We do not see it this way, but we are cautious about the boundaries needed for a closer interest in people at work. People are the main resource: it is sensible, indeed essential, to take care of them, to develop their skills and to make them feel good about work. If there is no sense of purpose and satisfaction at work then it is more likely that energy will be dissipated in disputes and bad feeling. Across the wider society, few workers derive any satisfaction or enjoyment from work; they work because they have to live. In education, there is the possibility of gaining continued and substantial pleasure from work. However, this can be exaggerated and reversed into a myth which can negatively affect a stressed teacher, the myth that working with young people is inherently rewarding and enjoyable.

Looking after somebody also means looking after oneself. Unhappy, stressed workaholics are not good role models for young people and are unlikely to retain the good humour and positive attitudes required. There is no merit in any occupation in allowing it to damage you or others. In the last resort teaching is an occupation to be followed professionally. This does not mean that we are advocating a very limited view of work demands. Hard work can be and usually is good for people. One of the best ways to stop worrying about tasks that have to be done is to do them. The problems come when the quality of work is poor and the stress symptoms take over. Innovation demands an investment of time and emotion and the first two or three years of turning a system round are stressful and relatively unrewarding. In this period, mutual regard and support are essential. They are also an excellent foundation for long-term progress and satisfaction.

Looking after people in an organisation means that the organisation recognises that the people are likely to experience negative life events and stresses that have nothing to do with work: illness and bereavement in the family, divorce and so on. While most people recognise that these affect their work, they frequently do not tell people at work about their problems, for fear that this will undermine their credibility. A voyeuristic element can intrude. Yet without talking problems through, all sorts of negative cycles can deepen and gain momentum. A supportive organisation will create opportunities for all within it to talk about such events and how they cope with them as part of the informal routines of the day, with limits that recognise the autonomy of the individual distinct from the working self, and the core role of the school as educator.

Situation 10.2

An experienced and very capable teacher in a high school had a series of misfortunes: illness in the family, money worries and marital arguments. The result was greatly increased alcohol consumption over several months. This did not seem to affect their teaching or efficiency but it was clear and widely known in the school and local community that the teacher was drinking heavily every evening.

How could this be resolved? In an unsupportive school, the response to the first complaint or gossip would be a formal warning interview. This would probably make matters worse and could undermine the will to keep up the very high standards of teaching and efficiency.

In a more supportive school, isolation would be less likely. Peer support would emphasise the immense respect due to the teacher, and keep the problems in some kind of perspective. It might also prevent the teacher reaching a stage at which complaints were likely. The issues might be discussed. The sharing of negative life events would be part of peer support and practical although limited help would be offered. It would be stressful but it would not be terminally so for the teacher's contribution to the school.

If these stresses and life events are not talked about, and respected, the people in the organisation will not be treated as people but rather as machines. Smail argues for the need for a revisiting of the whole concept of taking care:

We suffer pain because we do damage to each other, and we shall continue to suffer pain as long as we continue to do the damage. The way to alleviate and mitigate distress is for us to *take care of* the world and the other people in it, not to treat them.

(Smail, 1987: 1)

An innovating school can be a place of challenge, of positive stress; but if this is added to only by negative stress and insufficient care and support, then burn-out is more likely to occur. This needs to be on the agenda when new staff are inducted and has to be discussed by the leader of the organisation. People need recognition, even when they may be doing a job to less than perfect standards. There must be an appreciation that they are trying and want to persist in improving the quality of what they do. The importance of praise and positive reinforcement has been well recognised in the business world for a number of years now.

Positive reinforcement is practised in many Japanese, British, French and other non-American corporations, often with considerable influence on employee motivation and performance.

(Morgan, 1986: 120)

Praise when delivered should never be hollow or empty and is thus best delivered using specific terms, spelling out precisely what actions have been valued. Of course this is also the most powerful way of changing children's behaviour, giving them at the same time extremely clear messages and positive attention. We are not here implying that managers need to be paternalistic and treat all staff like children, but we are reminding the reader that we all have a part of us that is still very much a child, with needs for praise and recognition. We continue to strive for love and attention, in all its symbolic forms, all our lives.

Improving and maintaining the physical environment is something that educators recognise as important and teachers of very young children in particular have developed skills in the creation of attractive and appropriate environments. Looking after the environments of classrooms and staff areas takes time and effort but is an important sign of looking after staff. What is to be avoided is the quality of environment reflecting someone's status, with most of the teachers lacking desks or bookcases, a staff room that is disorganised, untidy, poorly furnished or dirty, while the managers have offices which are furnished, maintained and cleaned to higher standards. Positive environments do not consume resources, nor need to be luxurious. Negative environments consume resources, are not looked after and deteriorate. A positive environment shows some ownership of public areas, tidiness, absence of unnecessary noise or other unpleasantness. Standards need to be as high as or higher than at home. Achieving these standards starts with management and is maintained by all. Formal arrangements for maintaining a positive environment are required and this needs to be one of the objectives for school development. Staff attendance is encouraged by good environments.

Looking after yourself and others and having in turn the reasonable expectation of some support makes a school a rewarding place in which to work. People need to be challenged to produce their best in order to be looked after; it is not in their interests to stagnate. Recognising and celebrating success helps in the caring for people as does being aware of the boundaries of work demands.

Leadership: change starts at the top

A useful place to start is to brainstorm what looking after oneself and others might involve for a senior manager or headteacher. Start by listing what a good school might be doing to look after its children. The research on school effectiveness and ethos is an even more specific prompt to this process. What daily actions might be described as 'looking-after' actions? There are many such: promoting wellbeing by setting or negotiating appropriate tasks; asking for opinions and giving encouragement; trusting, giving recognition and praise, and discussing common problems in an atmosphere of co-operation not competition; allocating time to leisure, making time to talk casually, ensuring pleasant working conditions, learning and using people's names; being open about your own needs, listening to others, opening up issues, avoiding either/or decisions, being supportive, using genuine humour.

Managing stress

A lot has been spoken and written about stress in the last thirty years, but many would find it difficult to produce a clear definition. What is stress? Whilst stress and tension are a normal part of everyday life how much does it take to do us harm? How can we recognise, monitor and learn to manage and cope with stress on a day-to-day basis?

There have been a number of theories of stress. The early theories looked at stress as the load, demand or pressure put on people. Questions were subsequently asked about the elastic limit of people, their rate of wear and tear in response to such stimuli. Emotional and bodily reactions to pressure have been differentiated and long-and short-term effects studied. The most recent theories tend to reflect the dimensions of pressures, reactions and personal coping resources of individuals in the context of real-world situations. Thus Cox (1989) defines stress as 'a phenomenon arising from a comparison between the demand made on a person and the ability to cope'.

Stress in organisations undergoing change may be inevitable but it is essential that this is not ignored by anyone in the system. It is important for individuals to be aware of what stresses them and what effects this has on them. Individuals need to be aware of their own personal resources and particularly those that are helping them manage their stress levels effectively. They also need to know what they can do to strengthen their coping actions. Everyone at some stage will require support or systematic help in stress management and anyone involved in school change would do well to be fully conversant with this area. The process of change is often not as rational as is sometimes assumed and emotional issues can become fundamental to the success or failure of a venture.

It is possible to improve the management of stress. The first stage is to identify stressors or stress inducers. In other words, it is important to list first what stresses you, under the headings of:

work
money
career
relationships
changes
health
family
decisions

A significant number of individuals in any organisation at any time will be experiencing stress that is not work-related but which can be projected onto the work situation. Relationship stress, financial stress, housing stress and health concerns are common and serious sources of stress. There will be a significant number of individuals who are not able to sleep well or eat appropriately and who may be lapsing into habits that have negative health and functioning consequences.

For many individuals, such stress may be endemic but too serious and threatening to discuss or even face up to, producing poor functioning at work and negative, pessimistic views. If a stressor is minor, a person can identify it and adopt a strategy to manage that stress effectively. It may not go away, but it will be managed. With multiple stresses, or with single sources of stress that are major and threatening, the person may be unable to face up to the situation and may deny the stress or reformulate it externally, project it on to an entirely different situation for which that individual is not responsible. In addition, children and parents may have their own stresses which they may project on to the school situation. Headteachers, educational psychologists and managers in education can all too easily become the convenient dumping ground for all these stresses, reformulated into educational and behavioural 'problems'. If the headteacher cannot solve all these problems, then she or he has failed, yet the formulation and purpose of these problems and their origin mean that no solution will ever be accepted. It is essential that educational managers are aware of these issues and of the positive ways forward and of the key preventative strategies.

A particular source of psychological stress for many people working with and in schools relates to personal *drivers*, the deep rooted ideas that drive us along. Unconscious drivers may include constructs such as:

- I must be the most successful.
- I must always do my best.
- I cannot accept anything less than perfect.
- I must help.
- I must rescue.
- I must always be in control.
- I can change others.

Hawkins and Shohet (1989) attempt to explore some of the complex motives for wanting to enter the helping professions, very relevant to those in teaching. They reflect on what Jungian psychologists call our 'shadow' side, and point to the importance of becoming aware of this so that we have less need to make others into parts of ourselves that we cannot accept. The out-of-control pupil should not have to carry our own craziness, while we pretend to be completely sane, rational and in control. They suggest that focusing on our own shadow may lead us to being less prone to self-important fantasies of changing others or the world, when we cannot change ourselves.

> How often we find ourselves caught in the shadow side of helping, letting ourself and others think we are special, creating that illusion, and then being disillusioned when people want to take us down a peg or two. The idea that we are helpers as opposed to a channel for help is a dangerous one. We want the praise for the success, but not the blame for failure.
>
> (Hawkins and Shohet, 1989:9)

Many of us want to help and even heal the children, families and adults that we are involved with during our work in schools, a desire shared by helpers and non-helpers alike. This drive does not always allow us to accept our own vulnerability, or to accept that we, too, are often being helped and healed by those we work with. Our strivings for power to better carry out what we are deeply motivated to achieve are an enormous area of psychological stress, particularly when our ability to give is thwarted by our own needs not being acknowledged or satisfied.

The effects of stress

The next stage in effective stress management is to examine and discuss the effects of your stress inducers on you with someone you trust, who is ideally not directly involved in your stress situation.

When faced with excessive levels of perceived challenge, by contrast our metabolism switches into its emergency mode: digestion is inhibited, excretion disrupted, and adrenalin released into the bloodstream together with cortisone and other hormones. This, the flight/fight response, was a life saver for primitive man in his natural habitat; not so in the boardrooms and offices of today.

(Simpson, 1987: 125)

Short-term responses to stress, or stress signals, can be physiological, psychological or behavioural. Physiological effects may include anything from increased breathing rate to constipation or diarrhoea. Psychological effects may range from anxiety to irritability. Behavioural effects include heavy smoking, over-indulgence in alcohol or food, difficulty in concentrating, displays of excessive emotion, becoming a workaholic.

Psychological effects, when we are overstressed during periods of uncertainty, for instance, lead us to worry or imagine potential disasters. Many people are able to create what Simpson calls 'mental videos' of impending doom, and are able to play them obsessively to themselves. Some people need to identify what are often termed by psychologists faulty thought patterns, which in themselves can cause undue stress. Worry that becomes obsessively pessimistic or irrational can become destructive.

Some faulty thought patterns that can take over at such times are: selective envy (the grass is always greener on the other side): catastrophic extrapolation, imagining that small problems will grow with catastrophic results: polarized blaming, unfairly blaming oneself or others; homogenising, making a general judgement and systematically misinterpreting future events in support of that judgement: and projection, basing your thoughts on the fatally flawed belief that other people think and feel as you do.

(Simpson, 1987: 126)

We will all almost certainly tend to one form or another of faulty thinking at some stage in our lives, a feeling of being totally useless, unimportant or unloved, or persecuted by those around us. Simpson goes on to describe the all too familiar situation in which a problem goes round and round in your brain, typically keeping you in mental turmoil half the night. Our anxiety distorts our perception, we become more irrational and so more and more unlikely to reach a solution, simply guaranteeing ourselves a sleepless night.

Longer-term stress signals can be considered under the headings of medical and behavioural effects and these may arise from the regular occurrence of short-term effects. While many of the effects are immediate and of short duration, prolonged daily increases in blood pressure, for example, can lead to a medical condition of hypertension. Other medical effects include dizziness, ulcers, palpitations, heart and artery disorders, neck and back problems and insomnia. Behavioural problems range from avoidable absence from work and total exhaustion to drug dependence and sexual disorders.

Stress can be dangerous. It also seems to be person-specific. What stresses one person does not affect another and the effects of stress for one person are different for another, even though they may be involved in the same situation. Stress and performance are commonly depicted in an inverted 'U' graph showing that in the early stages of low stress an individual may be understressed. This progresses to the peak of performance where a person is optimally stimulated, but is then followed by a decrease in performance if there is continued stimulation or stress. The first stage is characterised by boredom, fatigue, frustration or dissatisfaction. The second with creativity, rational problem-solving, progress, change and satisfaction. Finally the third stage of overstimulation is characterised by irrational problem-solving, exhaustion, illness and low self-esteem. As can be understood by this, effective stress management is all about achieving a very delicate balance. Thus it is with change: too much and there is too much stress and poor performance all round; not enough and there is stagnation, people become bored, frustrated and dissatisfied.

Stress in school organisations

The demands an organisation makes upon an individual constitutes a significant source of stress. When stress becomes debilitating both the individual and the organisation suffer.

> Workers who are stressed most often act out this stress on their colleagues. They can become irritable with the secretary, angry with their boss and non-cooperative with their colleagues. Fights can develop about who is responsible for what, and arguments over duty rotas. Team meetings begin to start later and later.
>
> (Hawkins and Shohet, 1989: 121)

Groups and teams within organisations need to take stock of how they are functioning, individually and as a whole unit, for what the team does not contain will soon spill over into the rest of the organisation or department. Communication channels are usually the first to suffer, and individuals and teams will be quick to get into negative projections and blame aimed at management, other teams or other parts of the organisation.

One area of particular relevance to teacher stress is that of person–job fit. When the job fit is good there is a balance, stress being acceptable and coping not compromised. It is important that there is a balance between the actual and perceived demands of the work and the perceived ability to cope. When there is an imbalance the individual experiences emotional and physiological effects accompanied by cognitive and behavioural attempts to reduce the stressful nature of the demand. This is the individual's attempt at coping. One of the authors recently asked a senior teacher at a comprehensive school undergoing enormous stress what he had found most stressful over the last year. After a few moments the teacher replied: 'It was that I had no sense of purpose. I didn't know what was expected of me and I didn't know who to relate to.'

This teacher further reported that he thought he was heading for a breakdown. Is it any wonder with such a lack of clarity to his work in school? We suspect this experience is becoming increasingly common.

It would seem imperative to monitor the organisation's demands on staff, particularly in terms of a mismatch between the demands on teachers and the abilities of individuals to meet these. Accurate assessment and monitoring at a group and individual level can be an extremely proactive measure and can lead to early and effective preventative actions to reduce problems.

Ways forward

- List your own stressors.
- List the effects of these stressors on you under the headings: physical, psychological, behavioural.
- Monitor in writing the occurrence of these and other stressors and their effects over a two-week period.
- Discuss with a trusted friend or colleague what you have discovered about yourself and your responses to stress.

It is beyond the scope of this book fully to detail ways of coping with stress, but there are many sources of practical advice. Enough is now known about stress for us to go further in preventing its potentially negative impact on our lives. While stress, like conflict, is in many ways both natural and healthy, too much can cause problems in the short and long term. We believe it is important for individuals, teams, and organisations to be aware of stress, to change the way that stress is responded to and to strengthen personal and interpersonal resources.

Typically, most staff in schools have their own coping actions in relation to stress, including avoiding confrontations, relaxing after work, rationalising, trying not to worry, working even harder, trying to see the funny side, letting off steam at colleagues, talking through situations, thinking about positive future events. These are more or less conscious strategies which vary in effectiveness for individuals. More systematic approaches may be needed.

Problem-solving approaches to stress reduction are appropriate for individuals as well as organisations. Typical steps include the following:

- Analyse what the sources of stress are for you in and out of the work place, and what stress impact these are having in the short and long term.

- Define which sources of stress are changeable and which are not.
- List what personal and interpersonal resources you have to draw on and what could be added to this list.
- Develop a stress management plan with these elements:
    specific priority goals, likely to achieve success and written in unambiguous performance terms;
    a time scale;
    a required action (it may be necessary to brainstorm ideas and strategies in consultation with others, expert or non-expert, to get the best out of this section of the plan);
    the personal and interpersonal resources needed.

With such an approach the emphasis is on heightening awareness and recognition of stress inducers and personal stress signals or effects, with a view to dealing with the causes of stress and taking positive action in a planned way. This might lead individuals to try to rearrange their lives so that they feel more fulfilled. It might lead to more active attempts to resolve relationship difficulties by talking them through, or by learning to express emotions such as anger in a more direct but constructive way. You might even plan to counter some of your own personal drivers for power or to help and heal by giving yourself regular written and spoken reminders of your own vulnerability or more reasonable demands on yourself.

I can only do my best; it will not always be perfect.
I cannot always change the world.

A practical strategy may be very appropriate for individuals facing particular problems that are stress related. Consider the suggestion made by Simpson for the sleepless person caught with a troubled mind that is 'looping' in the night.

To break out of the loop, dramatic action is required. If you are in bed, you should get up: in the end you are likely to lose far less sleep this way . . . . Having got up, make yourself a drink, sit down and write a brief description of the problem, followed by all the solutions or the partial solutions you can think of . . . . The point is to get the fuzzy ideas out of your head and clear ones on to paper, [to] substitute rational analysis with tangible results. Do not go back to bed until you are exhausted of ideas, or just plain exhausted.

(Simpson, 1987: 127)

Simpson here catches the thrust of problem-solving approaches to stress reduction. His approach works just as well at an organisational level. Organisational plans to reduce stress might include the following goals:

- staff to relax more when in the staff room

- staff to take less work home
- reduce stress-related absenteeism
- increase the level of play in team meetings
- staff to learn and use improved breathing techniques during the school day.

The culture of the healthy organisation and its leadership needs to take stress very seriously and its systematic counteraction and prevention especially in the context of ongoing change.

Dietary experts suggest that we should eat less saturated fats and more high fibre food. They also point out that excess caffeine, nicotine and concentrated sugar in the body can increase stress levels. Sleep is extremely important, with six to eight hours being the minimum necessary for most people. Sleep needs to be full, relaxed and long enough.

Rest itself is highly underestimated in schools and other organisations. Pausing and resting during the day can actually lead to fewer illnesses. Your body needs variation in its working rhythm rather than the typical pattern of working at full speed all day until you collapse at the end of the day in an exhausted heap. In person-pressured jobs it is important sometimes to get away from people, to find a quieter place to be in, however briefly. More energy can be gained from five minutes of meditation, self-hypnosis, deep muscle relaxation or deep breathing than from a much longer break.

Taking exercise can lengthen your life and help you cope with stress. Three twenty-minute sessions a week can build up your flexibility, muscle tone, strength, general state of well-being and cardio-vascular system. Exercise relieves tension, improves physiological condition, heart and breathing systems, provides greater oxygen to your body tissue and improves ability to cope with stress. Sports known to have the most positive effect on your cardio-vascular system include swimming, jogging, cycling, skiing, squash, aerobics. Vigorous walking, yoga, tennis, football and so on are close behind.

Relaxation requires a special mention as it has been found to have great preventative power in relation to illnesses and stress. It is a much more potent antidote to stress than many so-called relaxing activities such as drinking coffee or tea, having a snack or a smoke. There are a number of deep relaxation techniques that are very beneficial to adults and children. These include deep breathing exercises, positive visualisation, autogenic, deep muscle, biofeedback, and self-hypnosis. Yoga is an excellent and sophisticated approach to the relaxation of mind and body and has its roots going back centuries.

True relaxation contains the following elements: slower heart rate, deeper, more even breathing, muscles loosened and relaxed, hands and feet feeling warm and heavy. As a result the body has energy and feels refreshed.

Most deep relaxation exercises involve lying down or sitting in a very comfortable position. You can teach yourself, attend classes, listen to tapes, or have a friend or partner take you through some instructions.

Managing the stress of change

Change will bring its own stress, as we have already outlined. Losing someone through death or separation, entering a new relationship, starting to live with someone for the first time, beginning a new job are all recognised to be sources of intense personal stress. Supporting staff through organisational change in the face of many national and international changes in education and society is bound to be stressful as we will explore next. Here we wish to pose some questions to promote reflection at individual, team and organisational levels with particular reference to change.

Self-reflection

- Did I want this to happen?
- Am I proactive in new situations?
- What do I want from this situation?
- How can I help myself to deal with the stress of this change?
- What are my feelings telling me about where I am?

Reflection on new situations:

- What has changed?
- What are the implications of the change?
- What transition has really taken place?
- How am I expected to behave in this situation?
- Can I try out the new situation in advance?

Reflection on other interpersonal resources:

- To whom can I talk about my concerns and worries?
- On whom will I depend in a crisis?
- To whom do I feel close?
- Who makes me feel valued and competent?
- Who can effectively challenge me to take a proper look at myself?
- With whom can I share good news?
- Who will give me constructive feedback?

Reflecting on the past

- Can I easily let go of past situations?
- Am I thinking that this should not have happened to me?
- Is there anything similar that has happened to me?
- Have I done anything in the past that might help me now?

A model of stress that is multicausal is valuable in organisations. Essentially, this states that a single source of stress, even a severe stress such as a bereavement, can be survived, with support. Indeed, managing and experiencing stressful events or situations is part of life experience and can make us confident and mature in the long term. Multiply sources of stress and the situation becomes dangerous. The concern must be to manage stress effectively in helping professions in the knowledge that in working with people, a stressed individual will have plenty of opportunities to project that stress on to others. It is rather like having the flu and passing it around. The challenge for promoting change in schools is to overcome short-term stress and to ensure that the benefits of change are positive and seen as such.

Support and supervision

Many other kinds of support are waiting to be introduced or applied effectively and routinely in the education system. In this respect, education is behind other professions. Recognising stress as part of the job, as a part of dealing with people, requires organisational structures to help address these issues. Talking through difficult situations and one's feelings about them is important and needs to be part of the organisation. With appropriate supervision too, the consciousness grows that complaint about others, seeing things in terms of blame or, less often, praise is not helpful or realistic. Supervision can deal with the feelings about our work and ourselves which we all have and which have to be dealt with. Aggressive behaviour promotes counter-feelings of aggression which we will benefit from identification and resolution; unresolved feelings of aggression have no part in any positive organisation, least of all in schools.

Feelings of failure can be damaging to individuals and their work yet we all feel failures on occasions in our working lives. Retaining feelings of personal failure is again something that supervision can address.

> Schools are social organizations. Without interdependent and collaborative relationships among people, they are nothing but wood, concrete, and paper. Many of the difficulties experienced by staffs, during periods of change, may be traced to the culture of the school. Thus, most deliberate attempts at school improvement affect not only the principal and the faculty, but also the relationships between them and their collective relationships with the students and parents.
>
> (Schmuck, 1990: 899)

Unfortunately the staff of schools in many countries are notorious for finding it difficult to collaborate effectively or to help each other. In any consideration of looking after humans it is necessary to reflect on what have often been referred to as helping relationships. It is these which should characterise relationships within excellent schools where change is being brought about successfully. If individuals can effectively help each other, feel supported and work together with appropriate and regular professional supervision the change process will take care of itself with very little need for top down impetus.

What do we mean when we talk of effective helping relationships?

By this term I mean a relationship in which at least one of the parties has the intent of promoting the growth, development, maturity, improved functioning, improved coping with life of the other. The other, in this sense may be an individual or a group. To put it in another way, a helping relationship might be defined as one in which one of the participants intends that there should come about, in one or both parties, more appreciation of, more expression of, more functional use of the latent inner resources of the individual.

(Rogers, 1961: 39–40)

Rogers is here defining a relationship which has at its heart the very essence of effective support and development. We argue here that successful organisational change rests on such relationships existing between key participants in the process as these will encourage reflection, problem-solving, professional development, feelings of well-being and purpose. Such relationships need to exist at every level in the school hierarchy, between peers, between headteacher and deputies, deputies and middle management, deputies and staff, teachers and children and so on. Such relationships should usefully also be extended to those outside the organisation who work with it as advisors or consultants or as parents. Rogers goes on to set out the characteristics of the helping relationship. He illuminates the importance and complexity of letting ourselves experience positive attitudes of warmth, caring, liking, interest and respect towards other people without letting our fear suppress the free experience of these feelings. He describes the all too familiar reaction of building up distance between ourselves and others, a form of aloofness, a 'professional' attitude, an impersonal relationship. He stresses the importance of suspending judgements of other people, and encourages us to enter fully the world of feelings and personal meanings, to see things as others do. Ultimately he believes in the immense potentiality of every living person's capability for creative inner development. His hypothesis, which he has drawn from attempts to work with troubled, unhappy, maladjusted individuals, goes like this:

If I can create a relationship characterized on my part by:

a genuineness and transparency, in which I am my real feelings;

a warm acceptance of and prizing of the other person as a separate individual;

a sensible ability to see his world and himself as he sees them;

Then the other individual in the relationship will:

experience and understand aspects of himself which previously he has repressed;

find himself better integrated, more able to function effectively;

become more similar to the person he would like to be;

be more self directing and self confident;

become more of a person, more unique and self expressive;

be more understanding, more acceptant of others;

be able to cope with the problems of life more adequately and more comfortably.

(Rogers, 1961: 37–8)

What more could any of us ask of relationships in schools? Rogers makes very powerful claims for the effectiveness of this approach to relationships, everyday as well as therapeutic, and many have successfully followed his lead in work with adults and children. The approach has clear implications for the support and development of individual teachers, parents and pupils. Many educational psychologists recognise the strengths of this humanistic approach to the counselling and support of adults and children with its emphasis on warmth, empathy and genuineness. Since the 1960s much work has been done by Rogers and others to develop approaches to individual helping, therapeutic and supportive relationships (Hughes, 1990) but the points made still remain important landmarks for anyone seriously addressing this area.

Effective support in practice must involve staff in giving each other quality time to listen to each other. Whether they are using Rogers' own non-directive strategies of reflecting back, following the direction of his clients in relation to their personal constructs and feelings, or whether the approach is more directive and challenging, support is crucial. It is worth reflecting on the times that you have felt most supported by your colleagues or managers. Can you remember the events, what was said, why it felt good, who was involved and exactly what was done?

An infant teacher known to us recently listed the times she felt most supported:

- during an appraisal interview.
- during a staff meeting when her headteacher publicly praised and detailed the work she was doing.
- when late on a Friday her headteacher helped her put a display up on the wall so that she could get home at a reasonable hour.

Support needs to be real. It is not enough to believe in the principles of support, it must be lived out in practical ways even when time constraints appear to stand in its way. Support needs to be thought about in the same way as brushing your teeth. You do it because you think it is important. There is no neat list of what constitutes effective support for colleagues, but if one were to exist it might include the following:

- good listening for enough time, in a situation that has privacy, confidentiality and comfort as its key components. Listening skills will need to include positive non-verbal communication in areas such as posture, vocal tone and eye contact.
- practical helping
- promoting, sponsoring, acknowledging and praising
- counselling when appropriate
- non-verbal support: smiling, nodding, thumbs up and so on
- granting time to work on something.

The leaders of organisations such as schools are crucial as models of effective support for others to imitate or criticise. However, being an effective headteacher demands seemingly contradictory styles in different situations. This role demands accountabilities not only to teachers but also to the LEA, to parents, governors and children, with inevitable conflicts in relation to who to support and who to 'tell', direct or challenge in some situations.

> *the head will need to be able to adopt a variety of roles:* he or she will at various times be acting as an appraiser (of staff and pupil work); an adviser/counsellor (to staff and pupils); an organiser (of timetable, curriculum, resources); a linking agent (between staff within the school, between staff and other teachers, between staff and pupils, and staff and parents); an expert (on curriculum content or teaching techniques); a promoter (of an idea, etc.); a legitimator; or a devil's advocate (to test out commitment to a process or the logic of an idea). In effect the one individual is expected to be an innovator, a change agent, an evaluator and a friend!

> (Day *et al.*, 1990: 133)

We believe that this apparently impossible job can be done coherently, without losing a supportive emphasis. Leaders need to be trusted and to learn to trust others working under their leadership. An often-repeated observation is that of teachers reporting that they felt especially supported and trusted when they were left to carry out an initiative of their own without being fettered by over-cautious management. Freedom granted in the face of power held by others still seems to carry a universally positive feeling. Supervision, whilst present in most helping professions such as social work, psychological and psychiatric services, is strikingly absent for most of those involved in the education of children, despite the emotive and difficult nature of most of it and the constant need for change and professional development. Whilst appraisal is becoming increasingly prevalent and developed (Poster and Poster, 1990), individual and group supervision is noticeable by its absence. Hawkins and Shohet (1989) outlined the increasing importance for all those involved in the helping professions to be involved in regular individual and team supervision. Following Winnicott's concept of the *good-enough mother,* they suggest that supervision can help the *good-enough* helping professional to 'survive the negative attacks of the client through the strength of being held together within and by the supervisory relationship'. Perhaps this is what the teacher, manager, leader and change agent need, to become 'good-enough'? Many teachers have severe self-doubts arising from unresolved, disturbing situations encountered with pupils, parents or other staff. It is in such situations that supervision could be particularly useful.

> The supervisor's role is not just to reassure the worker, but to allow the emotional disturbance to be felt within the safer setting of the supervisory relationship where it can be survived, reflected upon and learnt from.
>
> (Hawkins and Shohet, 1989: 3)

Hawkins and Shohet point out that there is a need for those involved in supervision to integrate educative, supportive and managerial roles into a supervisory relationship approach. However, there are many blocks to supervision occurring anywhere, let alone in schools. These include previous negative experiences of supervision, personal inhibitions, organisational, practical and cultural blocks, together with confusion between appraisal and supervision.

This is yet another area where it is important to be proactive if obstacles are to be overcome. It may be from reflecting on your own support system that you find the motivation to promote the development of supervision in your school or organisation.

If you are involved in supervising, you will need a clear supervisory contract, within one of the following categories: tutorial, training, consultancy or managerial supervision. You may be involved in peer supervision or in supervising a less experienced colleague, leading to either a vertical or horizontal supervisory contract.

Supervisory styles are individual, but Hawkins and Shohet describe a developmental approach which one of the authors has found extremely relevant to working with individuals and groups of teachers in relation to meeting the emotional and behavioural needs of pupils. The following is our adaptation for use in schools of the model which was initially developed for use with therapists:

- reflection on the pupil giving concern, with accurate observations and description of various aspects of the child's life
- exploration of strategies and interventions used by the teacher
- exploration of the counselling and/or teaching process and relationship
- focus on the pupil's and the teacher's transference and counter-transference
- focus on the here-and-now process as a mirror for the there-and-then process
- focus on the supervisor's transference and counter-transference
- sharing of understandings and hypotheses
- shared brainstorming of strategies for supervisee to select from, about the way forward with the pupil.

Feedback is the process of telling other individuals how they are experienced. This is an area that is fraught with difficulties and anxieties, as anyone on the receiving end can easily be reminded subconsciously of being told off as a child. As it is so emotive, feedback is usually badly given. Hawkins and Shohet suggest that feedback is *clear*, rather than vague and faltering; *owned*, rather than preaching at people or implying a statement of absolute truth; and *regular*, rather than being saved up for rare occasions. They go on to suggest that it should also be *balanced* between the positives and negatives and finally that it should be *specific*, rather than generalised.

Feedback should be received as if you were receiving a gift. Put in your pocket and keep those bits which you value and discard the rest. Thank the person giving the feedback, and try to avoid defensive reactions or responses; this feedback is simply the person's own experience of you. It is worth asking for feedback that you are not given but would like to hear.

Supervisory intervention skills can be learned in training. Heron (1975) describes six categories:

- prescriptive: giving advice, being directive
- informative: providing instruction and information
- confrontative: challenging, giving direct feedback
- cathartic: releasing tension, abreaction
- catalytic: being reflective, encouraging self-directed problem-solving
- supportive: being approving, confirming and validating.

When supervising groups, it is important to set ground rules regarding the giving of feedback, the avoidance of being patronising, the equal sharing of time and so forth. Each session can begin by checking out what needs people are bringing to the group, as long as individuals are clear about what they want from the group. The processes can reflect what was outlined above for individual cases or can broaden out to consider issues or organisational problems. Teams can be usefully supervised by outside consultants as they review their functioning. This may be important if emotive areas such as what is appreciated and found difficult by individual members of a team is going to be on the agenda.

Essentially we would agree with Hawkins and Shohet that all organisations including schools should strive to become learning cultures, each with its own statement of policy on supervision that states clearly why it is important, who should receive supervision from whom, when and with what frequency supervision should happen, how supervision should be carried out and with what sort of style and approach.

ACTION PLAN

- Reflect on the human factors associated with change in your own school culture. What is the history of change here? How have individuals been looked after traditionally? What are the key sources of stress in the school? How are these being experienced, by whom and with what short- and long-term effects?
- Reflect on the management of change to date. What more effective ways might there be to positively lead and manage individuals and teams?
- How are you taking care of yourself? How are other individuals in the organisation being looked after? What could be changed to improve the quality of this care?
- Develop your own stress management plan and encourage others to do the same.
- Develop your own and the school's support and supervision structures, both formal and informal. Reflect on the quality of relationships and communication at every level.
- Consider piloting, establishing and maintaining a supervision system.
- Plan personal priorities within the organisation and encourage others to do so.
- Create and maintain an attractive and pleasant working environment.
- Define limited and attainable goals and develop your understanding of change strategies.

Chapter 11

Surviving imposed change

In this chapter we look at some of the stark realities of change in the 1990s. We will explore the context and occurrence of some of the unprecedented changes being imposed upon schools at this time and will highlight implications. We will then consider how it is possible to assert your school philosophy and carry out effective change in the face of this.

THE CONTEXT OF CHANGE

In the 1990s, schools in Britain and elsewhere face imposed change of an unprecedented nature. In the context of the 1988 Education Reform Act the Department of Education and Science in Britain recognised that in schools there are:

uncertainties about the precise nature of the changes they are required to implement;
anxieties about their ability to cope within the timescales set for implementation;
difficulties in allocating enough management time to these problems.

(DES, School Management Task Force, 1990: 10)

Asserting your philosophy amid imposed change

Never before have so many changes been faced simultaneously by schools and with so little control over which will be taken on. Why now?

Governments tend to favour three forms of economies:

free enterprise economies
socialist economies that emphasise public funding
mixed economies.

In Britain until the 1970s a mixed economy was favoured, consisting of a highly valued set of public services working alongside a free enterprise business and manufacturing world. Education, like health care, transport and energy, was characteristic of the public services. These services had a well researched and established tradition and were supported by a set of beliefs in what was being done. There was an acceptance of the public service ethos in Britain and it was known to have its own ethic and to be well motivated by a sense of good will amongst its participants. Rights of individual citizens, children and adults, to such public services went unquestioned.

The arrival of a radical conservative government in Britain and a similarly right-wing government in the United States was to set the scene for much stronger moves towards a free enterprise culture where market forces could be brought to bear on public as well as private services. The idea began to be promoted and eventually to take hold that it was inefficient and unfashionable to fund public sector work or industry. The government's fiscal policies reflected the notion that there was no need to give public services and industry money just for the sake of it. The 1980s saw threats to many areas of public funding including health, social and educational services, and moves towards focused financing and the encouragement of opting out of state control. Some areas of the public sector were deliberately abandoned or starved, whereas many private sector developments were actively rewarded. Interestingly, this process was paralleled as the cold war began to thaw and Eastern Europeans cast off their own socialist economies in favour of the highly coveted free but competitive enterprise of the West.

British education, long an area of substantial expenditure, was one of the most important and early targets of this change of approach. Politicians levelled serious criticisms at the door of educationists with particular reference to standards of teaching and education, lack of choice for parents and the dependency of schools on centralised local authorities. Legislation and focused financing were to be the tools to bring about change in schools and brought the advent of free market forces in the world of education. The role of the local authority would no longer be that of universal provider. Competition is the spur to notions of efficiency and value for money wherever it operates.

Thus the Education Reform Act was underpinned by ideology that reflected a free market economy which supported competition, privatisation and efficiency and came closer than almost any conservative legislation to setting up the ideal 'night-watchman' style state. In such a situation the state sets minimum standards and provides minimum financing and then monitors the results. If this is the broader context, exactly what changes are being imposed upon schools?

THE CHANGES TAKING PLACE

The pace and intensity of imposed change has sent many reeling, resigning or retiring. The following is a list of some of the key changes being dealt with in schools in the early 1990s:

- implementation of a national curriculum
- assessment and testing for all pupils at ages 7, 11 and 14
- local financial management of schools
- delegated budgets to schools
- new examination syllabus and exams
- teachers pay and conditions of service
- appraisal schemes
- records of achievement
- technical, vocational and educational initiative
- integration of pupils with special needs
- reduction in the support role of local authorities
- increased parental choice of school and involvement in school government.

At the same time central government has made it easier for parents to access private education and has attempted the development of new privately run and generously funded city technology colleges. It has also made it possible and financially rewarding for schools to opt out of local authority control and achieve grant-maintained status. Teachers are obliged to go on training days to learn more about the delivery of the new initiatives, leaving every school in great and regular need of supply teachers.

Of course, not all changes can be laid at the door of conservative governments. Society has changed ideologically, technologically and demographically but education has not always reflected the diversity of these changes. There have been significant cultural changes to many schools' catchment areas. Individual child and family needs have changed enormously in the last twenty years. These developments are reflected to some extent in curriculum developments in areas such as personal and social education. Increasingly the community is looking to local schools to meet all the needs of its children whatever their culture, creed, need or disability. However, the extent of changes in and around schools has not helped increasing numbers of pupils formally excluded from schools or those who are non-attending. Pupils have their own ways of protesting against change, even if they experience its effects indirectly, by voting with their feet or with their behaviour.

School managers have been encouraged to work in increasingly open and facilitative ways, with a collegiate style rather than traditional line management becoming the preferred approach. Managers in schools have had to take on more responsibilities, particularly financial, with the thrust of legislation encouraging maximum decentralisation of schools. Accountability has increased rather than diminished with this development, particularly to parents and school governors who are getting increased information on school performances and power in relation to school management.

> Leaders in the 1990s must ensure that their schools have annually reviewed, publicly available school-development plans, systematic teacher appraisal, a school marketing policy, efficient monitoring and assessment procedures for the National Curriculum – and all this whilst managing 'directed time', professional development days and a 'real' school budget.
>
> (Day *et al.*, 1990: 1).

School managers have over the last ten years found themselves caught in many dilemmas: implementing imposed change, supporting stressed staff, negotiating with staff unions over the changes in pay and conditions of service of their members, attempting to increase democratic processes whilst maintaining a clear form of leadership, trying to be independent whilst needing local authority support, and so on.

You may find it helpful to list the changes you have been involved in, indicating those you have some control over, those you are pleased about, those which are causing you most stress and those you have to learn to live with.

Another useful activity is to create a *rich picture*, on one half of a sheet of paper, of the changes that are stressing you and the school and, on the other, the areas of support and solid foundation on which you and the school depend. Is there a balance? Can you make more of some of your existing supports and inspirations?

Clearly British schools have had a lot of change to put up with but changes in school management have been occurring in other countries also. In Australia, school councils have been given the power to set educational policies within government guidelines, with a view to increasing the school responsibilities for budgeting. They have also had to face a new curriculum framework set by the government with a particular priority for the redress of disadvantage. The United States has been influenced not only by political ideology but also by research on school effectiveness and school improvement. There has been, since the 1980s, a move towards a more decentralised system of education with an emphasis on localised school-site management and the principle of every school becoming self-directed (Beare *et al.*, 1989).

THE IMPLICATIONS OF IMPOSED CHANGE

* Nobody likes being told to do something.
* Nobody likes having to do things, even if they actually agree with them, especially if they have reacted against or have felt alienated from the change process.
* Nobody likes being consulted but not listened to.

Imposed change at the intensity of recent years has reached a level that few can comfortably tolerate. Morale in the profession has sunk to an all-time low and stress levels risen to an all-time high. Teacher stress has been surveyed since the mid-1980s in a number of studies, each of which has consistently shown increasing numbers of teachers avoiding attending school, increased incidence of physical and psychological difficulty including alcoholism, mental breakdown, marital disharmony and break up, long-term sickness and burn-out. Increasing numbers of teachers have left teaching altogether and many more are expressing dissatisfaction with their jobs.

Of concern to us in this book are the psychological implications for positive school change when individuals sense a loss of direction, when they become reactive and locked in to crisis management. Clearly the negative implications of change can mean that self-motivated or self-imposed change activity ceases or is considerably reduced. Individuals may lose their vision or it may become somewhat blurred, a feeling of pessimism may overwhelm them and they may feel defeated or develop a strong dislike of certain children, parents or other staff. All these are well recognised manifestations of learned helplessness or stress, brought about by change overload and criticism.

An organisation, being made up of individuals, will soon begin to creak if change pressures upon them are too great. Loss or non-appearance of key individuals will affect its processes and development, and staff stress and conflict between individuals or with management in either an organised or a spontaneous way can severely damage the operation of the organisation. The organisation may be seen itself to begin to be operating in a disoriented way, with no sense of direction. Crisis management, knee-jerk reactions leading to increased exclusion of usually the most vulnerable children, low performance and attainment, absenteeism and behaviour difficult to manage are just some of the indicators of an overstretched, non-coping school.

Imposed changes often cause paper overload which has the effect of increasing a general feeling of not being able to cope. Paper overload also appears to have a negative effect on communication; for, although people are sent information for a purpose, they can lose any sense of priority and may cease even to read it. Communication itself soon becomes problematic in overstretched organisations, messages becoming unclear and conflict rife.

The implications of excessive imposed change are thus clear and stand in the way of those who wish to assert their own school philosophy. Given these obstacles, is it possible to turn them into opportunities?

Asserting your school philosophy

To assert successfully your school philosophy amid imposed change you need to consider at least four dimensions:

vision and objectives
assertiveness and leadership
organisational culture
buffering and protecting.

Vision and objectives

In most work since the late 1970s in the area of leadership and effective schooling one comes across the importance of vision. There is a growing body of evidence that outstanding leaders have a vision for their organisation. For instance Bennis and Nanus in their study of ninety transforming leaders in a vast variety of settings described vision as:

> a mental image of a possible and desirable future state of the organisation . . . as vague as a dream or as precise as a goal or mission statement . . . a view of a realistic, credible, attractive future for the organisation, a condition that is better in some important ways than what now exists.
>
> (Bennis and Nanus, 1985: 189)

Individuals are often cited who, under extreme oppression, and certainly amid imposed changes and negative external forces, have been able to assert their vision in an extremely powerful way with immense impact on the organisation or groups of whom they are leaders. Examples include Gandhi, J.F. Kennedy and of course Martin Luther King Jnr, with his 'I have a dream' vision. Individuals in many settings have inspired others with their vision or have faced considerable oppression as a result of this. Many visions whilst appearing impossible to achieve have, in the fullness of time, been attained, for instance putting a man on the moon. Whilst you may not have a vision as creative as this for your school, it is crucial for you or your headteacher or the management of your school to have a clear sense of vision at this time. The vision needs to be a clear statement or philosophy that is clearly communicated, delivered and acted upon.

Successful heads are *goal-orientated* insofar as they have a vision of how they would like to see their school develop. Thus they give the school a sense of direction and are capable of operationalising their goals and values both through a long term strategy and at the level of their day to day action. They engage in 'purposing' which Vaill (1984) defines as ' . . . that continuous stream of action by an organisation's formal leadership which has the effect of inducing clarity, consensus and commitment regarding the organisation's basic purpose.'

(Coulson, 1986: 85)

Vision is an ever-recurring theme in studies of effective schooling, and in discussion of excellent leadership in education. Visions may be verbalised or written and may include such statements as:

> Our school provides education for all children in our community independent of whatever culture, difficulty or disability they may represent and we aim to maximise the potential of each and every individual.

Alternatively a vision may be communicated in the terms of a specific mission statement such as: 'We aim by the end of five years to have doubled the number of contacts we have with parents in our community.' We would argue that it may be worthwhile unpacking a superordinate vision into more specific short-term objectives or mission statements. These objectives could address specific areas of school functioning such as the following:

support for teachers
recruitment
curriculum development
parental involvement
positive behaviour management
personal and social education
quality of teaching and learning.

In this way a vision could be unpacked and specific objectives set out which can then be drawn into a school's development plan. Specific objectives can then be worked to consistently and precisely in a systematic way and can be clearly communicated to all those who are involved inside and outside the school.

Your school's vision is only as valuable as the way it is communicated to staff, to pupils, to parents, to your LEA and to other significant actors in the social world of the school. It is essential that key people are communicated with and involved in a school's vision. This may be quite independent of their status within the school. One comprehensive school known to us, probably reflecting the practice of many other schools throughout the country, actively involves the school caretaker in a vision of a school where *all* are involved in the teaching and learning process. This caretaker has brought his dog into science lessons and has been actively involved in helping pupils with experiments at other times.

'Don't worry about the outside of the building, come in and meet the people.'

This quotation from a headteacher says a lot about the philosophy of this school. It seems important that a vision is not only communicated and expressed effectively, but that key individuals are committed to it and in effect 'live it'. Such commitment can then readily lead to joint action towards the achievement of a shared vision and the achievement of specific objectives in its furtherance. Thus, a school committed to the fullest collaborative involvement of deputies and staff members in decision-making may be characterised by cross-hierarchical working parties addressing specific areas of the school's functioning in which very important decisions are made.

Being actively proactive in the face of change is encapsulated in the act of stating and holding on to a vision for your school. At times you may feel that your vision is beginning to look like General Custer's battleworn flag when all around the arrows are flying. Beare *et al.*, (1989), describing a number of generalisations that appear to shape leadership in schools where excellence is valued, make the point that attention should be given to institutionalising vision if leadership of the transforming kind is to be successful.

This generalisation points to the importance of what Burns (1978) called 'transforming leadership', when the headteacher has a vision for the school, that she or he is able to articulate in such a way that others become committed to it and day-to-day activities are imbued with meanings and values. It is necessary, of course, that the vision be sustained or institutionalised, with its meanings and values embedded in the culture of the school. Beare *et al.* go on to quote Starratt (1986) who produced a model for leadership described as the 'communal institutionalising of a vision'. The model suggests the following characteristics:

- the leader's power is rooted in a vision that itself is rooted in something basic to human life
- the vision illuminates the ordinary with dramatic significance
- the leader articulates the vision in such compelling ways that colleagues share the vision and it illuminates their ordinary activity with dramatic significance
- the leader implants the vision in the structures and processes of the organisation, so that people experience the vision in the various patterned activities of the organisation
- the leader and colleagues make day-to-day decisions in the light of the vision, so that the vision becomes part of the culture of the organisation
- all the members of the organisation celebrate the vision in ritual, ceremonies and art forms.

Vision has enormous potential for maintaining a philosophy or further developing a set of purposes in a school situation. The belief and purpose it embodies can reflect the children's enthusiasm that the school tries to promote. It is clear that vision can empower people to change and paint a clear picture of where an organisation is heading. Confused people are often poor adapters to change, whereas a vision can provide a clear picture of an organisation's strategic focus. A good vision can include deeply felt values and can allow individuals to convert threat into opportunities. However, it is clear from work carried out by Hargreaves (1991) and others that schools do not always match up to these lofty notions of vision. Many schools in Britain at this time feel threatened and confused. Vision and developmental planning are often not seen as essential parts of a school's process but rather as a 'trick' of the LEA. It is clear that at this time in Britain a great number of schools are not expressing vision but are busy reacting to and suffering the negative effects of imposed and excessive change as mentioned in the earlier section.

How can vision once communicated become a tangible reality? It is clear that vision must be well communicated, engender commitment and ideally become institutionalised within the organisation if it is to have any impact. Ultimately there must be specific outcomes that are visible manifestations of the vision itself and thus it may be very worthwhile to have specific objectives which can become performance indicators for the successful achievement of the vision. Thus improvements and changes in the following may be a clear indication of movement in the desired direction:

- improved academic performance
- school ethos obvious to visitors
- attendance at school improved
- the visual look of the environment of the school obviously improved
- pupils when interviewed or spoken to reporting that they feel valued by staff
- behaviour improved in and around the school and community, and exclusions reduced.

It would seem that in the delivery of the school vision, philosophy must permeate public, private and personal dimensions to such a degree that there is carry-over from one generation of pupils to the next. Specific manifestations of the vision may include mottoes, Latin verses, or badges and other insignia worn or displayed around the school. Explicit symbols of what is valued in the school may relate to rituals and specific celebrations of success and effort which together can clearly underline and help with the achievement of the details that make up the school's vision.

Thus, while many schools have a long way to go in clarifying and expressing their sense of vision, it is clear that there is considerable evidence of the effectiveness of this strategy even amid imposed change. Ultimately school leaders need visions that include images of a desirable future state that embody their own view of what constitutes excellence in their school as well as in the broader educational scene and in society in general.

Assertiveness

A non-assertive person is easy to recognise, but are we as clear about what a non-assertive school organisation or its management looks like? We know what it is like to meet people who assert clear beliefs and philosophies, but schools which assert beliefs, values and philosophies are less readily identifiable.

We hold that the psychology of assertiveness is highly relevant to organisations and the people who work in them and that it is appropriate for beliefs and philosophies to be clearly articulated to those who threaten or attempt to erode them. It is important for visions and specific objectives or goals to be pursued unswervingly but at the same time for a new flexibility to become evident with a new set of effective processes for dealing with and promoting change. On the one hand, individuals will need to learn to say no more effectively in some situations, and organisations may need to learn a new confidence in sticking to their guns. On the other hand, newer more flexible approaches involving changes to the organisational and leadership culture will be essential as well as ways of buffering outside impositions. It is not just in the market place that schools may find themselves having to be assertive, but also within their local community, wider society and the whole field of education itself if important beliefs and values are to be retained and not squeezed out by other forces.

School leaders may well find themselves asserting educational values over economic values. Thus negative constructs such as 'pupils with special needs are high cost, low value' will need to be countered with much more powerful moral and educational values about the rights and needs of individual young people independent of their culture or difficulties. Many schools are aware of the need to assert themselves and the market-place analogies often used in the wider society have not been lost on schools. Other reasons for an assertion of a basic educational philosophy can easily be identified. Assertive people are those whose opinion and commitment to a course of action are important. They are likely to be fulfilled, more optimistic and have track records of success. There are assertion skills which are valuable in the classroom for teachers, and which teachers can foster in children. It is possible that these may also improve the quality of life of the school as an organisation. Teachers need to make full use of all the advice and ideas contained in contemporary psychology literature in the area of assertiveness.

Organisational culture

'The way we do things round here.'

It is vital that not only is the organisation noticed for what it wants to be, but also that there is an organisational culture geared up to manage change effectively. It may also be essential to have effective leadership, styles of more open management and whole-school approaches in a range of areas. These elements should help your school stand up to against and smoothly move through imposed change. Let us take a closer look at any helpful ideas we can learn from the effective schooling research and from the international school improvement project (ISIP).

While in Britain and elsewhere schools may have in common the government-imposed changes and changes in society, they differ from each other widely in effectiveness. Recent research on effective schools in Britain (Rutter *et al.*, 1979; Mortimer *et al.*, 1988) and the United States (Purkey and Smith, 1983) illustrates that certain internal conditions are typical in schools that achieve higher levels of outcomes for their students. These studies indicate that schools can and do make a difference to pupil achievement and that these differences in outcome are related to variations in the school climate, culture or ethos and their quality as social systems. Hopkins points out that:

> The research suggests that teachers and schools have more control than they may have imagined over their ability to change their present direction and become efficient and effective agents of pupils' learning and development.
>
> (Hopkins, 1990: 190)

Typical organisational factors that are seen as characteristics of effective schools are cited by Purkey and Smith (1983) and include:

- curriculum-focused school leadership
- supportive climate within the school
- emphasis on curriculum and teaching, for example, maximising academic learning
- clear goals and high expectations
- a system for monitoring performance and achievement
- on-going staff development and in-service planning
- parental involvement and support
- LEA support.

There are clearly other factors that put meaning and life into the process of change within school including those identified by Fullan (1985), among them a feel for the process of leadership, a guiding value system, intense interaction and communication and collaborative planning and implementation. These process factors are meant to provide means of achieving the organisational change by lubricating the system and somehow fuelling the dynamics of interaction.

Within the effective schools' movement there has been a recent paradigm shift, to use Kuhn's term (1970), towards thinking about schools and other organisations as organisational cultures. This is a departure from the domination of the metaphors of organisation as a machine or even as a living organism (Beare *et al.*, 1989; Morgan, 1986). With this in mind Beare and his co-writers argue that it appears that the acknowledged 'best' schools have developed a culture, milieu, an environment, atmosphere and a *cultus corporis* which in many ways influence how well children learn. In Edmonds (1982) the effective school appears to be a concentrated culture based upon a core assumption about its prime function being instruction and learning.

> Coherence like this within subjects, across subjects, across year groups, among classroom approaches, does not emerge by chance. It is driven by a common vision about education, about the school and about what the school's programmes are for. It comes from a collectivity of people who have devised a collective vision or picture together.
>
> (Beare *et al.*, 1989: 19)

The international school improvement project has, according to Hopkins (1990), placed considerable emphasis on process rather than product, particularly in relation to teaching–learning processes, the evaluation of improvement strategies and the notion of quality schooling. School improvement is seen as emerging from a 'relatively autonomous school' existing within a supportive educational environment sustained by the local education authority (Schmuck, 1984). The ISIP project teams have also emphasised the importance of the process of innovation. Miles (1986) describes the process as beginning with the initiation phase of innovation which needs to be clearly articulated, have an active advocate, a forceful mandate and be backed up by extensive training. Through the implementation phase the change needs to be well co-ordinated, have adequate and sustained support, have control increasingly spread throughout the school, and provide rewards for all those involved. During the institutionalisation phase, the change needs to be embedded in the school organisation, tied into classroom practice and have widespread use in school, LEA and be supported by a cadre of local trainers.

Hopkins (1990) believes that there is a need to establish a synthesis between school improvement and knowledge and research about effective schools. For our purposes this work gives some valuable clues to the importance of an effective organisational culture that is both strong enough and flexible enough to withstand and promote change processes.

One very important notion which we have already referred to, in this chapter and elsewhere, is that of effective leadership within the organisational culture, particularly as it engenders more open styles of management and the sharing of the functions of leadership. Let us examine in more detail what is known about leadership with particular regard to the effective assertion of a school's philosophy and amid imposed change. Leadership is clearly a crucial factor in determining organisational effectiveness. Peters and Austin (1985), looking at leadership in a number of settings report the following:

> For the last twenty five years we have carried around with us a model of *manager* as cop, referee, devil's advocate, dispassionate analyst, professional, decision maker, naysayer, pronouncer. The alternative we now propose is *leader*, (not manager) as a cheer-leader, enthusiast, nurturer of champions, hero-finder, wanderer, dramatist, coach, facilitator, builder. It's not a model of what might be or a prescription for the impossible. We've learned it in real time, from people who've done it in glamour industries and those who've won in extremely adverse situations – in low growth industries or the public sector. From all these people we have learned nothing about magic. We've learned, instead, of passion, care, intensity, consistency, attention, drama, of the implicit and explicit use of symbols – in short, of leadership.
>
> (Peters and Austin, 1985: 265)

Effective leadership in schools appears to be characterised by the following:

- inspired mission
- involvement of others in change
- listening and responding
- skilled communication
- ability to stand back
- obviously caring
- emphasis on teacher quality
- enthusiastic but judicious approach to innovation
- keeping paper work to a minimum.

Southworth (1990) attempts to answer the question: what does an effective primary headteacher appear to look like? He draws together a number of principles derived from a range of sources (Coulson, 1986, 1988; DES, 1987; ILEA, 1985; Mortimer *et al.*, 1988; Nias *et al.*, 1989; Southworth, 1988). Effective headteachers appear to emphasise the centrality of teaching and learning by way of their own teaching commitment and their persistent interest in children's work and development. They are also seen to pay attention to teachers' plans, practice, reflections and evaluations. Effective headteachers ensure that there are explicit curricular aims, guidelines, and consistency, continuity and coherence in pupil record-keeping. Such headteachers will act as exemplars by regularly teaching, leading assemblies and generally working long and hard for the school. They will ensure that their teachers have some non-contact time and set high expectations for themselves, children and staff. They will encourage and develop others to lead and accept positions of responsibility and will attempt actively to involve the deputy head in policy decision-making, so that they operate as partners. Teachers, and sometimes others, are actively involved in curriculum planning and school organisation and a consultative approach generally tends to be adopted towards decision-making.

Effective headteachers appear to be conscious of the needs of the school and of individual teachers for in-service training and professional development. They tend to be considerate towards staff, offering psychological support and taking an interest in them as people. They appear to be willing, on occasions, to help reconcile and make allowance for personal or professional role conflicts. They constantly enquire into many aspects of the school as an organisation and will be found touring the school before, during and after school hours, visiting staff in their classrooms and work places and attempting to perceive the school from different perspectives. They often seek to manage 'by wandering about', making every effort to observe and listen wherever they go. They attempt to develop and sustain a whole-school perspective, a shared and agreed vision of effective practice to be adopted by and become the staff's collective mission. They will nurture and maintain a school culture and ensure that the school has an explicit and understood development plan and a sense of direction in anticipation of future developments. Effective headteachers will involve parents and governors in the work and life of the school and are effective communicators of the school's successes and challenges, presenting a positive image of the school, staff and children.

One principle that emerges strongly is the notion of shared leadership or leadership density. Teamwork some argue, should be *forced* on to as many organisational situations as possible. Whether this is overstating the position or not, the idea that every individual in a school organisation has the potential for leadership has considerable mileage. It is certainly true that all members of staff are at some point managers and at some point leaders, as they move between the functions of classroom management, classroom and school development, the tasks of classroom and school maintenance.

An effective, flexible organisational culture, containing excellent leadership, open management and some of the cultural principles of effective schooling as outlined above, should stand a school in good stead in relation to surviving imposed change. Such schools are likely to be bigger than any change that is thrust upon them.

Buffering and protecting

Having considered positive ways of asserting your philosophy, let us now see what steps you can carry out to buffer the psychological impact of imposed change upon your organisation and its members. Clearly, getting it right in relation to having a clear vision, specific objectives, effective leadership and assertiveness skills, and an open flexible organisational culture will in their own right be effective buffers and means of protection. However, there are also other strategies and tactics.

Anticipating change is a very effective way of being proactive in a changing situation. Effective predictions can lead to actions to help minimise the impact of the change when it actually occurs. Predictions may lead to planning organisational responses to likely events in the near future; and the building up of alternative plans of action can make the organisation and its members all the more ready to act effectively when the change occurs. Systematic problem-solving as an approach to dealing with change processes is probably one of the more healthy perspectives and set of processes to use.

It is important to consider proactively how stress, which appears to be such an inevitable implication of imposed change, will be dealt with. Although stress is a normal and natural part of everyday life, there are few schools in Britain that seriously and strategically plan for stress management even though many are only too well aware of its impact. If we are serious about stress management what do we need to do in our schools?

Improved systems for the regular supervision and support of individual teachers, in situations where emotive and practical issues can be discussed individually or in small groups, do much to build up their resources to manage their own stress levels as well as to improve the quality of teaching and learning and caring. This process does not have to be hierarchical although it does have to be valued by school leaders. Peer appraisal schemes, peer supervision and peer group support groups may all be helpful. One of the authors is at present working with a support group of teachers looking at intervention issues brought up by pupils presenting emotional and behavioural difficulties in an area of high social disadvantage. This group has been able to spend time reflecting on how past unresolved situations and feelings about individuals, both child and adult, can be transferred to new problem situations intensifying emotions and causing knee-jerk reactions rather than planned responses.

Only by being offered an opportunity to reflect more objectively on such common transference experiences can individual teachers begin to understand themselves and their pupils more fully, with a view to more rational, balanced and appropriate actions. Sadly such opportunities are rarely available to teachers, despite the recognition of the importance of regular structured supervision by the majority of other public services who deal with emotional and social needs of adults and children.

Leaders within a school offering facilities for genuine psychological support who are prepared to listen to staff and to offer empathy and quality time for discussion of difficulties and issues tend to be highly valued by the school's members. Opportunities for deep relaxation during the school day are virtually impossible to find in any school in Britain. These opportunities could be planned for and built into the schedule of the working week if valued and considered worthwhile enough by the school's management. Many American and British business companies have realised the importance of effective stress management and particularly the effect of deep relaxation even for short periods of five to ten minutes to introduce more of a healthy cycle and rhythm to the working day with its consequent positive influence on job-related performance and activity for the rest of the day. Other stress management techniques, including healthy foods, exercise and other forms of relaxation, are acknowledged as important in many school situations, but again these are seldom acted upon during the general course of the working day. One of the authors is currently introducing a yoga teacher in a local school whose staff are exploring their approaches to stress in the 1990s.

We still need to do much, in Britain and elsewhere, to empower our teachers. We need to view leadership and management as means of offering individual staff members the opportunity to share in leadership tasks, by working collaboratively in teams in which all are expected to contribute and by creating situations where colleagues' talents can be unlocked and self-esteem lifted. We need to rethink our rigid vertical hierarchies and move towards more flexible roles with more horizontal teams and the opportunities for new relationships. An effective framework needs to be established which is underpinned by written policy statements in all major areas of curriculum and school functioning. Strategies and survival guides need to be created that can be used in all areas of the school. Effective meetings, task groups and other forms of grouping need to be encouraged. Communication and reporting, and more accurate judgement about progress are important, as are monitoring, evaluation and planning cycles. All these, combined, will be important ways of holding together the infrastructure to withstand imposed change and other external pressures.

ACTION PLAN

- Take a reading of changes that are presently occurring and those that are likely to occur in the future.
- Reflect upon how effectively your school is buffering these changes and how individuals are being protected from negative implications of them.
- Clarify and communicate your vision-engendering commitment, joint action and whole-school approaches.
- Set out objectives in the key areas of school functioning.
- Pay attention to change processes you are making use of.
- Assert your school philosophy using psychological assertiveness techniques, but keep flexible and do not forget to listen.

- Develop leadership skills in your organisation and the sharing of these.
- Develop an organisational culture with an effective school ethos.
- Plan for personal empowerment and support for individual members of your organisation.

Conclusion
Speculating about future change

We have looked at the importance of and potential for asserting a school philosophy amid imposed change with the help of psychology. We have argued that it is essential to look after other people as well as yourself if change is to take care of itself, there being a limit to the amount and type of change any of us can stand. We have looked at how to evaluate and monitor achievements and development with a view to the next cycle of planning and change. A number of strategies for facilitating change have been detailed and discussed including professional development, in-service training, policy development, consultation and negotiation. We have highlighted the need to establish a successful synthesis between all of these processes if change is to take place coherently and smoothly. Prior to this we examined the question: where do you want to go? We looked at making the links between fostering children's learning and helping a school develop and at the importance of vision, and the setting of attainable and short-term objectives. We began by considering how a school might go about finding out where it is at now and raised the essential question: why change now? We stressed the importance of managing and planning change proactively and described in detail approaches to the evaluation and review of an organisation's functioning.

Gamblers and investors

Finally, we pose the question: are you a gambler, an investor or a saver? Gambling is the taking of risks in order to give some chance of gain. Investing is the retention of resources from consumption to buy resources that may be productive and rewarding in the future. There is a degree of risk in investment in that the rewards are deferred and cannot be guaranteed. Investment is different from saving; saving refers to the retention of resources while investment refers to the use of savings.

We believe that humans are strongly attracted to gambling and to saving. Gambling usually involves a strong focus on the reward and minimal focus on the possible risks. Essentially, gambling is the giving away of a resource with the hope that it will be returned multiplied. Investment is similar in many ways; the hope is that the investor has some operational control over the resource and its use and of course, some investments are a lot safer than others.

We believe that the best investment is in people and improving schools is the improvement of the personal effectiveness of the people, especially the teachers. If teachers feel well regarded, seen as an asset by the school, treated with respect and given access to ways of improving their skills, the school may retain staff for a little longer than average. This may sound a relatively modest outcome, but turnover is necessary and schools and school identity should be greater than the role of any individual or group. Few successful investments involve no change between sectors or stocks, but rather a process of predicting positive long-term trends. When staff have positive experiences in a school or other organisation they also have enhanced skills and confidence and may be good candidates for promotion. This kind of movement can be seen as unfortunate in the short term but in the long term it can work to spread the good reputation of the school, especially if staff who have left go on to key positions.

Investment in the creation of a learning culture which intrinsically values change may be a long-term vision that requires long-term planning. Short-term, returns may not be as immediately obvious as the lucky win after a quick gamble, but ultimately the wise investor will be the richer.

Accurate and successful investment requires lucky or precise anticipation of future events. Speculating about future change can be a very challenging exercise and any one school has to take account of not only the local context but also the international scene. Historical, sociological, political and psychological considerations will all have a bearing on speculating about the future and the planning that takes place as a result of this. Let us conclude with some of our own speculations about the future which may or may not influence investors reading this book.

It is likely that the dawning of the twenty-first century will bring a number of changes, the seeds of which can already be detected. Information technology is likely to be one of the key areas of development. Interactive videos, massive information databases accessed from classrooms and homes and the use of desktop computers from the beginning to the end of a school career in virtually all areas of learning are highly likely in the future. Access to high quality up-to-the-minute information from international sources will become critical and highly valued and will deeply impinge on what pupils are expected to memorise. Processes rather than content will dominate the efforts of teachers.

It is also possible to detect a move in the direction of all pupils' rights being offered more legal protection to ensure appropriate opportunities for all. This may bring more litigation, but will also strengthen further the access of all vulnerable groups to quality education firmly rooted in their local communities. All pupils, however severe or disturbing their difficulties, will be educated in their local school by right and will be supported effectively once there.

Further evidence of the effectiveness of parental participation in children's learning is likely to strengthen and increase active parental involvement both in and out of schools across the world. Much more intense learning activity is likely to occur in the home and local community away from schools, facilitated by information technology and new access to information. Adult learners are much more likely in the future to be members of classrooms in which children are being educated and this in turn will positively impact upon the classroom climate and behaviour.

Schools may become increasingly independent and clearer about their individual strengths but at the same time a new sense of inter-school co-operation may eventually grow out of the ashes of a period of painful competition.

Without doubt schools will become much more sophisticated about the process of change they are engaging in. Leadership will be further devolved and strengthened as a result. Schools will develop their loose–tight properties, having a very tight clear sense of direction and standards whilst at the same time having in-built teams working in very loose, creative and spontaneous ways. Staff will be more valued and more effectively taken care of as a new ethos of schools as truly nurturing places for everyone finally begins to emerge. This 'taking care' will start with senior staff and flow through to parents and children.

Learning in all schools is likely to become increasingly pupil-centred and at the same time much more relevant and meaningful to the needs of younger and older people in the twenty-first century. Individual progress will be much more closely monitored and recorded and parents will have intimate and direct access to information on their children, facilitated ultimately by pupils recording much of their work using personal computer or terminals linked to mainframe computer systems. High density compact disks and new forms of hightec recording tapes will follow pupils through their educational careers.

Learning will ultimately become more overtly a lifelong occupation for the majority of the population and schools will become the nerve centres within the community for this activity as well as increasingly important social centres within the community.

Changes in these directions will not happen overnight and will be fraught with problems, pain, contradictions and new challenges. There will be times of self-questioning and doubt and the quality of human relationships will no doubt determine the course of whatever methods or approaches are adopted.

A lot will be asked of leaders and managers today and tomorrow if our transition into the next century is to be educationally smooth and prosperous. Let us hope they will be prepared.

Bibliography

Acklaw, J. (1990) 'Change and the management of educational psychology services in England and Wales', in *School Psychology International*, 11: 3–7.

Adams, J.L. (1986) *The Care and Feeding of Ideas: A Guide to Encouraging Creativity*, Reading, Mass.: Addison-Wesley.

Adams, R.S. with Chen, D. (1981) *The Process of Educational Innovation: An International Perspective*, London: Unesco Press.

Ainscow, M. and Muncey, J. (1984) *SNAP, Special Needs Action Programme, Revised Edition*, Cardiff: Drake Associates.

Ainscow, M. and Tweddle, D.A. (1977) 'Behavioural objectives and children with learning difficulties', *Association of Educational Psychologists Journal*, 4(5): 33–7.

Allsop, P., Jacques, K., Lofthouse, M., and Newlands, P. (1989) 'Changing Patterns of Inset Provision: An Ilustration', *International School of Educational Management*, 3(1): 27–9.

Asmussen, S. (1987) *Applied Probability and Queues*, Chichester: Wiley.

Aubrey, C. (1988) 'Organisational school psychology and school consultancy', in Jones, N. and Sayer, J. (eds) *Management and the Psychology of Schooling*, Lewes, Sussex: Falmer Press.

Audit Commission (1986) *Making a Reality of Community Care, A Report by the Audit Commission*, London: HMSO.

Bailey, A.J. and Braithwaite, R.J. (1980) 'Inservice education and the promotion of change in a secondary school', *British Journal of Teacher Education*, 6, 3, 203–13.

Baldridge, J.V. and Deal, T.E. (eds) with Ancell, M.Z. (1975) *Managing Change in Educational Organisations. Sociological perspectives, strategies and case studies*, Berkeley, Calif: McCutchan.

Bandura, A. (1978) 'The self-system in reciprocal determinism', *American Psychologist*, 33: 344–58.

Barton, L. (1988) *The politics of Special Educational Needs*, Lewes, Sussex: Falmer Press

Bassett, G.W. (1970) *Innovation in Primary Education*, London: Wiley-Interscience.

Bayley, S. and Tarrant, A. (1990) 'Equal Opportunities', *Essex Perspectives*, Chelmsford: Essex County Council.

Beare, H., Caldwell, B., and Millikan, R. (1989) *Creating an Excellent School: Some New Management Techniques*, London: Routledge.

Beer, M. and Walton, A.E. (1987) 'Organisational change and development', in M.R. Rosenzweig and L.W. Porter (eds) *Annual Review of Psychology* 38: 339–67, Palo Alto, Calif.: Annual Reviews Inc.

Belloc, N.B. and Breslow, L. (1973) 'Preventative medicine', in *The International Journal of Health Services*, 3: 7–21.

Bennett, R. (1990) *Choosing and Using Management Consultants*, London: Kogan Page.

Bennis, W.G. and Nanus, B. (1985) *Leaders*, New York: Harper & Row.

Bennis, W.G., Benne, K.D., Chin, R. (eds) (1969) *The Planning of Change* (2nd edtn), New York: Reinhart and Winston.

Berne, E. (1964) *Games People Play*, New York: Grove Press.

Bolam, R. (1986) 'School improvement: the national scene'., *School Organisation*, 6(3): 314–20.

Bolam, R. (1979) 'Evaluating In-service Education and Training: a National Perspective', *British Journal of Teacher Education*, 5(1): 1–15.

Bollington, R., Hopkins, D. and West, M. (1990) *An Introduction to Teacher Appraisal: a professional development approach*, London: Cassell Educational.

Boyd, B. (1985) 'Whole School Policies', *Forum for the Discussion of New Trends in Education*, 27 (3): 5–10.

Bruner, J. (1975) 'The ontogenesis of speech acts', *Journal of Child Language*, 2: 1–19.

Buchanan, D. and Huczynski, A. (1985) *Organisational Behaviour*, Englewood Cliffs, NJ: Prentice-Hall.

Burns, J.M. (1978), *Leadership*, New York: Harper & Row.

Caldwell, B.J. and Spinks, J.M. (1986) *Policy Making and Planning for School Effectiveness*, Hobart, Tasmania: Education Department.

Campbell, R. (1985) *Developing the Primary School Curriculum*, London: Holt, Rinehart & Winston.

Caplan, G. (1970) *The Theory and Practice of Mental Health Consultation*, New York: Basic Books.

Carver, F.D. and Sergiovanni, T.J. (1969) *Organizations and Human Behavior: Focus on Schools*, New York: McGraw-Hill.

Casdagli, P. and Gobey, F. (1990) *Only Playing Miss*, Stoke on Trent: Trentham Books.

Checkland, P.B. (1981) *Systems Thinking, Systems Practice*, London: Wiley.

Chevalier G. (1956) *Clochemerle*, Paris: Quadridge d'Apollon.

Chisholm B. (1986) *Preventive Approaches to Disruption*, Basingstoke and London: Macmillan Education.

Clark, P.A. (1972) *Action Research and Organizational Change*, London: Harper & Row.

Conoley, J.C. (ed.) (1981) *Consultation in Schools: Theory, Research, Procedures*, New York: Academic Press.

Coulson, A.A. (1986) 'The Managerial Work of Primary School Headteachers', *Sheffield Papers in Education Management, No. 48*, Sheffield City Polytechnic: Department of Education Management.

Coulson, A.A. (1988) 'Primary school headship: a review of research', paper presented to *BEMAS Conference on Research in Educational Management and Administration*, University College, Cardiff.

Cox, T. (1989), *Stress*, Nottingham: Nottingham University Stress Research Unit.

Crossley, M., Smith, P. and Bray, M. (1985) 'INSET: Prospects and Practice in Developing Countries', *Journal of Education for Teaching*, 11: 120–32.

Dalin, P. (1978) *Limits to Educational Change*, London: Macmillan.

Dalin, P. and Rust, V.D. (1983) *Can Schools Learn?*, Windsor: NFER-Nelson.

Day, C., Whitaker, P. and Johnston, D. (1990) *Managing Primary Schools in the 1990s*, 2nd edn, London: Paul Chapman.

Deal, J.V. and Deal, T.E. (1975) *Managing Change in Educational Organisations*, Berkeley, Calif.: McCutchan.

Deal, T. and Kennedy, A. (1982) *Corporate Cultures: the rites and rituals of corporate life*, Reading, Mass.: Addison-Wesley.

De Caluwe, L., Marx, E., and Petri, M. (1988) *School Development: models and change*, Leuven: OECD, ACCO.

DES (1972) *Teacher Education and Training*, A Report by a committee of enquiry appointed by the Secretary of State for Education and Science under the chairmanship of Lord James of Rusholme (James Report), London: HMSO.

DES (1978) *Enquiry into the Education of Handicapped Children and Young People* (Warnock Report), London: HMSO.

DES (1981) *The 1981 Education Act*, London: HMSO.

DES (1987) *Primary Schools: Some Aspects of Good Practice*, London: HMSO.

DES (1988) *Education Reform Act*, London: HMSO.

DES and Welsh Office (1988) *National Curriculum Task Group on Assessment and Testing*, London: HMSO.

DES, School Management Task Force (1990) *Developing School Management: the way forward*, London: HMSO.

Dessent, T. (1987) *Making The Ordinary School Special*, Lewes, Sussex: Falmer.

Dror, Y. (1973) *Public Policy Making Re-examined*, England: Leonard Hill Books.

Duignan, P.A. and MacPherson, R.J. (1989) 'Educational leadership: an Australian project', *International School of Educational Management*, 3(1): 12–23.

Edmonds, R.R. (1982) 'Programs for school improvement: an overview', *Educational Leadership*, December.

Engelmann, S. and Carnine, D. (1982) *Theory of Instruction: principles and applications*, New York: Irvington.

Farrell, P. (ed.) (1985) *EDY. Its Impact on Staff Training in Mental Handicap*, Manchester: Manchester University Press.

Fisher, R. and Ury, W. (1981) *Getting to Yes: negotiating agreement without giving in*, Boston: Houghton Mifflin, London: Hutchinson Business (1986).

Fox, M. (1989) 'The EPS: a quality service', unpublished paper for Essex Educational Psychology Service.

Frederickson, N. (1988) 'Continuing professional education: towards a framework for development', *Management and the Psychology of Schooling*, Lewes, Sussex: Falmer.

Frederickson, N. (ed.) (1990) *Introduction to Soft Systems Methodology and its Application in Work with Schools*, London: University College.

Fullan, M.G. (1985) 'Change Processes and Strategies at the local level', *Elementary School Journal*, 85: 391–421.

Fullan, M.G. (1986) 'Improving the implementation of educational change', *School Organization*, 6(3): 321–6.

Fullan, M., Anderson, S. and Newton, E. (1986), *Support Systems for Implementing Curriculum in School Districts*, Toronto: OISE.

Gaine, C. (1988) *No Problem Here: a practical approach to education and 'race' in white schools*, London: Hutchinson.

Galbraith, J.R. (1977) *Organisation Design*, Reading, Mass.: Addison-Wesley.

Gale, A. (1991) 'The school as organisation: new roles for psychologists in education', *Educational Psychology in Practice*, 7 (2) 67–73.

Gardner, W.I. and Cole, C. (1988) 'Self Monitoring', in E.S. Shapiro and T.R. Kratochwill (eds) *Behavioural Assessment in the Schools*, New York: Guilford Press 206–46.

Garratt, B. (1987) *The Learning Organization*, London: Fontana.

George, M., Hawkins P. and McLean, A. (1988) *Organizational Culture Manual*, Bath: Bath Associates.

Georgiades, N.J. and Phillimore, L. (1975) 'The myth of the hero innovator and alternative strategies for organisational change', in C. Kiernan, and F.P. Woodward, (eds) *Behaviour Modification with the Severely Retarded*, Amsterdam: Associated Scientific Publishers.

Gergen, K.J. (1985) 'The social constructivist movement in modern psychology', *American Psychologist*, 40: 266–75.

Gilham, B. (Ed.) (1978) *Reconstructing Educational Psychology*, London: Croom Helm.

Gordon, D. (1984) *The Myths of School Self-renewal*, New York: Teachers Press.

Gorrell-Barnes, G. (1985) 'Systems theory and family theory', in M. Rutter and L. Hersov (eds) *Child Psychiatry: modern approaches*, Oxford: Blackwell.

Gould, A. and Shotter, J. (1977) *Human Action and its Psychological Investigation*, London: Routledge & Kegan Paul.

Goulet, R.R. (1968) *Educational Change*, New York: Citation Press.

Gray, P. and Lindsay, G. (1991) 'What price success? Appraising research in field settings', in P. Gray and G. Lyndsay (eds) 'Research and its relation to policy, *Education and Child Psychology*, 8(1): 75–82.

Gregory, R.P. (1988) *Action Research in the Secondary School: the psychologist as change agent*, London: Routledge.

Gutkin, T. and Curtis, M. (1990) 'School-based consultation: theory and techniques', in C. Reynolds and T. Gutkin (eds) *The Handbook of School Psychology*, 2nd edn, New York: Wiley.

Hall, G.E. and Hord, S.M. (1987) *Change in Schools: facilitating the process*, Albany, NY: State University of New York Press.

Handy, C. (1984) *Taken For Granted? Looking at Schools as Organisations*, London: Longman for the Schools Council.

Handy, C. and Aitken, R. (1990) *Understanding Schools as Organisations*, London: Penguin.

Hargreaves, D. (1974) 'Do we need Headteachers?' in *Education*, 2(1): 24–7.

Hargreaves, D. (1978) 'What teaching does to teachers', *New Society*, 9 March, 540–2.

Hargreaves, D. (1991) Lecture at Leicester University on 'Managing Change in Schools'.

Haring, N.G., Lovitt, T.C., Eaton, M.D. and Hansen, C.L. (1978) *The Fourth R: research in the classroom*, Columbus, Ohio: C.E. Merrill.

Harris, T.A. (1970) *I'm OK You're OK*, London: Pan.

Hastings, C., Bixby, P. and Chaudhry-Lawton, R. (1986) *Superteams: a blueprint for organisational success*, London: Fontana.

Hawkins, P. and Shohet, R. (1989) *Supervision in the Helping Professions*, Milton Keynes: Open University Press.

Hegarty, S. and Evans, P. (eds) (1985) *Research and Evaluation Methods in Special Education: quantitative and qualitative techniques in case study work*, Windsor: NFER-Nelson.

Hellawell, D.E. (1986) 'The management of change and the training of headteachers in Western Europe', *Collected Original Resources in Education*, 10 (2).

Hentsche, G.C. (1975) *Management Operations in Education*, Berkeley, Calif.: McCutchan.

Heron, J. (1975), *Six Category Intervention Analysis*, Guildford, Surrey: University of Surrey Human Potential Resource Project.

Hersey, P. and Blanchard, K. (1988) *Management of Organizational Behavior: utilizing human resources*, 5th edn, London: Prentice-Hall.

Herzberg, F. (1966) *Work and the Nature of Man*, New York: World Publishing Co.

Holly, P. (1986a) *The Teachers' GUIDE*, CIE/TRIST Working Paper, Cambridge: CIE.

Holly, P. (1986b) 'Soaring like turkeys', – the impossible dream?', *School Organization*, 6(3): 346–64.

Hopkins, D. (1985) *School Based Review for School Improvement*, Leuven, Belgium: ACCO/OECD.

Hopkins, D. (ed.) (1986): *In-service Training and Educational Development: an international survey*, London: Croom Helm.

Hopkins, D. (1990), 'The international school improvement project and effective schools: towards a synthesis', *School Organisation*, 10(2,3): 179–94.

Hord, S. (1987) *Evaluating Educational Innovation*, London: Croom Helm.

Houghton, R.S. (1987) 'Some factors affecting the implementation of educational change', *Educational Change and Development*, 8(1): 11–14.

House, R.J. and Singh, J.V. (1987) 'Organizational behaviour: some directions for I/O psychology', in M.R. Rosenzweig and L.W. Porter (eds) *Annual Review of Psychology*, 38, 669–718. Palo Alto, Calif.: Annual Reviews Inc.

Hovey, S, (1986), 'Teachers at the center', *American Educator*, Fall.

Hughes, J.N. (1990), 'Brief Psychotherapies', in T.B Gutkin and C.R. Reynolds (eds) *The Handbook of School Psychology, 2nd edn, New York: Wiley*.

Hutchins, D. (1985) *Quality Circles Handbook*, London: Pitman.

ILEA (1985) *Improving Primary Schools*, Report of the Committee on Primary Education (Thomas Report), London: ILEA.

Illback, R.J., Zins, J.E., Maher, C.A. and Greenburg, R. (1990) 'An overview of principles and procedures of program planning and evaluation', in C. Reynolds and T. Gutkin (eds) *The Handbook of School Psychology*, 2nd edn, New York: Wiley.

Isenberg, D.J. (1984) 'How senior managers think', *Harvard Business Review*, 62: 80–90.

Johnston, G. and Yeakey, C. (1986) *Theory: developments in the field of educational administration*, Lanham: University Press of America.

Jones, K., O'Sullivan, F. and Reid, K. (1987) 'The challenge of the "New INSET"', *Educational Review* 39(3): 191–202.

Joyce, B.R. and Showers, B. (1980), 'Improving in-service training: the message of research', *Educational Leadership*, 37: 379–84.

Kanter, R.M. (1983) *The Change Masters: corporate enterpreneurs at work*, London: Counterpoint, Unwin.

Katz, J.H. (1978) *White Awareness: handbook for Anti-racism Training*, Norman, Okla.: University of Oklahoma Press.

Katz, D. and Kahn, R.L. (1978) *The Social Psychology of Organizations*, New York: Wiley.

Kelly, G.A. (1955) *The Psychology of Personal Constructs*, New York: Norton.

Kemmis, S. and McTaggart, R. (1981) *The Action Research Planner*, Victoria, Australia: Deakin University Press.

Kennedy, C. (1987) 'Innovating for a change: Teacher development and innovation', *ELT Journal*, 41 (3): 163–71.

Kouzes, J.M. and Posner, B.Z. (1987) *The Leadership Challenge: how to get extraordinary things done in organizations*, San Fransisco: Jossey-Bass.

Kuhn, T, (1970) *The Structure of Scientific Revolution*, Chicago: University of Chicago Press.

Leithwood, K. (1979) 'Helping schools change: strategies derived from field experience', Occasional Paper 20, Ontario: OISE.

Lewin, K. (1952) 'Defining the field at a given time', in D. Cartwright (ed.) *Field Theory in Social Sciences*, London: Tavistock.

MacBrien, J. and Foxen, T. (1981), *Training Staff in Behavioural Methods: the EDY in-service course for mental handicap practitioners*, Manchester: Manchester University Press.

McConkey, R. (1986) *Working with Parents, for teachers and therapists*, London: Croom Helm.

McConville, R. (1991) 'Reflections on an EPS research project: "Indicators of special educational needs"', in P. Gray and G. Lyndsay (eds) 'Research and its relation to policy', *Education and Child Psychology*, 8(1): 44–50.

McLean, A. and Marshall, J. (1988) *Working With Cultures. A Workbook for People in Local Government*, Luton: Local Government Training Board.

McMahon, A., Bolam, R., Abbott, R. and Holly, P. (1984) *Guidelines for Review and Internal Development in Schools, a primary handbook*, York: Longmans in association with Schools Council.

Manning, R.C. (1988) *The Teacher Evaluation Handbook*, Engelwood Cliffs, NJ: Prentice-Hall.

March, J.G. and Simon, H.A. (1958) *Organizations*, New York: Wiley.

Marsh, P. and Campbell, A. (eds) (1982) *Aggression and Violence*, Oxford: Basil Blackwell.

Maturana, H. and Varela, F. (1980) *Autopoiesis and Cognition: the realization of the living*, London: Reidl.

Miles, M. (1986) 'Research findings on the stages of school improvement', New York: Centre for Policy Research.

Miller, A. (1989) 'Paradigms Lost: what theory informs educational psychologists in their use of behavioural approaches?', *Educational Psychology in Practice*, 5(3): 143–7.

Minuchin, S.H. and Fishman, C. (1981) *Family Therapy Techniques*, Cambridge, Mass.: Harvard University Press.

Morgan, G. (1986) *Images of Organisation*, London: Sage.

Mortimer, P. and Mortimer, J. (1989) 'School focus of inservice training, England and Wales: the challenge to higher education', *Journal of Education for Teaching*, 15(2): 133–9.

Mortimore, P., Sammons, P., Stoll, L., Lewis D. and Ecob, R. (1988) *School Matters: the Junior Years*, Wells: Open Books.

Mortimore, P. (1991) Presentation in the Institute of Education marking the 25th anniversary of the training of Educational Psychologists at the Institute of Education, University of London.

Mulford, B. (1987) *Indicators of School Effectiveness*, Australian Council of Education Administration Monograph Series.

Mussen, P.H. (ed.) *Carmichael's Manual of Child Psychology*, 3rd. edn, vol. l, New York: Wiley.

Myers, M. (1985) 'System Supplied Information (SSI)', Unpublished materials from the University of Birmingham.

Newton, C. and Tarrant, A. (1988) 'Objectives for work in schools', in *Essex Perspectives*, Chelmsford, Essex County Council.

Newton, C. and Tarrant, A. (1990) 'Objectives for change in educational organisations', *Educational Management and Administration*, 18(3): 61–7.

Newton, C. and Taylor, G. (1991) 'Working with parents to promote learning' in *Network*, Nottingham: Nottinghamshire County Council.

Newton, C., Collins, M., Gray, P. and Barber, P. (1991) 'Researching and developing provision for under 5s with special educational needs in Nottinghamshire', presentation paper at the Annual Conference of the Association of Educational Psychologists, Exeter.

Nias, D.J. (1987) 'The primary school staff relationships project: origins, aims and methods', *Cambridge Journal of Education*, 17(2): 89–103.

Nias, D.J., Southworth, G.W. and Yeomans, R. (1989) *Staff Relationships in the Primary School: a study of school cultures*, London: Cassell.

Oldroyd, D. and Tiller, T. (1987) 'Change from within: an account of school-based collaborative action research in an English secondary school', *Journal of Education for Teaching*, 12(3): 13–27.

Osborne, A. (1987) 'Professionals, managers and comprehensive schools: Part 2', *Educational Change and Development* 8(1): 4–10.

Patton, M.Q. (1980) *Qualitative Evaluation Methods*, Beverley Hills and London: Sage Publications.

Peters, T. (1988) *Thriving on Chaos: handbook for a management revolution*, London: Macmillan.

Peters, T. and Waterman, R. (1982) *In Search of Excellence*, London: Harper & Row.

Peters, T.J. and Austin, N. (1985) *A Passion for Excellence: the leadership difference*, London: Fontana.

Pfeffer, J. (1981) *Power in Organizations*, Marshfield, Mass.: Pitman.

Phi Delta Kappa (1980) *Why Do Some Urban Schools Succeed? The Phi Delta Kappa Study of Exceptional Urban Elementary Schools.* Bloomington, Ind.: Phi Delta Kappa Press.

Philips, B.N. (1990) 'Reading, evaluating and applying research in school psychology', in T.B. Gutkin and C.R. Reynolds (eds) *The Handbook of School Psychology*, 2nd edn, New York: Wiley.

Piaget, J. and Inhelder, B. (1969) *The Psychology of the Child* (trans. Weaver, H.) London: Routledge and Kegan Paul

Pipes, R. (1981) 'Consulting in organisations: the entry problem', in J.C. Conoley (ed.), *Consultation in Schools: theory, research, procedures*, New York: Academic Press.

Plant, R. (1987) *Managing Change and Making it Stick*, London: Fontana/Collins.

Plas, J.M. (1986) *Systems Psychology in the Schools*, Oxford: Pergamon.

Pope, M.L. and Keen, T.R. (1981) *Personal Construct Psychology and Education*, London: Academic Press.

Poster, C. and Poster, D. with Benington, M. (1991) *Teacher Appraisal: a guide to training*, London: Routledge.

Priest, S. and Higgins, A. (1991) 'Resolving conflicts between pupils', DSDP Dissemination Conference paper, Chesterfield, Derbyshire: Educational Psychology Service.

Purkey, S. and Smith, M. (1983) 'Effective Schools: a review', *Elementary School Journal*, 83: 427–52.

Purkey, S.C. and Smith, M.S. (1985) 'School reform: the district policy implications of the effective schools literature', *The Elementary School Journal*, 85: 353–89.

Quicke, J. (1982) *The Cautious Expert: a social analysis of developments in the practice of educational psychology*, Milton Keynes: Open University Press.

Ranson, S. (1990) *The Politics of Reorganising Schools*, London: Unwin Hyman.

Reed, J. and Jayne, E. (1986) 'Managing change in the primary school: what we have learnt about the role of external support', *School Organization*, 6(3): 339–45.

Reid, K., Hopkins, D. and Holly, P. (1987) *Towards the Effective School: the problems and some solutions*, Oxford: Basil Blackwell.

Reynolds, D. (1987) 'The effective school: do educational psychologists help or hinder?', *Educational Psychology in Practice*, 3 (3): 22–7.

Reynolds, D., Creemers, B., Peters, T. (eds) (1989) 'School effectiveness and improvement', proceedings of the first international congress, London 1988, Cardiff: School of Education, University of Wales.

Reynolds, C., Elliot, S., Gutkin, T. and Witt, J. (1984) *School Psychology – Essentials of Theory and Practice*, New York: Wiley.

Rogers, C. (1961) *On Becoming A Person*, London: Constable.

Rutter, M., Maughan, B., Mortimore, P. and Ousten, J. (1979) *Fifteen Thousand Hours: secondary schools and their effects on children*, London: Open Books.

Sarason, P. (1982): *The Culture of the School and the Problem of Change*, Boston: Allyn & Bacon.

Schein, E.H. (1987) *Process Consultation*, vol. 2, Reading, Mass., Addison-Wesley.

Schein, E.H. (1989) *Process Consultation: its role in organisation development*. Reading, Mass.: Addison-Wesley.

Schmuck, R. (1984), 'Characteristics of the autonomous school', in D. Hopkins and E. Wideon (eds) *Alternative Perspectives on School Improvement*, Lewes: Falmer Press.

Schmuck, R.A. (1990) 'Organization development in schools: contemporary concepts and practices', in Gutkin, T.B and Reynolds, C.R. (eds) *The Handbook of School Psychology, 2nd edn, New York: Wiley.*

Schon, D.A. (1983) *The Reflective Practitioner: how professionals think in action*, New York: Basic Books.

Schostak, J.F. (1986) *Schooling the Violent Imagination*, London: Routledge & Kegan Paul.

Sengupta, J.K. (1986) *Stochastic Optimization and Economic Models*, Dordrecht: Reidel.

Sidorsky, D. (ed.) (1977) *John Dewey: The Essential Writings*, New York: Harper and Row.

Simpson, B. (1987) 'Stressing the Positive', *Management Today*, Nov., 125–8.

Smail, D. (1987) *Taking Care: an alternative to therapy*, London and Melbourne: Dent.

Solity, J. (1991), 'Special Needs: A discriminatory concept?', *Educational Psychology in Practice*, 7(1), Harlow, Essex: Longman.

Southworth, G. (1990) 'Leadership, headship and effective primary schools', *School Organisation*, 10(1): 3–16.

Southworth, G. (1988) 'Looking at leadership: English primary school headteachers at work, *Education*, 3–13, 16, 2, 53–6.

Starratt, R.J. (1986) *Excellence in Education and Quality of Leadership*, Occasional Paper No. 1., Southern Tasmanian Council for Education Administration.

Stratford, R.J. and Cameron, R. (1979) *Aiming at Larger Targets*, BPS Division of Educational and Child Psychology Occasional Papers 5(2).

Theroux, P. (1983) *The Kingdom By the Sea*, London: Penguin.

Thomas, K.W. (1976) 'Conflict and conflict management', in Dunnette, M.D. (ed.) *Handbook of Industrial and Organisational Psychology*, vol. 2, Chicago: Rand & McNally.

Tizard, B. (1991) 'Educational Research and educational policy: is there a link?', in P. Gray and G. Lyndsay (eds) 'Research and its relation to policy', *Education and Child Psychology*, 8(1): 6–16.

Topping, K.J., (1986), *Parents as Educators: training parents to teach their children*, London and Sydney: Croom Helm.

Tough, A. (1979) *The Adults Learning Projects*, Research in Education Series, No. 1, 2nd edn, Ontario: OISE.

Tulder, M.V., S. Veenman and Sieben, J. (1988) 'Features of effective inservice activities: results of a Delphi study', *Educational Studies*, 14(2): 209–23.

Ury, W. (1991) *Getting Past No*, London: Century.

Vail, P.B. (1984) 'The purposing of high performing systems', in Sergiovanni, T.J. and

Corbally, J.E. (eds) *Leadership and Organizational Culture*, Chicago: University of Illinois Press.

Van Velzen, W.G., Miles, M., Ekholm, M., Hameyer, U. and Robin, D. (1985) *Making School Improvement Work: a conceptual guide to practice*, Leuven/Amersfoort: OECD.

Vygotsky, L.S. (1962) *Thought and Language*, Cambridge, Mass.: MIT Press.

Walker, R., Macdonald, B., Elliot, J. and Edelman, C. (1986) 'Innovation: the school and the teacher', *(1) Educational Studies, Curriculum Design and Development*, Unit 27 and 28, Milton Keynes: Open University Press.

Weindling, D. and Early, P. (1986) 'How heads manage change', *School Organization*, 6(3): 327–8.

White, D.R., and Haring, N.G. (1980) *Exceptional Teaching*. Columbus, Ohio: Charles E. Merrill.

Wilkinson, C. and Cave, E. (1987) *Teaching and Managing: inseparable activities in schools*, London: Croom Helm.

Wolfendale, S. (1987) *Primary Schools and Special Needs: policy, planning and provision*, London: Cassell.

Index